STANDARDIZING DIVERSITY

NATIONAL AND ETHNIC CONFLICT
IN THE TWENTY-FIRST CENTURY

Brendan O'Leary, Series Editor

STANDARDIZING DIVERSITY

The Political Economy of Language Regimes

Amy H. Liu

PENN

UNIVERSITY OF PENNSYLVANIA PRESS

PHILADELPHIA

Published by
University of Pennsylvania Press
Philadelphia, Pennsylvania 19104-4112

Printed in the United States of America
on acid-free paper

1 3 5 7 9 10 8 6 4 2

Library of Congress Cataloging-in-Publication Data
Liu, Amy H.
   Standardizing diversity : the political economy of language regimes /
Amy H. Liu. — 1st ed.
       p.   cm. — (National and ethnic conflict in the twenty-first century)
   Includes bibliographical references and index.
   ISBN 978-0-8122-4672-8
   1. Language policy—Southeast Asia—Political aspects. 2. Language policy—
Southeast Asia—Economic aspects. 3. Southeast Asia—Languages—Political
aspects. 4. Language policy—Political aspects. 5. Language policy—Economic
aspects. 6. Language and languages—Political aspects. 7. Language and
languages—Economic aspects. I. Title. II. Series: National and ethnic conflict in the
twenty-first century.
P119.32.S64L58   2015
306.44'9598—dc23   2014028635

CONTENTS

NOTE ABOUT INTERVIEWS

All interviews were conducted across multiple sites in 2008 and 2010. Indonesian interviews took place in Bali, Jakarta, and Yogyakarta. Malaysian interviews were conducted from Singapore via mobile or Skype video conferencing. In-person interviews were not possible. Research access into the country had been denied on the grounds of the "seditious" nature of the project. Per an amendment to the 1948 Sedition Act, "questioning" the country's language policies was an offense punishable by five years' imprisonment. Finally, Singaporean interviews were done in person in Singapore.

Given the possibility of the questions and answers being considered too sensitive, consistent with Institutional Review Board regulations, all interviews were conducted privately and quotes are given with names withheld.

PART I

Toward a Typology of Language Regimes

CHAPTER 1

Introduction

People, stop please! Look at yourselves. This is wrong.
What are words, after all, but a way to communicate, to bring us
    together?
But you, you're using them as weapons!
    —Niles Crane in *Frasier*, Season 9, Episode 18 ("War of the Words")

When the Dutch East India Company established Batavia (Jakarta) in 1619, present-day Indonesia was the site of numerous competitive and unstable kingdoms scattered across a broad archipelago. Over the following centuries, the Dutch presence gradually expanded throughout the region. The colonial authorities, however, did little to bring the islands together under one central administrative language, let alone the Dutch language. There was equally little planning about Dutch decolonization. When the Dutch surrendered in 1949 after a four-year nationalist insurrection, the new Indonesian government found itself with an empty treasury, presiding over a territory of more than 13,000 islands populated by speakers of some 712 languages (Bertrand 2003: 265). Given these conditions at its birth, theoretical expectations in political science would have suggested the following. First, the abject poverty prevalent across the islands should have increased the salience of ethnolinguistic cleavages (Lipset 1959). Second, the salience of these cleavages and their sheer number should have caused some sort of "growth tragedy"—poor education, political volatility, weak financial systems, distorted markets, large government debts, and underdeveloped infrastructure (Easterly and Levine 1997).

Indeed, Indonesia experienced horrific developmental pains, including Sukarno's "Guided Democracy" and Suharto's "New Order." The latter was born amid extensive anticommunist massacres in which the Chinese population was disproportionately targeted (Cribbs 2008). Casualty figures range from 78,000 to 1,000,000. Putting this in perspective, these massacres collectively rank eighty-first in a list of the one hundred deadliest atrocities in world history (M. White 2011: 476). However, the politics over language were not at stake. Moreover, Indonesia appeared to have overcome the poverty trap: its high (sometimes even double-digit) growth figures caught the attention of the World Bank before the dramatic implosion of the *rupiah* in 1997–1998. In 1993, the international financial institution published a report classifying Indonesia as a "High-Performing Asian Economy" (World Bank 1993: xvi). With this designation, Indonesia found itself in an elite grouping that included the "East Asian Tigers" of Singapore, South Korea, and Taiwan.

The East Asian financial crisis years (1997–1998) notwithstanding, growth levels in Indonesia continued to amaze outsiders. In 1999, Indonesia was included as a member of the G20, a grouping of finance ministers and central bank governors from the twenty largest economies (Kirton 1999). In 2005, Goldman Sachs placed Indonesia on its list of the Next Eleven (N-11) countries most likely to join the BRIC group (Brazil, Russia, India, and China) of fast-growing economies (O'Neill et al. 2005). Within the eleven, Indonesia was considered one of the top four, as evidenced by its presence in another popular acronym: MIKT (Mexico, Indonesia, South Korea, and Turkey). A few years later, the Economist Intelligence Unit followed suit with CIVETS (Colombia, Indonesia, Vietnam, Egypt, Turkey, and South Africa) (Moore 2012). Whether Indonesia would transform the BRIC into the BRIIC has become a standard trope in popular commentary (Day 2011).

The negative effects of ethnolinguistic heterogeneity are arguably "one of the most powerful hypotheses in political economy" (Banerjee, Iyer, and Somanathan 2005: 639, quoted in Habyarimana et al. 2007: 709). Yet that hypothesis cannot explain the economic miracle of postcolonial Indonesia. What explains Indonesia's counterintuitive economic success? Heterogeneity, linguistic or otherwise, does not necessarily doom a country's prospects. Rather, the answer lies in a country's institutions, in particular, its language regime. Language regimes are the rules that delineate which languages can be used when and where. In Indonesia, only one language was officially recognized. It was not, however, the language of the largest group (Javanese).[1] It was, instead, a lingua franca—the common language of trade among the merchants of the East Indies (Malay). This book argues that this linguistic arrangement has played a decisive role in counteracting the potentially negative economic effects of the country's heterogeneity. The use and development of this lingua franca helped build a larger "national" identity that accommodated multiple ethnolinguistic groups. The adoption of Malay—later renamed Indonesian (*basha Indonesia*) in 1945—provided coordination around a link language (communicative efficiency) without signaling coercive Javanization (collective equality).

Language regimes, however, are not exogenous: they are endogenous institutional choices. Why did the Indonesian government choose to recognize Malay instead of Javanese or some combination of Javanese and other minority languages? The answer, I suggest, is the high level of *politically relevant* linguistic heterogeneity. The extreme diversity constrained the government to behave judiciously with its language regime choices. It could not recognize every language, at least not with equal resources, and to impose Javanese would have polarized the population.

Inspired by the Indonesian example, this book asks: what explains language regime choice, and what are the economic implications of this choice? The answers require us to first define language. Specifically, how is a language different from a dialect, and when is a language simply—quoting Niles Crane—"a way to communicate, to bring us together" (i.e., a linguistic concept) versus a "weapon" (i.e., a political tool)?

Defining Language

Language is a "vehicle for the expression or exchanging of thoughts, concepts, knowledge, and information as well as the fixing and transmission of experience and knowledge" (Bussman 1996: 253). It is the "currency of human communities" (Ostler 2006: 9). It is the "glue that binds [people] as a community and allows [people] to communicate as friends [and] as neighbors, in commerce and in government" (Vo-Duc 2011). Not all languages, however, flow from "community-binding" efforts to glue together families and individuals. Phoenician, for instance, was a commercial language. At its height, Phoenician was used throughout the Mediterranean area by merchants and traders (Ostler 2006: 44–45, 68–78). There are also "sacred languages." Latin fulfilled this function in western Christendom, as did Greek in Orthodox Christianity. Similarly, Arabic was (and still is) a language of religion. By 712 CE, eighty years after Muhammad's death, Arabic had become an instrument for worship and had spread beyond the Middle

East (Ostler 2006: 97–98, 110–12). Languages spread by diffusion, but they also spread by the spear or the bayonet. Under Alexander the Great, the Greeks conquered the Persian Empire, and for an interval Greek replaced Farsi as a language of prestige (Ostler 2010: 75–77).

Languages Versus Dialects

What is the difference between a language and a dialect? In linguistics, one commonly employed distinction is that "a language is a collection of mutually intelligible dialects" (Chambers and Trudgill 1998: 3). Mutual intelligibility refers to the "ability of the users of one variety [language or dialect] to understand another variety" (Lewis 2009: "Language Information"). With this definition, all dialects are a subset of some language. This definition, however, is problematic for at least two reasons. First, the ability to understand may not be mutual. Speakers of one variety may be able to understand speakers of another variety better than vice versa. For example, Danish speakers understand modern Norwegian speakers better than Norwegians do Danish (Chambers and Trudgill 1998: 4), even though Denmark ruled Norway for centuries.[2]

Second, there is also a matter of degree. According to one source, "Values of less than 85% [of mutual intelligibility] are likely to signal difficulty in comprehension of the indicated language" (Lewis 2009: "Language Information"). To classify two varieties with 86 percent mutual intelligibility as "dialects" and two other varieties with 84 percent mutual intelligibility as "languages" seems arbitrary. Moreover, the 85 percent rule is not consistently applied. Chinese, for instance, is often considered a single language because of the common writing system across the eleven different major "dialects." However, the phonetic dissimilarities between Mandarin (which is actually the northern dialect, *beifang hua*) and the other larger dialects such as Cantonese (*guangdong hua*) and Shanghainese (*shanghai hua*)[3] render the dialects mutually unintelligible. In contrast, Portuguese and Spanish are considered "languages" (Lewis 2009). Yet because of their mutual intelligibility, the media in one language will at times make no attempt to translate, subtitle, or voiceover programs into the other (J. Jensen 1989).

An alternative distinction, coined by Marshal Hubert Lyautey of France, is that "a language is a dialect with an army and navy" (see Laponce 2006: 113). This political definition highlights the role of the state. It is the state that takes a folk dialect; standardizes the orthography, grammar, and alphabet; disseminates it systematically; and institutionalizes its use (Safran 2010). The rise of the *bei-*

fang dialect as "Chinese" happened in 1911 after the fall of the Qing Dynasty. The Republican government designated the northern dialect as the official language (*guo yu*), to the chagrin of the Shanghainese speakers (Kaske 2008). Several committees were charged with the task of standardizing the orthography, establishing a rubric for pronunciation, preparing a dictionary, and disseminating the changes in the education system (Kaplan and Baldauf 2003: 48–51).

The role of the state in differentiating between languages and dialects is appropriately reflected in what Laitin (1977: 3) once wrote: "The multilingual state faces the problem of which indigenous *language* should receive the most support; [supposedly] monolingual states often face the problem of which *dialect* of the shared language should be supported" (italicized in original source). This reasoning, of course, suggests that the "identification of 'a language' is not solely within the realm of linguistics" (Lewis 2009). Instead, politics matters. This book adopts this politically derived distinction. Specifically, I define a system of communication as a "language" if and only if it is considered as one by the relevant state.

As an example, consider Southern Min (Hokkien), one of the larger Chinese varieties spoken in the Chinese province of Fujian. In China, this speech pattern is considered a "dialect" (*hua*) and has played second fiddle to Mandarin Chinese since the aforementioned regime change in 1911 (Kaplan and Baldauf 2003: 49–51). Similarly, in Singapore, there is a large Chinese population, many of whom have ancestors from Fujian. In 1979, the Singaporean government launched an initiative to encourage the entire Chinese community, regardless of the dialect spoken at home, to learn Mandarin—not because it was just another Chinese *dialect*, but because it was one of the four official *languages* of the country [4] (Š. Ganguly 2003: 256, 259). The dominance of Mandarin over Southern Min and other dialects has been evident. Since the "Speak Mandarin Campaign," there has been only one instance—the SARS outbreak in 2003—when the government has officially used other Chinese dialects on public radio and television (E. Tan 2007: 91).[5] In contrast, in Taiwan, where Southern Min speakers are the numerical majority, their speech pattern has come to be recognized by the government as a "language" (*yu*). In fact, in response to the political dominance of Mandarin, the non-Mandarin native speakers renamed Southern Min as the "Taiwanese" language (*tai yu*). While its use was severely restricted for a number of decades, Taiwanese would begin assuming some equality with Mandarin in the early 1990s, not coincidentally a few years before the first democratic election in 1996 (Dreyer 2003: 399–404; Kaplan and Baldauf 2003: 55, 58–59). This discussion highlights the fact that despite the speech pattern of Southern Min being the same in all three contexts—China, Singapore, and Taiwan—the political landscape has determined whether it is considered a language or a dialect. Languages are inherently political.

Language as a Political Instrument

While the primary purpose of language—communication—is fundamentally apolitical, the necessity to "describe the nature of things" (Codevilla, introduction to Machiavelli 1532/1997: xxiii) makes language extremely political. Languages essentially become, as Machiavelli argued, "particular articulations of the universal struggle for primacy" (xxiii). Government recognition of one group's language but not another group's language is nothing short of political: it determines which "people have a legitimate claim to greater respect, importance, or worth in society than [others]" (Horowitz 1985: 220).

Language is political for at least three different reasons. First, it is a marker of ethnic identity. For many ethnic groups, language is "not just *a* marker, it is *the* marker: It determines who is and is not a member of the group, and what the boundaries of the group are" (M. Brown and Š. Ganguly 2003: 3, italic in original). Abkhazian, Catalan, Igbo, Quechuan, and Samoan are more than just "concrete acts of speaking, writing, or signing" (Crystal 2003: 255). They suggest a shared history and a common culture among the members of an in-group. In ancient Greece, for instance, "Greekness" (*tò Hellenikón*) was defined as having the same language[6] and the same blood (Ostler 2006: 232). Likewise, languages can identify the existence and difference of the members of an out-group. During Ceauşescu's dictatorship (1965–1989), the two million Hungarians, residing primarily in the Transylvania region of Romania, suffered. Their schools were closed, their language was banned in public, and a number of their coethnics were killed (Gilberg 1992: 293). Despite their Romanian citizenship, the Hungarians were targeted precisely because they were ethnically Hungarians.[7]

Second, language is political because it is a source of national cohesion. It is the "strongest and most lasting [bond] that can unite men" (Tocqueville 1835/2002: 29). Guaraní, Kurdish, Maori, Sami, and Tibetan are five of the many languages without a corresponding sovereign and independent state.[8] But they are still just as relevant—if not more—as vehicles for the promotion of a national identity. The Uyghurs in China speak a language akin to Turkish and use the Arabic script for written communication. The Arabic script, with its fundamental association with Islam, has allowed the language to be an important ethnic marker and in some instances a catalyst for demands for an independent Xinjiang (Bovingdon 2001: 95–139; Dwyer 2005: 28, 91–92). Similarly, the choice by the Moldovan Popular Front in the early 1990s to call their language "Romanian" was seen as a step toward the creation of a new Greater Romania (C. King 2000: 151–60).

Third, language is political because it is an instrument used to build a political community (Safran 2005). During the Tito regime, the Serbo-Croatian language was renamed the Yugoslav language (*jugoslavenski jezik*) to ensure that the country had a corresponding language. After the breakup, Croatian and Serbian were considered distinct languages in their respective new countries. Furthermore, the language spoken in Sarajevo—up to this point a mere dialect of Serbo-Croatian—was renamed Bosnian. In each case, the insistence on a distinct language was clearly a "political act" (Safran 2010: 63). Likewise, in Indonesia, the 1928 Youth Congress Proclamation of "one nation, one people, one language" (*satu nusa, satu bangsa, satu bahasa*) highlights the fundamental role of language in that case. The choice to subsequently rename Malay "Indonesian" was motivated precisely by the need to create a hitherto nonexistent nation (Bertrand 2003: 272–75; Montolalu and Suryadinata 2007: 40–41).

Ethnolinguistic Heterogeneity and Institutions

Central to any culture is its set of myths and legends. These myths and legends often involve some struggle between the gods (i.e., some supernatural forces) and the human population. One common outcome in these mythological struggles is an explanation for linguistic diversity. For example, according to Greek mythology, under the rule of Zeus, all people spoke one language and lived without any need for law. Zeus and the Pleiad Maia (a daughter of Atlas) had a son, Hermes, the patron of boundaries and commerce, among other things. Hermes, however, was filled with evil. His credentials included inventing writing and introducing a multitude of tongues. This, in turn, created nations and bred discord among humans. When the quarrels became too much, Zeus abdicated in favor of Phoroneus, who would become the first king of mortals (Frazer 1918: 150–51).

The Bible provides an alternative narrative. The people of the Shinar Plains were bonded by "one language and one speech." One day, they decided to build themselves "a city with a tower that reaches to the heavens." When God saw this, he responded, "If as one people speaking the same language they have begun to do this, then nothing they plan to do will be impossible for them. Come, let us go down and confuse their language so they will not understand each other." With that, the people stopped building the city and scattered across the world (Genesis 11:1–9, New International Version; also see Ether 1: 33–38, Book of Mormon).

Another account, in Hindu legend, tells there was a tree in the center of the earth. This tree was full of knowledge and almost reached the heavens. The tree, "holding my head in heaven," decided it would "spread my branches all over the earth, and gather all men together under my shadow, protect them, and prevent them from separating." Brahma, the god of creation, heard of this plan, and he realized the tree had to be punished for its pride. He cut off its branches. These branches were then cast down to earth, where they "sprang up as wata trees, and made differences of belief and speech" (A. White 1898: 172–73).

The common denominator across these three stories is not just the subject matter (language), but the theme: the root of linguistic diversity is some form of evil. The implications are far-reaching. Without the eradication of this evil, the world will continue to be a segregated place, where communities remain connected to each other through translations. Linguistic homogeneity—a desired outcome—is never attainable so long as mankind is evil. Even the notion of an international language complementing the mother tongue is radical. When attempting to create Esperanto, Ludwig Zamenhof acknowledged his efforts were likely to be viewed by skeptics as utopian and "utterly impossible of realization" (Zamenhof and Phillips 1889: 5). Furthermore, if linguistic heterogeneity is derived from evil, the effects of heterogeneity must then also be negative. Empirically, there is evidence to suggest this is the case. For example, the broader consensus in the political economy literature is that homogeneity is good and heterogeneity is bad. Specifically, high levels of ethnolinguistic fractionalization correlate with poor economic performance (e.g., Alesina et al. 2003; Brock and Durlauf 2001; P. Collier and Gunning 1999; Easterly and Levine 1997; Easterly 2001; Englebert 2000; Hall and Jones 1999; Rodrik 1999). Daniel Posner (2004) goes as far as noting, "Thanks largely to their article [Easterly and Levine (1997)], it is now *de rigueur* for economists to include a measure of ethnic diversity in their cross-country growth regressions" (849). This de rigueur applies well beyond economics. For example, heterogeneity[9] has been linked to democratic instability and civil wars (Annett 2001; Cederman, Wimmer, and Min 2010; Elbadawi and Sambanis 2002; Fearon 2004; Fearon, Kasara, and Laitin 2007; Reyna-Querol 2002). Similarly, it is often cited as an explanation for lower levels of social capital (e.g., Alesina and La Ferrara 2002; C. Anderson and Paskeviciute 2006; Costa and Kahn 2003; Delhey and Newton 2005; Knack and Keefer 1997; Putnam 2007; Rice and Steele 2001).

There are multiple explanations offered for this seemingly robust relationship between ethnolinguistic heterogeneity and some normatively bad outcome. James Habyarimana et al. (2009: 5–13) have compiled a list of eight mechanisms, categorized into three "families." The first family of mechanisms is preferences toward coethnics. There are a number of ways this preference can manifest itself, including taking the welfare of other coethnics into consideration, valuing the same outcome as coethnics, and choosing to work with coethnics. The second family concerns technology. Because ethnicity identifies a collective group, there is an inherent network. This network allows coethnics to function at a greater efficiency (efficacy), to gauge each other more accurately (readability), to interact more frequently (periodicity), and to find each other (reachability). The third family of mechanisms focuses on reciprocity; for example, coethnics "may be more likely to punish each other for failing to cooperate" (2009: 7).

Although by no means exhaustive, this list of families of mechanisms highlights the many avenues through which heterogeneity is expected to generate negative socioeconomic outcomes. Yet absent in all these accounts is the role of institutions. Institutions matter for ethnic conflict regulation (Horowitz 1985; Lijphart 1968). With the right set of institutions, the purported mechanisms of ethnicity (i.e., preference similarities, technologies, and reciprocity) can be "redirected" away from the negative effects and instead toward some normatively positive outcome.

Broadly speaking, the literature on ethnic institutions and conflict regulation[10] can be divided into two camps (see Reynolds 2002: vii). The first camp argues that moderation through power-concentrating institutions is the key to conflict regulation. For instance, Donald Horowitz (1991) argues that when electoral rules require plurality winners, or for groups to "pool" preferences to win a sufficient number of votes, parties have an incentive to adopt broad party manifestos (chaps. 7–8). Papua New Guinea, for example, is home to several thousand tribal groups. Not surprisingly, voting patterns have reflected these ethnic demarcations. But with the use of the alternate vote (a derivative of the plurality electoral rule) between 1964 and 1972, candidates who were able to secure substantial support beyond their tribes were the ones most likely to win (Reilly 1997: 1–11).

Another important power-concentrating institution is the presidential system. With the population at large deciding who occupies the most powerful seat in the country, candidates have an incentive to shy away from extremist positions.[11] Under such conditions, we are most likely to witness some convergence toward the median voter (Duverger 1963). In Nigeria, the presidential electoral rule requires not only that winning candidates have a plurality in votes but that these votes also reflect a geographical distributive spread. In Sri Lanka, the president is elected through the supplementary vote. In both examples, the rules for electing a chief executive clearly ensure that she is a "panethnic figure" (Horowitz 1991: 206).

The second camp asserts that consensus through power-sharing institutions generates possibilities for successful conflict regulation (McEvoy and O'Leary 2013). Proportional electoral rules create multiparty systems (Cox 1997; Duverger 1963; Riker 1982). Under most conditions, for all intents and purposes, this necessitates some sort of coalition-building. Arend Lijphart (1968) argues that in the Netherlands, list-proportional electoral rules have historically allowed the four politically relevant groups (Calvinists, Catholics, Liberals, and Socialists) to secure representation in the legislative body. This arrangement has forced the different elites to cooperate with non-coethnic elites. Similarly, parliamentary systems fuse the executive with the legislature. This means the former must govern at the mercy of the latter (Linz 1994: 13–14, 64–67). In Belgium, for instance, the executive must maintain the support of the cabinet, which by law requires as many Dutch-speaking as French-speaking ministers. This arrangement ensures that no prime minister promotes one language at the expense of the other (Lijphart 2002).

This book follows the trend in recognizing the importance of the way power—in this case, linguistic power—is distributed. But by focusing on how the balance of power among linguistic groups shapes institutional designs, I shift the attention away from the exclusive focus on the efficiency-enhancing properties of institutions (North 1990) to their distributional consequences (Knight 1992; Moe 2005). In doing so, this book highlights the limitations of the power-concentrating (i.e., "majoritarian" or winner-takes-all) versus power-sharing (i.e., consensual) institutional design dichotomy.

There is a third, distinct institutional arrangement, the neutralization of power through a third party,[12] and a fourth arrangement that is a hybrid of power-sharing and power-neutralizing. This book argues that designs that neutralize power to any extent through a third party may be as viable an alternative for regulating conflict as power-concentrating or power-sharing. Additionally, these institutional designs have features that can ameliorate the negative effects of ethnolinguistic heterogeneity and promote economic growth.

The Argument

Language is the "quintessential entitlement issue" (Horowitz 1985: 220). When a language is recognized, its speakers are empowered (Bourdieu 1991: 32–42). Thus, language regimes—by recognizing one language (or one set of languages) over all other languages—institutionalize the distribution of linguistic power. This distribution has long-term implications. Directly, the distribution can generate social capital and attract foreign capital; indirectly it can facilitate economic growth. This book identifies four types of language regimes, each characterized by a distinct distribution of linguistic power: power-concentrating, power-sharing, power-neutralizing, and neutralized-sharing. Of the four types, the latter two (power-neutralizing and neutralized-sharing) have the largest potential to minimize—if not reverse—the purported negative effects of ethnolinguistic heterogeneity.

Power-neutralizing language regimes are characterized by the use of a *lingua franca*. A lingua franca, such as Indonesian in Indonesia and Swahili in Tanzania, is an interethnic language (Crystal 2003). It is a language spoken by many but is the mother tongue of few. With this language regime, linguistic power is effectively removed from the hands of all concerned actors and placed in those of a neutral third party. The argument is that when countries such as Indonesia choose power-neutralizing language regimes—or even a neutralized-sharing hybrid—the potential of high growth levels is very real.

The effect is mediated through two different mechanisms. The first has to do with social capital. When a lingua franca is recognized, no potentially antagonistic group can lay claim to greater social importance (or subordination) than any other group. There is instead a sense of relative equality among the speakers of the different languages. There is equality in opportunity and proficiency. Theoretically, speakers of both the politically dominant and politically nondominant languages have similar resources to learn and master the same language. There is also equality in symbolism. The use of a lingua franca can remove perceptions of a status quo that favors the politically dominant. This can foster a sense of a state that is collectively shared and owned by all rather than controlled and represented by just one group.[13] And when there is this sense of a community larger than the boundaries of just one ethnolinguistic group, there is trust—arguably a necessary condition for economic growth (Knack and Keefer 1997; Ostrom 1990; Putnam 1993).

The second indirect mechanism has to do with foreign capital. Recognizing a lingua franca ensures there is one language that is spoken by the entire population. The presence of a language that cuts across linguistic group boundaries reduces transaction costs, specifically, translation volume. Translations are prone to error. A funny example involves an exchange between an Asian president and U.S. president Bill Clinton. The former, worried about his lack of English proficiency, had his aides teach him basic conversational English. The practiced routine was as follows. The Asian president would begin by asking Clinton, "How are you?" Clinton would no doubt answer, "Fine," and follow with the same question. The Asian president would then only have to say, "Me too." After that point, the two heads of state would then be able to speak privately through interpreters. However, when the two men met, the Asian president became confused and asked instead, "Who are you?" Clinton jokingly answered, "I'm Hillary's husband." The Asian president, not realizing the snafu, responded resolutely, "Me too" (Ignatius 2000). Whether or not the errors are funny, translations are costly in both money and time. The use of one language—provided it is accessible and proficiency is not difficult—reduces transaction costs. When there is such efficiency, a country may be much more attractive to potential foreign investors who are looking to keep transaction costs to a minimum. Here, foreign direct investments (FDI) are important because they can introduce the necessary capital, employment opportunities, and technology transfers for growth.

In this book I argue that because a lingua franca can generate social capital *and* attract foreign capital, its recognition can indirectly promote economic growth. Other language regime types, specifically power-concentrating and power-sharing, are either less conducive to community-wide trust or more costly to foreign investors. The precise mechanism, however, is different between the two language regimes. Power-concentrating language regimes, characterized by the exclusive use of one group's mother tongue, can perpetuate a sense of inequality. For speakers of nonrecognized languages, there is inequality of opportunity: members of the politically dominant group can speak their language publicly or privately and have it be recognized officially, but members of the other groups cannot. There is also inequality in linguistic proficiency: members of the politically dominant group can naturally speak their language with greater ease than everyone else. Additionally, there is a symbolic inequality in power dynamics: the exclusive recognition of one language can exacerbate perceptions of ethnic chauvinism on the part of the politically dominant group (and of inferiority among all other groups).

If language regimes are like electoral rules in that they institutionalize power distribution, then power-concentrating language regimes are akin to their plurality (winner-takes-all) electoral rule cousins. While both are efficient, they can also be highly unfair. Neither plurality electoral rules nor power-concentrating language regimes take into consideration "second place," regardless of the numerical differential (vote share or group size) between first and second place. Effectively, these rules are likely to breed tyrannies of the majority (Madison,

Federalist 51). It follows that while power-concentrating language regimes may attract foreign capital because of their efficiency-enhancing properties, they can have a negative effect when it comes to generating social capital.

Power-sharing language regimes are characterized by the recognition of multiple mother tongues. In principle, power-sharing language regimes establish equality between the different languages. By law, a politically nondominant language is considered equal to a politically dominant language. Like proportional electoral rules, power-sharing language regimes are perceived as being fair. Those in "second place" and even those behind second place are given proper acknowledgment. This equality, however, comes at a heavy cost: inefficiency. Power-sharing language regimes necessitate translations between each pair of languages. When compounded, these translations are both costly and time consuming—just as consensual governments born out of proportional electoral rules are especially prone to gridlock because of the larger number of veto players (Tsebelis 2002: 84–85, 91–115). The argument, then, is that power-sharing language regimes have a positive effect on social capital but possibly a negative one on foreign capital.

If the distribution of linguistic power matters directly for social capital and foreign capital and indirectly for economic growth, this raises a second—albeit antecedent—question: What explains the origins of language regimes? Language regimes are not exogenous; they do not appear out of thin air. Rather, language regimes are endogenous; they are institutional choices. Consistent with David Laitin's *Language Repertoires and State Construction in Africa* (1992), this book adopts the position that these choices are the result of strategic interactions. Where the book departs from Laitin is in a conceptualization that allows for multiple minority groups with the possibility for opposing preferences. It also offers a novel explanation for how three different factors—cultural egoism, communicative efficiency, and collective equality—can constrain the government to choose one language regime rather than another.

I argue that language regime choices are strategic responses to a country's politically relevant linguistic heterogeneity (see Cederman, Wimmer, and Min 2010; Posner 2004). This heterogeneity is important for three reasons: *cultural egoism*, from having one's language recognized as being prestigious; *communicative efficiency* in minimizing translation costs between different languages; and legitimacy derived from *collective equality*. When the politically relevant linguistic heterogeneity level is low, the language of the politically dominant group prevails. A group under such conditions has little incentive to not concentrate linguistic power in its own language. To share or neutralize linguistic power would inevitably involve forfeiting the exclusive symbolic superiority of the group's culture. Just as the superordination of a language is the superordination of its people, the reverse is also true: the subordination of a language can be felt as the subordination of a people (Safran and Liu 2012: 269–92). To recognize a second language would suggest equality of the two different languages.

What happens when politically relevant linguistic heterogeneity levels are not low? Under such conditions, the government is constrained to distribute linguistic power differently. It must make concessions. Sharing and recognizing the mother tongues of other groups is one possibility. By sharing, the politically dominant group loses some cultural egoism benefits and has to pay some efficiency costs. But in exchange, there are benefits to a collective equality: members of the politically nondominant group are more likely to view the government as representative. Such equality benefits, however, are worth little when politically relevant linguistic heterogeneity levels are high. The recognition of too many languages can be detrimental: the trivial cultural egoism benefits are easily outweighed by the significant efficiency costs. At some point, it is simply neither practical nor possible to power-share. For instance, it is possible to run an education curriculum in three languages: Switzerland is an example. But it is not possible to run a curriculum in thirty languages—or three hundred languages. Resources are finite. Moreover, from a political standpoint, if each politically relevant linguistic group is conceptualized as a veto player, the choice to power-share with some languages but not others may actually prove more contentious than just strict power-concentration.

Consequently, under such conditions of high heterogeneity, the optimal choice is the recognition of a lingua franca. Admittedly, forfeiting recognition of one's mother tongue hurts cultural egoism, but the benefits in return are substantive. There are two types of benefits. One is greater communicative efficiency. The use of a lingua franca to cut across all linguistic groups can reduce the need for translations, thereby better facilitating communication. The other benefit is a perception of collective equality. Recognizing a third party's language creates a sense of relative equality. No group emerges as an absolute winner, and no group is singled out as an exclusive loser. In effect, it creates a sense of a collective community.

The implication is intriguing. If lingua franca recognition is an optimal choice under high levels of politically relevant linguistic heterogeneity, and if this recognition can generate social capital and attract foreign capital, then this would suggest that with the proper set of institutions, extreme ethnolinguistic diversity is not an obstacle but a catalyst for economic growth.

Admittedly, economic growth is not the only outcome of importance. In fact, in some scenarios, it can be of secondary relevance. This is especially true when governments use economic performance to justify linguicide in retrospect (Skutnabb-Kangas 2000: 436–67). When governments promote one group's language in the name of "modernization," much as the U.S. government did with English in the Philippines in the early 1900s (Hau and Tinio 2003: 340–41),[14] this denies the speakers of all other languages the right to use their own mother tongue to the fullest extent. This is problematic because to destroy a language is to destroy a rooted cultural identity (Fishman 1991). This destruction need not be large scale or violent like the Armenian massacre in 1915 Ottoman Turkey. It can be gradual. It can also be the product of seemingly innocuous government policies. A language—even one that currently has a sizable population of native speakers—can risk extinction when the children no longer learn it and instead choose to study the growth-promoting language. In the absence of government efforts to reinforce literacy in the threatened language, the language can face "intergenerational disruption" and die (Fishman 1991: 81–121).[15] In Indonesia, for example, the emphasis on learning Indonesian (Montolalu and Suryadinata 2007: 46–48) and the increasing popularity of English (*New York Times*, July 26, 2010) have put many of the diverse languages at risk (Lewis 2009).

Scholars such as Kukathas (2003: 15–18), Laitin and Reich (2003), and Waldron (1995) have championed the rights of minorities to use their own languages. Will Kymlicka (1995) goes one step farther with his theory of multinationalism. Since no language regime can be apolitical, nations should have the right of self-government. Such arrangements guarantee language security (Mowbray 2012: 1–13). In the absence of these political rights, continued use of the politically dominant language or even a lingua franca can induce a natural linguistic shift, which can render the minority language extinct in a few generations.

While language justice is normatively important, note that this book gives more consideration to economic growth. This is not to say the rights of minorities to use and protect their own languages have no role in this story. On the contrary, as will be evident in Chapters 5 and 6, language regimes that are perceived to be fair create a sense of a collective community larger than ethnolinguistic group boundaries. This community, in turn, plays an essential role in social capital development. Where this book departs from Kymlicka is in the belief that the recognition of a nonminority language need not be linguistically repressive. Instead, the use of a lingua franca, when implemented correctly, can facilitate justice and counteract the negative economic effects that the country's heterogeneity might otherwise have brought about.

Plan of the Book

Chapter 2 discusses in detail the different language regime types. Because ultimately the objective is to understand the politics behind language regime choice and the economic implications of this choice, the chapter's focus is on providing a precise conceptual typology of the variation in language regimes. For this typology there are two dimensions of interest:

(1) The number of recognized languages: one versus multiple; and
(2) The nativity of the recognized language: mother tongue of a domestic population versus lingua franca.

When combined, these two dimensions yield a two-by-two table and four corresponding language regimes of interest: power-concentrating, power-sharing, power-neutralizing, and neutralized-sharing. When operationalizing, I focus *not* on the official language(s) of the state but on the language(s) of public education. In Chapter 2, I discuss two samples (one quantitative: Asian countries 1945–2005; and one qualitative: Malaysia and Singapore) and the language regime variations in each.

I then seek to provide an explanation for the variance, and to answer the question: what explains language regime choice? In Chapter 3, using Indonesia as a motivating example, I argue that language regimes are political institutions. When choosing language regimes, governments must balance the three Es: cultural egoism, communicative efficiency, and collective equality. Which of the three components weighs most heavily, I shall show, depends on the level of politically relevant linguistic heterogeneity. When heterogeneity is low, linguistic power is concentrated.[16] When countries are more heterogeneous, the exclusive recognition of the politically dominant language is rendered difficult. Under such conditions, linguistic concessions must be made. One possibility is the recognition of multiple mother tongues.[17] Another is the choice of a power-neutralizing language regime. The last possibility is a hybrid of the other two (neutralized-sharing). The argument is that at extreme levels of heterogeneity, power-sharing is highly inefficient; instead, the recognition of a lingua franca—either exclusively or in conjunction with other mother tongues—is an optimal choice.

Chapter 4 empirically examines the arguments developed in Chapter 3. The first test assesses the preliminary validity of the argument. The statistical tests, using two newly constructed measures of language regimes, offer strong evidence confirming the link between politically relevant linguistic heterogeneity levels and language regime choice. The second test is a controlled comparison of two countries (Malaysia and Singapore) over two periods in each. Process-tracing in each of the two periods in the two countries (for a total of four causal-process observations) seeks to establish whether governments are choosing language regimes in response to the purported mechanisms: cultural egoism, communicative efficiency, and collective equality.

If language regimes are the rules that delineate which languages can be used when and where, what are the economic implications—if any—of these choices? Drawing on Indonesia again, Chapter 5 argues that language regimes that recognize a lingua franca can have a positive effect on economic growth. The effect, however, is indirect and achieved through two different mechanisms. One is through social capital, primarily generalized trust and secondarily altruism. Language regimes that guarantee equality facilitate the development of a collective community beyond linguistic group boundaries. Where there is a community, there can be trust. And where there is trust, there can be growth (Knack and Keefer 1997; Ostrom 1990; Putnam 1993).

The other mechanism involves foreign capital. When language regimes reduce the linguistic barriers to conducting business, transactions become (more) efficient. This efficiency is important because it can make a country attractive to foreign investors who have an incentive to minimize transaction costs whenever possible. And where there are foreign investors, there may be useful capital, worthwhile jobs, and technology transfers. Additionally, provided there are other favorable institutional and external economic conditions, there may also be growth. Since power-neutralizing, and to some extent neutralized-sharing, language regimes can both generate social capital and attract foreign capital, economic growth levels are more likely to be robust in countries where a lingua franca is recognized.

The next two chapters empirically test this claim. Chapter 6 focuses on the social capital mechanism; Chapter 7 on the foreign capital mechanism. Both chapters begin with statistical tests to examine the prima facie evidence. Again, I use two different measures for language regime and a number of different model specifications. The results show that power-neutralizing language regimes generate social capital, attract foreign capital, and therefore indirectly account for economic growth levels. After the statistical tests, the attention shifts to the two case

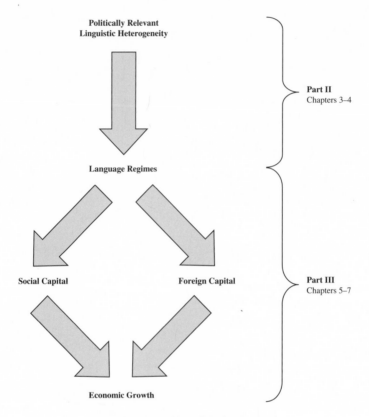

Figure 1.1. Plan of the book.

studies. The purpose of the controlled comparison of Malaysia (1971–) and Singapore (1965–) is to establish that the hypothesized mechanisms are actually in play. In other words, have—and if so, how have—the language regime choices in the two countries affected generalized trust and FDI levels? Note that Indonesia is never used as a case for empirical testing as that is the case from which the arguments are generated (see D. Collier, Seawright, and Munck 2004: 44). The relationship between Part II (Chapters 3–4) and Part III (Chapters 5–7) is depicted in Figure 1.1.

The conclusion summarizes the arguments and findings of the previous chapters and addresses two broader implications. One of the core innovations of this project is the identification of an alternative institutional arrangement for the distribution of power. The institutions literature has been broadly dominated by two types of designs (Reynolds 2002: vii): power-concentration versus power-sharing. However, there is a third possibility as well. Power-neutralization happens when power is removed from the hands of all relevant actors and placed figuratively in the hands of a third party. This arbitration-like arrangement is certainly not exclusive to language regimes.

By focusing on power-neutralizing language regimes and observing their positive implications for economic growth, this book challenges the heterogeneity-is-bad premise commonly found in the political economy literature. Contrary to the claims of Easterly and Levine (1997), countries are not trapped by their ethnolinguistic heterogeneity. Even those dealt a bad hand have institutional mechanisms to reverse the negative effects of diversity. One such institution is language regime. If power-neutralizing language regimes can generate high levels of growth, and if power-neutralizing language regimes are optimal choices under extreme levels of heterogeneity, this would suggest diversity is actually good for growth.

CHAPTER 2

Typology of Language Regimes

The United States has no official language, at least not at the federal level. Yet Sections 203(c) and 4(f)(4) of the federal Voting Rights Act require states and political subdivisions (e.g., counties) with a "language minority group" more than 5 percent or 10,000 of the voting age citizens to "conduct elections in the language of [that minority group] in addition to English." This is a legal rule. In Canada, the Francophone community is concentrated mostly in and around Quebec. Yet the Charter of Rights and Freedoms, Part 1, Section 23, guarantees citizens of Canada whose first language is either English or French "the right to have their children receive primary and secondary school instruction in that language"—regardless of the province of residency. This is a constitutional rule. In India, the official language is Hindi in the Devanagari script. Yet Part 17 (Chapter 2) of the constitution allows each state to "adopt any one or more of the languages in use in the state"—inclusive of Hindi—in any official capacity. This is also a constitutional rule. Additionally, also in India, the constitution (Article 343) recognizes English as an official language—but only for a period of fifteen years. Yet every fifteen years Parliament votes to reestablish the temporary status of English for another fifteen years (Stuligross and Varshney 2002: 439).

Language regimes specify which languages can be used when and where. They may also specify how a language is to be used, for example, in which script it will be composed, which grammatical rules will be followed, or which rules of transliteration will be followed in legal texts. These rules in aggregate—language regimes—"are [a set of] humanly devised constraints that shape human interaction" (North 1990: 3) and are "shared by the members of the relevant community" (Knight 1992: 2). Public officials assume the same language(s) will be spoken by *everyone* in government services; educators expect the same language(s) will be taught *every day* in the classrooms; and average citizens behave as if the same language(s) will be used *everywhere* to disseminate information. Fundamentally, language regimes are institutions: they are rules with enforcement mechanisms.

Language regimes, however, are not just institutions. They are *political* institutions (see Kymlicka 1995: chaps. 1–2). They are political because they determine which—if any—linguistic group shares in the "authoritative allocation of values" (Easton 1953: 129) that defines a political system; which linguistic group(s) "can do what to whom" (Lenin 1905: 190–97); and which linguistic group(s) "gets what, when, and how" (Lasswell 1936: 1). These decisions are contentious. King County in Washington State, for instance, is required by the Voting Rights Act to provide Chinese language ballots. Yet, in the September 17, 2002, primary election, only twenty-four of these ballots were used (Iwasaki 2002). Regardless why the other 9,976 and more eligible Chinese voters did not use these alternative ballots, this discrepancy between rights and reality highlights the political nature of language regimes.

To make sense of the different types of language regimes, this chapter begins with a conceptual typology (see D. Collier, LaPorte, and Seawright 2012). There are two dimensions of interest: (1) the number of recognized languages: one versus multiple, and (2) the nativity of recognized languages: mother tongue of domestic population versus lingua franca. Taking these two dimensions together yields a two-by-two table, from which I identify four language regime types: power-concentrating, power-sharing, power-neutralizing, and neutralized-sharing.

The chapter then shifts to a discussion about data. There are two types. Quantitatively, there are two newly constructed measures: one quadrachotomous and one continuous. The two measures seek to operationalize different concepts. One is about the presence or absence of lingua franca recognition; the other, the degree of lingua franca recognition. The sample for this quantitative dataset is all Asian countries 1945–2005. Qualitatively, the data on language regimes come from a cross-national comparison of Malaysia and Singapore over time. By focusing on four causal-process observations (D. Collier, Brady, and Seawright 2004: 252–63), one may draw the distinction between de jure and de facto language regimes.

Dimensions of Language

If language is power, then one way to conceptualize language regimes is to focus on the nature of the distribution of this power. When examining distribution, there are two dimensions of interest. The first dimension, as illustrated in Figure 2.1, is the number of recognized languages. At one end, only one language is

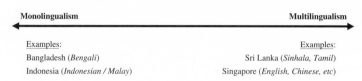

Figure 2.1. Dimension 1 (number of recognized languages).

recognized. Theoretically, monolingualism is efficient (Laitin 1988; Pool 1991): it minimizes transaction costs. When communication between two individuals necessitates translation, this incurs some cost. This cost is certainly not trivial. Consider an extreme example. The European Union (EU) allows for multiple official languages. When the EU consisted of only fifteen members, annual translation costs were officially estimated at €686 million. But with the expansion, these costs have risen to more than €1,123 million—a sum sufficient to pay 10 percent of the commission's workforce (Ginsburgh and Weber 2011: 163–64).

Translations are not only financially costly. They are also time consuming and vulnerable to errors. These errors, in turn, can have significant ramifications. For example, in 1969 when U.S. president Richard Nixon pressed Japanese prime minister Eisaku Sato to reduce textile exports, the latter answered, "I will try my best" (*Zensho simasu*). However, once translated, the response became "Yes, I agree." So when export levels remained unchanged, Nixon allegedly retaliated. He withheld information about secretary of state Henry Kissinger's secret trip to China (*Orlando Sentinel*, April 11, 1993). Another example is from the 2011 Southern Sudanese Independence Referendum. Before the referendum, in an interview with Agence France-Presse (AFP), UN Secretary-General Ban Ki-Moon said in English, "We will work hard to make this unity attractive." AFP, however, translated the statement into French as "We will work hard to avoid a possible secession" ("Nous allons travailler dur pour éviter une possible sécession"). This mistake caused an international stir: Southern Sudan's president Salva Kiir Mayardit accused the UN of interfering and reneging on its role as a "guarantor" of the free choice of either unity or secession as outlined in the 2005 Comprehensive Peace Agreement. Only after lengthy reassurances by the head of the UN Mission in Sudan that Ban was misquoted and a UN-issued public statement denying intentions of interference, did those tensions finally cool down (Lynch 2010). When legal or technical texts undergo transformations, it is not only poetry that may get lost in translation. In sum, translations are costly, and these costs only escalate—exponentially—as the number of recognized languages increases.

In contrast to monolingualism, at the other end is the recognition of more than one language (inclusive of bilingualism). In principle, multilingualism produces a sense of equality and fairness. In fact, in some policy circles, it touches on the normative notion of language justice (van Parijs 2011). Freedom House, for instance, considers the ability of an individual to conduct her daily life in the language she chooses a "human right" (McColm 1990: 19–20). Likewise, a number of international policy directives (e.g., the European Charter for Regional or Minority Languages of the Council of Europe and the 1992 UN Declaration on Minorities) require states to accommodate minority language speakers in the areas of government administration and public education (Hogan-Brun and Wolff 2003: 3–15). When Slovakia passed the 2009 language law that imposed a financial penalty for the use of a non-Slovak language in official functions, Hungarian president Sólyom László argued that the "forced attempt at assimilation" of the Hungarian minorities in Slovakia contradicted the human rights laws of the EU (*European Radio Network*, August 4, 2009).[1] Likewise, rhetoric from some members of the European Parliament suggested the policy did not "correspond to European standards" and was a step back toward a "totalitarian state" (EPP Group in the European Parliament, press release, July 9, 2009). Although some of these charters and conventions are legally nonbinding, the normative argument is that minorities are less likely to be disenfranchised (Fidrmuc, Ginsburgh, and Weber 2007) and more likely to be confident in political institutions (Liu and Baird 2012) when their languages are recognized by their government.

Orthogonal to the first dimension is the second: the nativity of the recognized language (see Figure 2.2). At one end, the language is considered the mother tongue of a significant portion of the domestic population. A population is considered significant if either (1) there are more than one million speakers or (2) the speakers constitute at least 1 percent of the country's population. This criterion was established by the Summer Institute of Linguistics (SIL). SIL was founded in 1934 to document Central American languages to facilitate translations of the Bible. Since then, SIL has developed a database cataloguing languages of the world (*Ethnologue*). Today, *Ethnologue* (Lewis 2009) is arguably the most comprehensive encyclopedic reference to date (see Ginsburgh and Weber 2011: 30).

At the other end of the nativity dimension is what sociolinguistics calls a lingua franca. A lingua franca is a third party's language, a language of interethnic communication (Crystal 2003: 271). In other words, it is a language spoken by many but is the mother tongue of few—if any. There are three—although not always mutually exclusive—sources for a lingua franca (Ostler 2010: 66). The most common is conquest. Between the sixteenth and eighteenth centuries, the use of

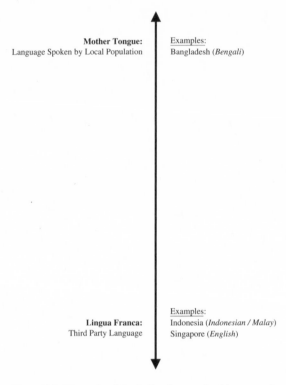

Figure 2.2. Dimension 2 (nativity of recognized languages).

Portuguese was extensive along the coasts of Asia. The prominence of Portuguese as a lingua franca is most impressive not just for its geographic spread but also for its continued use even after the decline of the Portuguese empire. The Dutch, who replaced the Portuguese in Southeast Asia, for example, opted to maintain the linguistic status quo. Not only did commerce continue in Portuguese but so did church services (Ostler 2010: 395–403). Another example of a conquering lingua franca is Russian. In contrast to the Portuguese who settled for spices and souls, the spread of Russian was strictly the result of Cossack military expansion (fourteenth to eighteenth centuries). And even though it "never became a prestige language" and "remains a highly ideological language," Russian is still a language of practical communication today in some parts of the former Soviet Union (421–46)

In addition to colonialism, religion can also be a source for a lingua franca. Consider the status of Arabic. The use of Arabic in lands far beyond the Middle

East coincided with the spread of Islam. Unlike its Protestant counterpart, Islam has held firmly to the principle that the words of Allah as revealed to Prophet Mohammad, the Qur'an, can be neither changed nor successfully translated (Ostler 2006: 94–96). Another example of a religious lingua franca is Sanskrit. When the emperors of the Maurya Empire (321–185 BCE) unified the Indian subcontinent and when Ashoka embraced Buddhism, the use of Sanskrit was promoted (Thapar 2012). The language—and its script—would eventually expand throughout Asia with traders and missionaries (Ostler 2006: 174–79).

The third source for a lingua franca is commerce. The rise and prominence of Phoenician in the second and first millennia BCE is one example. Phoenician was a language spoken in multiple cities along the coast of present-day Lebanon. These cities were not political units, but rather economic centers. As merchants from these cities traded across the Mediterranean as far as Northwest Africa and the Iberian Peninsula, their language would also spread (Ostler 2006: 44–46, 68–72). Malay is another example of a commercially derived lingua franca. Malay was the language of merchants in the East Indies. Malacca, strategically located on the Strait of Malacca, played a primary role in this linguistic spread. The use of Malay—specifically "bazaar Malay"—further expanded when the Dutch East India Company monopolized trade in the archipelago in the seventeenth and eighteenth centuries (Bertrand 2003: 269). Practical motivations (e.g., the ease of using a regional language for commercial transactions throughout the East Indies) and political considerations (e.g., a general unwillingness to use Dutch with colonial subjects) led the Dutch to expand the role of Malay as a lingua franca (Bertrand 2003; Ostler 2006: 400–401).

There is one important caveat when it comes to identifying a language as a lingua franca. No language is a lingua franca in all contexts (Ostler 2010: xvii–xviii). For instance, in the aforementioned examples, Portuguese was a lingua franca in the East Indies, but it was not the language of "interethnic communication" in Portugal. Instead, it was the language of the majority. Likewise, Malay was a language of trade in Southeast Asia; but it was also the language of the majority in the Thai-Malay Peninsula. As another illustration, consider the status of English. In the present day, it is hard to dispute that English is the language of globalization. From Singapore to South Africa, it is the lingua franca. But the same cannot be said in the United Kingdom. There, English remains the language of the numerical and politically dominant majority. Even with the revival of Gaelic (Crowley 2005) and Welsh (Cardinal and Denault 2007), it is still not the language of a third party. Likewise, English is not considered a lingua franca in either the United States or Australia. In both countries, English is the mother tongue of the majority. The distinction is important because the origins of English use—and the identity of its present-day speakers—outside England are different (Ostler 2006: chap. 12; 2010: chap. 1). To put it in primordial terms, in the American and Australian cases, English is the language of one ethnic group. In contrast, in Singapore and South Africa, there is no (significant) English ethnic group. In these cases, English became the language of interethnic communication upon independence.

In addition to English, two other languages proved challenging for conceptualization and coding. The first is Arabic. Classical Arabic is the dialect of the Prophet. The prestige of the Qur'an makes it a lingua franca for Muslims. And while countries of the Middle East and North Africa—from Morocco to Egypt to Saudi Arabia—have designated "classical Arabic" as their official language, it is not a true lingua franca in the sense of English in Singapore or South Africa. There are two related reasons. First, classical Arabic is not the mother tongue of any Arab. This is an extreme case of what sociolinguists call diglossia. Diglossia is a situation where two dialects, sometimes mutually unintelligible, operate simultaneously in a society. The dialect of higher prestige is used most often by the government, in the education system, and in formal texts. In contrast, the dialect of lower prestige is generally spoken by the broader population (Ferguson 1959). Other examples of diglossia include Chinese, Greek, and Hebrew. However, Arabic is arguably the only present case of such extremity. For instance, while Mandarin Chinese is the dialect of higher prestige and the lingua franca of the Chinese community, it is still the mother tongue for a sizable subpopulation (Kaplan and Baldauf 2003: 47). The same cannot be said for classical Arabic (M. Ibrahim 1985; Matthews 2007). Second, because of diglossia, the de facto official language is the Arabic dialect of the politically dominant. In Egypt, the dialect of larger communication is Egyptian Arabic; and in Jordan, it is Levantine Arabic (Leclerc 2010). The use of the politically dominant "dialect" as an official language in a country with heterogeneity of dialects renders that dialect the politically dominant "language" in these cases.

The other language of a more subjective nature is Russian. Two policies from the Soviet era made coding difficult. First, there were mass migrations, some forced and others voluntary. As a result of these movements, there were sizable Russian populations outside of Russia when the Soviet Union collapsed (Fierman 2006; Laitin 1998; Lieven and McGarry 1993). Second, although Russian was never declared the exclusive official language of the Soviet Union, its status as first among equals was undisputed. For instance, Russian was a compulsory subject in all schools (Grenoble 2003). The first policy rendered Russian a language of the minority in the non-Russian Soviet republics; but the second policy meant Russian became the medium of interethnic communication (Pavlenko 2006). Here, we see the uniqueness of Russian. Very few other colonial languages—if any—were both a minority language and a language of interethnic communication simultaneously in the same country, not even English. This tension is highlighted, for example, in Turkmenistan's 1990 Language Act. As stipulated in Article 1, Turkmen is the official language. But as noted in Article 2, Russian is the language of "inter-national communication." In the former Soviet states, I consider Russian—because of the sizable population—a minority language unless the constitution explicitly acknowledges it as a lingua franca, as is the case in Turkmenistan.

Language Regime Type

Having discussed the two dimensions of interest—number and nativity of recognized languages—I can now identify the different types of language regimes. Combining the two dimensions generates a two-by-two *conceptual typology*. Note that a conceptual typology aims to "explicate the meaning of a concept [in this case, language regime] by mapping out its dimensions, which correspond to the rows and columns in the typology" (D. Collier, LaPorte, and Seawright 2012: 218). Conceptual typologies are distinct from *explanatory typologies* where the rows and columns are the explanatory variables (218).

As illustrated in Figure 2.3, each language regime is characterized by its placement along two dimensions: how many languages (monolingual versus multilingual) along the horizontal axis and whose language (mother tongue of domestic population versus lingua franca) along the vertical axis. In all, there are four types of language regimes, each characterized by a unique distribution of linguistic power: power-concentrating, power-sharing, power-neutralizing, and neutralized-sharing. I discuss each regime in turn.

Power-Concentrating Language Regime

The language regime in the first cell is power-concentrating. These regimes are characterized by the concentration of linguistic power in the mother tongue of one domestic group. The one mother tongue is usually—if not always—that of the politically dominant group. With a few exceptions, the politically dominant

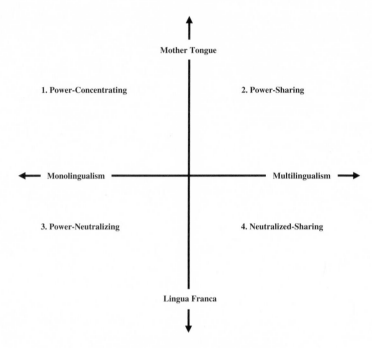

Figure 2.3. Language regime classification.

group is also numerically the largest group. In Bangladesh, for instance, all linguistic power is concentrated in Bengali, a language spoken by 80 percent of the population. Ever since its secession from Pakistan, the government has promoted only Bengali. There have been no attempts whatsoever, legally or symbolically, to allow other languages (e.g., Chittagonian and Sylhetti) to be used in the courtrooms or the classrooms (Callahan 2003). Likewise, in Nepal, during the monarchy period (1954–1990), Nepali (43 percent) was the exclusive language of the government, courts, and police. The trend was paralleled in the education curriculum. The 1971–1976 National Education System required Nepali as the medium of instruction even in English private schools. Furthermore, publications in other native languages of Nepal (e.g., Bhojpuri, Magar, Maithili, and Newar) were discouraged if not banned (Eagle 2000).

Here, it is important to bear in mind that the definition of a power-concentrating language regime is strictly about the choice to recognize one mother tongue. It is not about the actual demographics of the country. For instance, ex ante expectations would suggest a country with a more homogeneous population (e.g., Korea, 99 percent Korean) would have an easier time than the likes of Nepal adopting a power-concentrating language regime. In fact, the former has no incentive to choose a language regime that is not power-concentrating. Consequently, an argument can be made that to include these virtually impossible negative cases (the Koreas) with the Nepals can end up introducing bias in subsequent analyses (Mahoney and Goertz 2004).

While language regime choice was probably less contentious in Korea than in Nepal, there are at least three reasons to combine these two types under the same classification. First, just because a country is homogeneous does not translate automatically into a lack of politics over language regime choice. Both the North and South Korean governments chose to standardize Korean. But how this standardization developed was quite different on the two sides of the thirty-eighth parallel. In the North, Chinese characters and vocabulary were completely eliminated. Before 1991, the one other language allowed in any capacity was Russian. Since 1991, Chinese and English have replaced Russian. In contrast, in the South, there was also an initial effort to remove Chinese characters. When that policy failed, the government issued a list of 1,300 commonly used Chinese characters that would be taught in schools. Supplementing the Chinese was the teaching of English (Kaplan and Baldauf 2003: 34–45). Removing the likes of the Koreas from any sample simply because they are demographically homogeneous risks overlooking potential important politics.

Second, just because a country is currently homogeneous does not guarantee it has always been so. Identities are malleable; they can also vary in their intensity (see Abdelal et al. 2009: 2–4). To assume homogeneity exogenously over time disregards the very fact that the homogeneity could have been endogenously created. Consider Thailand. One of King Chulalongkorn's (1868–1910) major efforts was to promote the "Thai-ness" of the people. This included designating central Thai (15 percent) as the sole language of the kingdom. This was no easy feat considering that at the time, the demographic landscape was an amalgam of languages (e.g., Chinese, Khmer, and Lao) and dialects (e.g., central, northern, northeast, and southern). Moreover, the largest group was the northeasterners (33 percent), who, despite having a mother tongue named "northeastern Thai," spoke a language that was actually more akin to neighboring Laotian. Over the ensuing years, all schools including the monastic institutions adopted the central government curriculum. The King's successors continued in the same vein. One of the palace decrees did away with prefixes that described regional origins. Consequently, central Thai would come to be regarded as standard Thai. Varying degrees of coercion supported the efforts at linguistic standardization. Rebellions were rarely—if ever—a match for the better-equipped and better-organized Siamese military

(Liu and Ricks 2012: 498). The efforts by the palace to cultivate a new Thai identity have been a success. Today, 90 percent of the population claim standard Thai as their primary language (Keyes 1997, 2003; Wyatt 1969). Here, the Thai case highlights the malleability of group identity. To assume a country has always been homogeneous risks conflating the choice of language regime (e.g., power-concentrating in late nineteenth-century Thailand) with the outcome.

Even if a country's homogeneity were apolitical and constant, this raises a third concern over measurement. At what point is a country considered (1) to be sufficiently homogeneous that it is an impossible negative case versus (2) to have a large majority constrained by some minority preference(s)? In the absence of a prior, this cutoff is simply atheoretical. Even if an arbitrary threshold were to be set (e.g., 90 percent majority), this fundamentally would not eliminate the two larger theoretical concerns mentioned above. Given this discussion, when a government recognizes only the mother tongue of one group, and exclusively one group, this language regime is considered power-concentrating, regardless of the country's linguistic homogeneity or whether this monolingualism is the product of coercive assimilation. This is not to say that a country's demographic composition has no bearing on whether a government chooses a power-concentrating language regime. The effects of this variable will be examined in great detail in the empirical tests.

Power-Sharing Language Regime

In the second cell, the language regime is considered power-sharing. These regimes are characterized by the sharing of linguistic power across multiple mother tongues. Here, what is of primary interest is simply *whether* multiple languages are being recognized and *not how* the recognition of one language compares to the recognition of another language (i.e., whether the recognition afforded is equal and fair). Consider three examples of power-sharing, where multiple languages are recognized but the degree of recognition across the languages is different. The first is Canada. There, linguistic power is shared at the *federal* or *national* level between English and French, as stipulated by the Charter of Rights and Freedoms. The two languages are considered equal in all official capacities, from public services to judicial proceedings, from parliamentary debates to classroom teachings. By law, an English speaker in New Brunswick and a French speaker in Alberta have the same right to have any official paperwork and procedure be in their mother tongue.[2] In this example, we can think of the Canadian language regime as being collectively power-sharing where minority languages are protected.

Now consider the second arrangement. In Switzerland, per the 1848 Constitution, linguistic power is shared at the federal level but not at the *cantonal* level. Each canton has the right to choose its official language(s) from the menu of four: French, German, Italian, and Romansh. While all four languages are official at the aggregate national level, there is no guarantee that a speaker of French enjoys the same rights (i.e., having her language recognized as official) in each canton. Put differently, although the languages are considered equal, the power-sharing arrangement in Switzerland is slightly different from that of Canada. In this scenario, the recognition of multiple mother tongues is more like that of partition, where each group has equality in how it treats language matters within its own jurisdiction.

Finally, in the third example, in Malaysia today, only one language is recognized as official for all government services: Malay (majority language: 62 percent). But within the education curriculum, linguistic power is shared across three languages: Malay, Chinese, and Tamil. The latter two are spoken by the two largest minority populations. Without a doubt, when compared to either Canada or Switzerland, this linguistic arrangement seems highly inequitable. This is more in line with what Brendan O'Leary, Ian Lustick, and Thomas Callaghy (2001) call hierarchical control regimes.

Yet, relative to the other Southeast Asian countries (most notably Burma and Thailand), the linguistic recognition afforded to the two minority languages in Malaysia today is substantial. For the purposes of this book, the fact that *some* linguistic power is shared with the non-Malay languages renders this language regime power-sharing. This is not to say that all power-sharing linguistic arrangements are the same or always equitable. This is especially pronounced in federations where the rules of language use can vary substantially across government levels or subnational units.[3] It was perhaps not a coincidence that all three examples cited here are federations. The empirical tests will take into consideration the effects of federalism.

Power-Neutralizing Language Regime

The third type of language regime is power-neutralizing. These regimes are characterized by the exclusive recognition of a lingua franca; no mother tongue is recognized (Cell 3). In Indonesia, Malay (subsequently renamed "Indonesian" in 1945) is the one and only language of the state. Today, it is the only language of public instruction at the primary, secondary, *and* tertiary levels of education. Similarly, in Papua New Guinea, a lingua franca reigns supreme. The country is home to over eight hundred languages, and, according to *Ethnologue*, is the most linguistically diverse place in the world (Lewis 2009). In spite of this heterogeneity, English, the language of the colonial authorities, is the exclusive language of government services and public education (May 2003). The status of English in Papua New Guinea classifies the language regime for the purposes of this book as power-neutralizing.

Note that even with a power-neutralizing language regime, fairness across all linguistic groups—at least in an absolute sense—is a rarity (if not an impossibility). Some groups have an inherent advantage because of the linguistic proximity between their language and the lingua franca. For example, one argument levied against Esperanto, a genuine language of interethnic communication, when it was first introduced (but ultimately never materialized) is that it is based on the grammatical structure of Indo-European languages. So while it may be an easy language for a Spanish-speaker to learn, the same may not hold true for a speaker of a Sino-Tibetan language (e.g., Chinese). Additionally, other groups will have an inherent advantage because of previous exposure to the lingua franca. In Indonesia, for example, although Malay had been a widespread commercial lingua franca in the region, the language did not necessarily reach equally to all the islands in the archipelago (e.g., Papua and Timor). For the purposes of this book, a power-neutralizing language regime is defined not by whether each linguistic group is equally advantaged (or disadvantaged) by the choice of a given lingua franca. Instead, what is of primary interest is that all relevant bargaining groups forfeit claims to their mother tongues and agree to the exclusive use of a lingua franca.

Neutralized-Sharing Language Regime

The last type of language regime is a hybrid: it recognizes both a lingua franca and a set of mother tongues (Cell 4). Here, which mother tongues and how many mother tongues are recognized have no bearing. All that matters is that at least one mother tongue is recognized. These regimes are akin to what Laitin (1992: 18–19) has characterized as a 3±1 language regime. In postcolonial countries, efforts at state rationalization often resulted in the recognition of the politically dominant mother tongue, a domestically regional mother tongue (if it is different from the politically dominant language), possibly an even more local language, and a lingua franca. The Philippine language regime is one example. The language of the politically dominant group in the Philippines is Tagalog (25 percent). In spite of the difference in name, present day Filipino—one of the two official languages—is Tagalog. English is the other official language. Both Tagalog and English dominate the education system in the Philippines (Gonzalez 1999; Kaplan and Baldauf 2003: 75, 77).

Another example of a neutralized-sharing language regime is India's. In India, the Eighth Schedule protects twenty-two indigenous languages. English is also effectively a permanent official language. Every fifteen years, Congress meets to renew the "temporary" status of English. This neutralized-sharing arrangement did not evolve overnight. In 1965, when the temporary status of English as an official language was set to expire, the national government pushed forward with policies designating Hindi, the plurality language (41 percent), as the sole language. In response, Tamil-speakers (7.4 percent) organized widespread agitation (Das Gupta 1970: 190–96). The result, after a lengthy period of mass violence and government-sponsored repression, was the adoption of the Twenty-First Amendment. The amendment would recognize fifteen state languages (Stuligross and Varshney 2002). Since then, seven more languages have been added to the list: Konkani, Manipuri, and Nepali in 1992 (Seventy-First Amendment); and Bodo, Dogri, Maithili, and Santali in 2003 (Ninety-Second Amendment).[4]

Note that neither the power-neutralizing nor the neutralized-sharing language regime precludes the recognition of multiple lingua francas. In Timor-Leste, there is more than one language of interethnic communication. On independence, there were four languages on the menu, of which only one was indigenous: Tétum. One lingua franca was Portuguese, the language of conquest. Timor-Leste had been a Portuguese colony dating back to the sixteenth century. The argument in favor of Portuguese was that it would connect the country to a larger economic alliance that included Brazil and Portugal. Another lingua franca was Indonesian. Indonesian was both a language of conquest (1975–2002) and a language of commerce. Use of the language would facilitate trade with the other Southeast Asian countries. The third lingua franca was English. English had the advantage of being the language of Australia, Timor-Leste's southern neighbor. It was also seen as the language of the global economy (Hull 2000; Mydans 2007). This discussion about Timor-Leste demonstrates clearly the various sources from which a lingua franca can originate and the prevalence of lingua francas.

The primary interest of this book is the choice to recognize a lingua franca. What explains why groups figuratively forfeit power—*any* power—to a third party language; and second, what are the effects of this forfeiture? But as discussed above, this choice can be either exclusive or in conjunction with minority languages. To test (1) whether *any* neutralization is better for economic growth than *no* recognition of a lingua franca; and (2) whether *more* recognition is better than *less* recognition, this book employs two different coding schemes (to be discussed later in the chapter).

Universe of Cases

To test arguments about language regime choice and the economic effects of that choice, this book employs multiple methods. The first is a large N statistical analysis of Asian countries (1945–2005). This test achieves two purposes. One is to demonstrate *whether* there is any face validity to the argument. If there is face validity—and depending on the results from the second test—the relevant regressions may be evidence of the generalizability of the argument. The second test is detailed process-tracing of two countries: Malaysia and Singapore. These two cases were selected from a pool of on-the-regression-line observations (Lieberman 2005: 436–38). Additionally, the two countries shared a similar colonial history and were in fact in the same political unit 1963–1965. This setup rules out a number of alternative explanations: factors that are the same between two cases by construct cannot explain why two cases have different outcomes (Przeworski and Teune 1970: 32–34; Seawright and Gerring 2008: 304–5). By focusing on the two cases (and over two periods in each case), I can demonstrate *why* the purported causal mechanisms were in play.

Quantitative: Asia 1945–2005

The quantitative sample includes all countries in Asia 1945–2005. Here, the scope of "Asia" is broadly conceived. Geographically, it spans from Cyprus[5] and Turkey in the west to Japan and the Philippines in the east; from Kazakhstan and Russia in the north to Maldives and Timor-Leste in the south. In all there are fifty-four countries in the sample for a theoretical total N of 2,185. The unit of analysis is *country-year*. Note that because of the temporal nature of the sample, the vast majority of the countries are third-world, postcolonial states.

The choice to focus on Asia was driven by several considerations. First, Asia is merely a geographical concept. It is the land mass east of the Urals and Volga; and it is the land mass separated from Africa by the Suez Canal. As a result of this exogenous identification, there is little, if any, common denominator. Asia, as defined, was historically the site of multiple competing imperial powers, and only recently has it been home to multiple nation-states (Darwin 2008). In this region, there is greater postcolonial diversity than in either Africa or Eastern Europe. This region is also home to greater linguistic and religious diversity than Latin America. In short, diversity is one of the few shared characteristics across these fifty-four countries, rendering the region a good sample of the world.

Consider Southeast Asia. In this subset of only eleven states, there is heterogeneity of languages and world religions (e.g., Buddhism, Catholicism, Hinduism, and Islam); of colonial legacies (American, British, Dutch, French, Japanese, Portuguese, Spanish, and no legacy whatsoever); of political systems (e.g., democracies, hegemonic parties, military juntas, and monarchies) and government ideologies; and of economic models and development (e.g., East Asian tigers, newly industrialized countries, and failed states).

This extensive cultural, political, and economic diversity makes Asia a good representative sample in which to compare and test the choice of language regimes and the economic effects of these choices.[6] This diversity helps reduce the likelihood of spurious correlations or selection bias because of some shared geographical, cultural, or political trait. While a global cross-national sample would be ideal, there was a practical constraint. Detailed yearly information on language regimes is frequently absent or inconsistent in African and Latin American countries. This fact not only makes data collection extremely difficult, but also raises a number of validity and reliability concerns. Asia is not free of quirks. There have been civil wars, and there have been failed states. In both instances, to identify the language regime was challenging. Moreover, the Asia sample boasts a few instances when the education system was completely shut down and schooling was outright banned. This is important, as the medium of instruction is a good measure of language regime type (more in the following section). In 1975–1979, the Khmer Rouge of Cambodia saw education as a tool of the bourgeoisie. In an effort to return the country to a classless agrarian state, books were burned and teachers were killed (Short 2006: chap. 9). The data after this period were less than clear. However, it was possible to triangulate from a number of sources to increase confidence in the validity of the measurement.

Qualitative: Malaysia Versus Singapore

From a theoretical standpoint, Malaysia and Singapore, two former British colonies in Southeast Asia, lend themselves naturally to a most similar design

(George and Bennett 2005: 153–60). Most similar designs use two or more cases that are largely similar on as many dimensions as possible. The key, however, is that these cases differ in the primary explanatory variable and in the outcome of interest. With such construction, any alternative variable that has the same value between the cases cannot logically be an explanation. For this book, Malaysia and Singapore offer such a design. Not only do the two countries share a number of similarities, they both also experience language regime changes after a critical juncture. These changes allow for an additional most similar design in each country over time. Altogether, the two countries with the two temporal periods offer a total of four causal-process observations (D. Collier, Brady, and Seawright 2004: 252–63).

Arguably, the most important factor in case selection has to do with relevance: was language even an issue? For instance, if there had been no discussion whatsoever about language in either case, then any examination of the politics surrounding language regime choice and the implications of this choice could be rendered spurious. In contrast, if language was an important matter, this makes the understanding of language regimes and its surrounding politics possible. As it turns out, in both countries, language was recognized as fundamental to state-building. It was a salient and urgent matter. Tunku Abdul Rahman and Lee Kuan Yew, the first prime ministers of Malaysia and Singapore, respectively, both elaborated at great length on this issue in their memoirs (see K. Y. Lee 1998, 2000; Rahman Putra 1978, 1986). Moreover, in Malaysia, language policies fall under the rubric of "sensitive issues." As suggested in the amendment to the 1948 Sedition Act, raising these issues can be construed as seditious—an offense punishable by five years' imprisonment. In short, the salience of this issue makes the study of language regimes in these two cases both easier and all that much more necessary.

Aside from relevance, the two countries have a number of similarities on what could be alternative explanations. For instance, the two countries are both culturally diverse. Demographically, the likelihood that any two people chosen at random will speak different languages is 0.747 in Malaysia and 0.773 in Singapore (Lewis 2009). Although Malaysia is indigenously more heterogeneous than Singapore, both countries were historical destinations for two groups of immigrants. First, the Chinese migrated to Southeast Asia in two waves. One wave was characterized by Hokkien-speaking men from the Fujian province who would marry local women (Skinner 1958). The second wave came from a variety of provinces in China, where dialects other than Hokkien were spoken. Moreover, those in the latter wave often remained intentionally self-segregated once they arrived in the new country (Amrith 2011: 38; Skinner 1963). Compared to the first wave, integration was minimal. Concurrent with the Chinese waves was a second group of immigrants. The British brought a large number of Tamil-speaking Indians to work on rubber plantations (Amrith 2011: 48). By the time of independence, the census in the two countries identified the same three demographic groups: Chinese, Indians, and Malays.[7]

In addition to cultural diversity, both countries have been ruled by a hegemonic party since independence (Przeworski et al. 2000: 23–28). In Malaysia, the United Malay National Organization (UMNO)-led Alliance Party and its successor, the National Front (Barisan Nasional), have always commanded a supermajority in Parliament. The only exceptions were in the 1969, 2008, and 2013 elections. With the exception of the 2013 election, the UMNO-led party has always won more than 50 percent of the vote and the majority of the seats. Likewise, the People's Action Party (PAP) has long dominated Singapore politics. The worst electoral performances to date were in 1991 and 2011 when the PAP won 60 percent of the votes. Aside from their hegemonic presence, the two parties share a number of other political features, including British-educated founding fathers, multicultural visions, and anticommunist ideologies.

There are other commonalities. One is wealth. While Singapore's economy has grown faster than Malaysia's and has shown few signs of slowing down, this trend ignores the fact that the economic state in both countries at independence was unimpressive. Neither country had a GDP per capita above US$435. Moreover, poverty rates were comparably high. Here, it is important to note that it is precisely the fact that Malaysia and Singapore started at similar points but have since diverged quite significantly that allows for these two cases to be used for testing how language regimes have generated different growth outcomes.

Another similarity between the two countries is their colonial legacy. The British were more likely than their continental European counterparts to leave behind quality institutions (La Porta et al. 1999; Przeworski et al. 2000: 122–28) and multilingual curriculums (Albaugh 2009). Here, any colonial explanation is limited at best. Both Malaysia and Singapore were British colonies.[8] Not only were they subjected to the same governing institutions, but the British strategy for transferring power to the national governments was similarly motivated in both: to neutralize the communist threat. London played an active role to ensure the survival of both states. In the Malaysian case, the British fought the communists in a twelve-year conflict known as the Emergency. In the other case, they helped negotiate Singapore's merger into the Malaysian Federation—a policy at the time believed to be the only mechanism to thwart a communist takeover.

Admittedly, there are differences. One such difference is size. Singapore is a city-state while Malaysia is anything but. One possible reason why size, conceptualized as either area or population, can matter is that smaller entities may be better advantaged to overcome collective action problems (Olson 1965: 53–57; Ostrom 1990: 38–45). However, there are at least two reasons why size is not a concern here. First, while Singapore is relatively smaller than Malaysia, from an absolute standpoint, it is a far cry from the small "groups" and "communities" championed by the likes of Olson and Ostrom. Its population of two million in the 1960s, now over five million, spread across an area larger than Washington, D.C., does not necessarily translate into any concrete advantage. Second, to focus only on size ignores the very fact that Malaysia, despite being a federation, is in some respect a very centralized country. In both countries, many policies—and certainly those that touch on language and education—are passed at the national level. Simply put, while Malaysia dwarfs Singapore in both area and population, there is little theoretical reason to believe size matters in this case.

Operationalism

According to sociolinguist Joshua Fishman (1989), there are at least three arenas where the choice of language use is both political and public: government services, mass media, and primary education. The emphasis in this book is on the third arena, specifically, public education. The focus on education is motivated by three considerations. First, the politics surrounding education reflect the government's "vision of the country's future" (Albaugh 2009: 394). Education is, after all, a "transmitter and perpetuator of culture" (Kaplan and Baldauf 1997: 123). Education provides the very foundation for government services and mass media. It is not a coincidence that in "every case in which any sort of official language policy activity has been undertaken, the education sector has been involved to some degree, often extensively" (Kaplan and Baldauf 1997: 8). In fact, there have been instances where the "entire burden of planning . . . has been allocated to the education ministry."

Second, education systems can be a prime instrument for the management of ethnic relations. Education can be used to assimilate minorities (Skutnabb-Kangas 2000: chap. 8). It can also be used to socialize students and construct new identities (Wortham and Rymes 2002: chap. 1). Assimilation, after all, can primarily be either "acculturation" or "fusion" (O'Leary and McGarry 2012). After his father's death, King Vajiravudh of Thailand (1910–1925) expressed concern that the failure to assimilate the Chinese population—the "Jews of the East"—into the larger "Thai" identity would threaten national unity. As a result, Chinese schools were required to use standard Thai as a medium of instruction (Vella 1978: 189–96). Likewise, in Turkey, the classification of Kurdish speakers as "Mountain Turks" in the 1930s and 1940s meant their linguistic differences were not recognized—and they were not protected under the 1923 Lausanne Treaty. The 1982 Constitution (Article 42) and its 2001 revision (Article 28) further institutionalized the ban on the Kurdish language (see Aslan 2007). Recently, however, the Turkish state, under the leadership of the Justice and Development Party (AKP), seems likely to soften its previously rigorous exclusion of the Kurdish language. Not all language-in-education policies, of course, are negative or exclusionary. Education can also be a vehicle for preserving an ethnic group. In 1979, the Afghan government implemented the 1975 Education Policy. This policy incorporated Baluchi, Turkmen, and Uzbek, three previously nonrecognized languages, into the primary education system (Cowen and McLean 1983). In Georgia and Iran, the Azeri culture is protected as well. The Azeri minorities in both countries have the option to receive schooling in their own language (Leclerc 2010).

The choice to focus on education here was also motivated by a third consideration. Education is a key forum for early human capital formation (Baum and Lake 2003). An educated workforce is a necessary but not sufficient condition for development. Directly, education increases human capital by teaching skills that enhance productivity (Gradstein, Justman, and Meier 2005: 2–4). Indirectly, education can close the gap in wage differentials (Birdsall, Ross, and Sabot 1997: 93). It is not a coincidence that education was the second largest expenditure (after defense) in Singapore, South Korea, and Taiwan—three of the economic "tigers" noted in the 1993 World Bank "East Asian Miracle" report. Literacy is clearly important, yet there has been very little discussion on the language of literacy. Thus it is imperative to have a measure of the type of language use in the classrooms.

In contrast to Joshua Fishman (1989) who looks only at primary education, this book expands the focus to secondary education. Moreover, for the case studies, the scope encompasses tertiary education. The rationale for looking beyond primary education is twofold. First, the validity of the measurement—distribution of linguistic power—is greater when the analysis is not artificially truncated at the primary level and the focus is instead across multiple levels of education. Consider two possible scenarios. In one, a singular mother tongue is used throughout the primary level. However, a lingua franca is the exclusive medium at the secondary level. In another, one mother tongue is the sole language of instruction at both the primary and secondary levels. If the focus were only on primary education, the two cases would both be considered "power-concentrating" when in reality the distribution of linguistic power is clearly different.

The second reason to incorporate secondary education has to do with the reliability of measurement. Given the comparative interest of this book, it is necessary to have a consistent unit of measurement. Unfortunately, the use of primary education is highly inconsistent. The number of years of primary education varies not only across cases but also within cases. Consider the United States for instance. In some districts, "elementary school" is five years; in others, six years. Furthermore, "middle school" or "junior high" provides additional discrepancy over whether it should be constituted as primary or secondary education. According to the U.S. census, this block of two or three years (another source of possible confusion) is considered a part of the primary education. Secondary education is defined solely as the four years of "high school." In contrast, the United Nations Educational, Scientific, and Cultural Organization (UNESCO) considers the "middle school" block as a part of secondary education. American primary education, according to UNESCO, is strictly six years. The American example highlights the potential for coding error. The likelihood of error only increases in cases such as China where the education system is divided into four tiers and in cases such as Thailand where the education system was significantly restructured (1978).

To ensure reliability, this book focuses on both primary and secondary education. The above reasons should in principle extend as well to tertiary education. However, tertiary education is not always widely available and easily accessible. This is especially true in poorer countries where tertiary education can sometimes look like a club good rather than a public good. The quantitative tests therefore do not include tertiary education. This concern, however, is less pressing in the cases of Malaysia and Singapore. Accordingly, the qualitative sections of this book do take into consideration university education.

Finally, the emphasis on public education (as opposed to private education) has to do with direct government control. In principle, public education is the "ideological state apparatus" (Althusser 1971: 141) that broadcasts the government's vision of which languages can be used, and which identities it wishes to encourage. In contrast, there are two types of private education. The first type is financed and controlled by foreigners. Examples include Chinese schools in Thailand run by Chinese businessmen; English schools operated by American missionaries in the Philippines; and French schools in Cambodia run by the French Embassy. The number of languages taught in such schools is far beyond the scope of interest for this book. Furthermore, in a number of countries (e.g., South Korea and Taiwan), only holders of a foreign passport may attend international schools. This effectively creates an educational sphere that is of little relevance to the analysis in this book.

The second type of private education is operated independently at the local level. Finances come not from the state but from wealthy donors, religious institutions (e.g., churches, mosques, synagogues, or temples), or tuition. In contrast to the international schools, locals may attend and pay their way through these schools. While these schools are private, they are still subject to the laws of the country. If the education ministry stipulates only a certain language may be used in the curriculum, the private school must operate in that one language. During the Nepalese monarchy, missionaries operated a large number of private schools. These schools, however, were by law required to use Nepali as the language of instruction (Eagle 2000). Likewise, in Sri Lanka in 1961, missionary schools were required to phase out English so that by the 1970s English would only be taught as a subject (DeVotta 2003: 130–31).

To measure language regime, this book focuses primarily on the medium of instruction. A careful distinction must be made here between language as a subject and language as a medium of instruction (Liu 2011: 129–30). The former is about the instruction *of*, the latter, instruction *in* (Mowbray 2012: 25–26; italics in original). The fact that a language is taught does not necessarily imply it is a language of instruction. With subject recognition, the entire education curriculum is taught and carried out in some language x. During an allotted period in the x-language curriculum (e.g., forty-five minutes a day, five days a week), students can learn another language y. The status of aboriginal languages in Australia is an example of subject recognition. Across the country, about twenty different aboriginal languages are taught, but only as subjects. As the Education, Training, and Employment Ministry recently reaffirmed, the language of "writing, arithmetic, and techniques" remains exclusively English (Leclerc 2010).

In contrast, a language is considered a medium of instruction if it is used to teach the nonlanguage classes (e.g., history, math, and sciences) specifically and to carry out the curriculum broadly. In the Australian example, English is a medium of instruction. Another example of medium recognition is the status of both English and French in Canada. Although French is the language of the minority (22 percent), French-speaking students have the right to be "educated in their own

language at public expense, even if they are in the minority in any given province"
(Schmidt 1998: 49). In theory, the law applies as well to English speakers in
Francophone Quebec.

Quantitative Measures

Focusing on the medium of instruction, this book employs two different quantitative coding schemes. The first scheme is a quadrachotomous categorical measure. It separates the power-neutralizing language regimes that employ a lingua
franca exclusively (e.g., Indonesia) from those that recognize a lingua franca in
conjunction with other mother tongues (e.g., India). By classifying language regimes that correspond to each of the four cells in Figure 2.3, this measure will
allow for the examination of the conditions under which governments neutralize
at all and whether *any* neutralization is economically better than *none*. A language
regime is coded as "power-neutralizing" if the only medium of instruction is a
lingua franca. If there is a lingua franca, but it is recognized in conjunction with
a mother tongue, then the language regime is considered a "neutralized-sharing"
language regime. So for instance, the language regime in Indonesia (lingua
franca only) is considered power-neutralizing, but the Philippines (plurality language and lingua franca) and India (plurality language, minority languages, and
lingua franca) are both coded as neutralized-sharing.

Among those not considered power-neutralizing, a language regime is coded
as "power-concentrating" if and only if one mother tongue is recognized; and
"power-sharing" otherwise. The Bengali language regime recognizes neither a
minority language nor English (lingua franca). The language of the majority
(Bengali) has been the sole language of primary and secondary education (Mohsin 2003). This coding scheme produces a four-point categorical variable.

In principle, all language regimes are power-concentrating, power-sharing,
power-neutralizing, or neutralized-sharing.[9] This coding scheme, while parsi-
monious, is also blunt. For example, English (lingua franca) was never the exclusive medium of instruction in Malaysia. But in 1972, as a part of the New
Economic Policy, English was gradually removed (Š. Ganguly 2003: 250–52).
The quadrachotomous categorical variable cannot capture this trend. Based on
the coding scheme, there would only be a change between 1978 and 1979 when the
conversion of all English secondary schools into Malay instruction was completed. What is needed is an alternative measure that can reflect these gradual
decreases in the use of English.

In response to this need, the second coding scheme is a continuous measure. Specifically, it measures the degree of power-neutralization ($x_{LF} : x_{LF} \in [0,1]$): the number of years a lingua franca (LF) is available as a medium of instruction in primary and secondary education ($n_{LF} : n_{LF} \in Z$) over the total number of years all languages—politically dominant (D), politically nondominant (d), and lingua franca—are available as mediums ($n_D + n_{d1} + \cdots + n_{d(k-1)} + n_{LF}$) in a given year. This is mathematically expressed as follows, where k is the number of linguistic groups in the country in year t:

$$x_{LF}(country\text{-}year\ t) = \frac{n_{LF}}{n_D + n_{d1} + \cdots + n_{d(k-1)} + n_{LF}}$$

$$= \frac{n_{LF}}{n_D + \sum_{i=1}^{k-1} n_{di} + n_{LF}}. \tag{2.1}$$

Theoretically and mathematically, the possible values for x_{LF} range from a minimum of 0 (no power-neutralization whatsoever) to a maximum of 1 (complete power-neutralization). A couple of illustrations may help. First, consider the language regime in Thailand. Ever since 1939, the Thai government has recognized standard Thai as the exclusive medium of instruction (Keyes 2003). This is the case at both the primary and secondary levels (for a combined twelve years of schooling). Substituting this information into the above Equation 2.1 yields the following values for every year (e.g., 1972) for the Thailand case:

$$x_{LF}(Thailand\text{-}1972) = \frac{n_{LF}}{n_D + \sum_{i=1}^{k-1} n_{di} + n_{LF}}$$

$$= \frac{0}{12+0+0} = 0.000. \tag{2.2}$$

Now consider the aforementioned Malaysian example. In 1972, Malay and English were both languages of instruction at the primary (six years) and secondary (seven years) levels for a combined total of thirteen years. In addition, Chinese and Tamil were also mediums of primary education. Substituting this information into Equation 2.1 yields the following degree of power-neutralization:

$$x_{LF}(Malaysia\text{-}1972) = \frac{n_{LF}}{n_D + \sum_{i=1}^{k-1} n_{di} + n_{LF}}$$

$$= \frac{13}{13+6+6+13} = 0.342. \tag{2.3}$$

But 1972 was the last year of full English-medium education. All English-medium schools would subsequently be converted into Malay-medium schools. In 1973, the government began with the first year of primary education. The conversion was completed in 1979. This change in language-in-education policy corresponds to a shift in the degree of power-neutralization:

$$x_{LF}(Malaysia\text{-}1973) = \frac{n_{LF}}{n_D + \sum_{i=1}^{k-1} n_{di} + n_{LF}}$$

$$= \frac{12}{13+6+6+12} = 0.324, \tag{2.4}$$

$$x_{LF}(Malaysia\text{-}1979) = \frac{n_{LF}}{n_D + \sum_{i=1}^{k-1} n_{di} + n_{LF}}$$

$$= \frac{0}{13+6+6+0} = 0.000. \tag{2.5}$$

Here, the decreasing emphasis on English in the Malaysian curriculum between 1972 and 1979 is appropriately reflected by the decreasing value of x_{LF}. This continuous measurement captures both expansions and contractions in the use of a lingua franca. This allows for the understanding of why some governments neutralize more than others, and subsequently, whether *more* neutralization is better than *less* for the economy.

The data for both measures are drawn from a mix of different sources. Jacques Leclerc's (2010) database on language policies (*L'aménagement linguistique dans le monde*), which covers all countries, provided the initial information for most entries. For missing data and to ensure validity, the coding from this database was supplemented with other secondary sources, including encyclopedias (*Encyclopedia of Education, International Encyclopedia of Higher Education*, and *International Handbook of Education Systems*), book series (the Language Policy and Planning series from Multilingual Matters and the Studies of Nationalities series from Hoover Institution Press), and several other individual books (M. Brown and Š. Ganguly 2003; Grenoble 2003; Kaplan and Baldauf 2003; and Landau and Kellner-Heinkele 2001).[10]

Qualitative Measures

In contrast to the coding scheme discussed above where the focus is on the de jure education laws, the emphasis in the case studies is on the de facto arrangement in the curriculum. Just because all languages are recognized equally by law as mediums of instruction does not imply that they are de facto equal. To identify which language, if any, is first among equals, the focus includes languages as subjects. Consider a curriculum where the politically dominant and politically nondominant languages are both recognized as mediums of instruction. Children from either linguistic group can attend school where they learn their history, math, and sciences in their mother tongues. But there is a caveat. The politically nondominant curriculum requires compulsory learning of the politically dominant language as a subject alongside the history, math, and science classes. The converse, however, is not true. Students in the politically dominant curriculum are not required to learn even the basics of the politically nondominant language. From a de jure standpoint, this language regime would be considered power-sharing in the quantitative analysis. But from a de facto one, the linguistic arrangement is more concentrated in the language of the politically dominant than shared equally across all groups.

Another way to gauge which language is first among equals is to identify the medium of instruction not only at the primary and secondary levels (as done in the quantitative sections) but also at the tertiary level. Given the relative scarcity of public universities (compared to elementary schools), the costs to operate them, and the human capital potential of university graduates, it should come as no surprise that tertiary education is the least diverse when it comes to language use in the classrooms. For instance, despite the number of bilingual charter schools in the United States, at the tertiary level the one and only medium of instruction is English. This arrangement reflects the linguistic reality of the country: English is the de facto official language. In short, the medium of instruction at the tertiary level provides an alternative indicator for identifying a country's de facto language regime.

As a preview, Malaysia and Singapore both started out with neutralized-sharing language regimes (Cell 4). There was some combination of a lingua franca with multiple mother tongues. But with time, the two language regimes would change in different directions. Malaysia's shifted to power-concentration in the politically dominant language; Singapore's, to power-neutralization with the exclusive use of a lingua franca (Cell 3).

Conclusion

Language regimes are political institutions. They institutionalize the distribution of linguistic power along two key dimensions: number and nativity of recognized
languages. In all, there are four types of language regimes. One concentrates linguistic power in the mother tongue of the politically dominant; another shares linguistic power across multiple mother tongues; the third neutralizes linguistic
power with the use of a lingua franca; and the fourth is a hybrid that recognizes
a lingua franca and some set of mother tongues. Regardless of its sources (e.g.,
conquest, religion, or commercialism), and whether it is recognized singularly
or in conjunction with other languages, the use of a lingua franca occurs at a
much greater frequency than is properly acknowledged. This is the case both
theoretically and empirically. Table 2.1 shows the distribution of linguistic
power among the 104 countries that secured independence between 1945 and
2000.

Almost half the countries (forty-eight) recognized a lingua franca in some
capacity at independence. Of the forty-eight countries, there were a few more
neutralized-sharing language regimes than power-neutralizing ones. Compare these
numbers to those for power-concentrating (twenty-four) and power-sharing
(thirty-two). This highlights the frequency of a lingua franca as an alternative
when distributing linguistic power. Third parties are important, yet they are often
ignored (for an exception, see Laitin 2000: 151). To ignore these languages of
interethnic communication merely relegates something of extreme substantive
importance to a residual category. In the next chapters, this book examines (1)
the conditions under which governments recognize a lingua franca and (2) the
economic implications of choosing either a power-neutralizing or neutralized-
sharing language regime.

Table 2.1: Global Distribution of Linguistic Power

Cell	Language regime	N (%)
1	Power-Concentrating	24 (23.1%)
2	Power-Sharing	32 (30.8%)
3	Power-Neutralizing	22 (21.2%)
4	Neutralized-Sharing	26 (25.0%)

Appendix

Source	Geographical and temporal coverage
Primary database	
L'aménagement linguistique dans le monde (Leclerc 2010)	All countries
Encyclopedia references	
Encyclopedia of Education (1971)	Cambodia, Iran, Pakistan, Sri Lanka (*all four countries temporal coverage -1971*)
International Encyclopedia of Higher Education	Iran, Iraq, Pakistan (*-1977*)
International Handbook of Education Systems	Afghanistan, Bangladesh, China, India, Indonesia, Israel, Japan, Jordan, Malaysia, Nepal, Oman, Pakistan, Saudi Arabia, Singapore, Sri Lanka, Syria, Thailand, Turkey, United Arab Emirates (*-1983*)
Book series	
Language Policy and Planning Series (Multilingual Matters)	Japan, Kazakhstan, Kyrgyzstan, Nepal, Philippines, Taiwan, Tajikistan
Studies of Nationalities Series (Hoover Institution Press)	Azerbaijan (*-1992*), Georgia (*-2003*), Kazakhstan (*-1995*), Uzbekistan (*-1990*)
Individual books	
Michael Brown and Šumit Ganguly (2003)	Bangladesh, Burma, China, India, Indonesia, Laos, Malaysia, Pakistan, Philippines, Sri Lanka, Singapore, Taiwan, Thailand, Vietnam (*-2003*)
Lenore Grenoble (2003)	Armenia, Azerbaijan, Georgia, Kazakhstan, Kyrgyzstan, Russia, Tajikistan, Turkmenistan, Uzbekistan (*-1991*)
Robert B. Kaplan and Richard B. Baldauf (2003)	Brunei, Indonesia, Japan, Malaysia, North Korea, Singapore, South Korea, Philippines, Taiwan (*-2003*)
Jacob M. Landau and Barbara Kellner-Heinkele (2001)	Azerbaijan, Kazakhstan, Kyrgyzstan, Tajikistan, Turkmenistan, Uzbekistan (*-2001*)

Sources listed include only those that cover more than one country. Unless otherwise noted, temporal coverage spans from 1945 or year of independence to 2005.

PART II

Language Regime Choice

CHAPTER 3

Language Regime Choice: Theory

What explains language regime choice? This chapter argues that when choosing language regimes, governments must balance between cultural egoism, communicative efficiency, and collective equality. Which of the three components weighs most heavily depends on the level of *politically relevant* linguistic heterogeneity, as I explain below. Discussion begins with Indonesia. Note that while Indonesia motivates the argument, the argument itself does not depend on the Indonesian case. The chapter then lays out the theoretical framework for language regime choice. For ease of interpretation, the discussion (i.e., core results and relevant figures) is largely nonformal; the technical write up has been kept to a minimum. For those interested, the game tree and proofs can be found in the Appendix to the chapter.

An Illustrative Case: Indonesia

During colonial times dating back to 1619, the Dutch—driven primarily by spice demands and secondarily by missionary agendas—invested little in the development of their colony in the East Indies. Western education, for instance, initially was available only in the Dutch language and exclusively to the children of Europeans (Drake 1989: 31–32; Groeneboer 1998: 137–46).[1] It was not until 1893 that schools began admitting indigenous students, but even then they were only accessible to a select group (namely children of traditional native leaders). The larger "schools of the people" (*Volksschool*) did not open until 1907 (Bertrand 2003). This policy of liberalization, however, was superficial and soon disappeared with the onset of the Great Depression and World War II (Reid 1974).

During the Japanese occupation (1942–1945), Dutch was banned and Japanese became the administrative language of the state. At first, the use of Malay was also proscribed. With an initial objective of assimilation throughout the archipelago, the Japanese had the hope of an education curriculum that would mimic that in Japan, including learning the Japanese language. These intentions, however, were quickly shelved as the war continued. Japan recognized that it needed to mobilize the local population to meet intensive capital and labor needs, and for this, Japanese was simply not the appropriate language. Instead, it was Malay. Consequently, there was a policy reversal: while Japanese continued to be taught in schools, all forms of propaganda media operated primarily in Malay. The use of Malay here would have long-term implications. It signaled for the first time the credibility of this lingua franca, certainly in comparison to Dutch (Bertrand 2003; Kaplan and Baldauf 2003; Montinola and Suryadinata 2007).

With the defeat of the Japanese, the Dutch returned and four years of fighting ensued. During this period, the Malay language served as a vehicle for the nationalist movement. It was articulated by the nationalist leaders—from Java, e.g., Sukarno (Adams 1966: 69–77) and Sumatra, e.g., Hatta (Penders 1981: 45–46)— as the language of the future Indonesian state. To challenge the growing momentum of the nationalist movement, the Dutch employed a strategy of divide and conquer: they sought to demarcate multiple ethnically oriented states and to recognize their languages. In Bali, the Dutch promoted the use of Balinese. Similarly, in West Java, the Dutch established the state of "Pasundan" where the Sundanese language reigned supreme (Bertrand 2003).

When the Dutch finally withdrew in 1949, the Indonesian government found itself "morally and mentally need[ing] repairs" and "overwhelmed on all sides" (Sukarno, quoted in Adams 1966: 264). With respect to language regimes, the past couple of decades had been turbulent and the future—with 712 languages—was no more promising. But it was during this "struggle for survival" that Malay (renamed Indonesian in 1945) was chosen. Although Malay is the mother tongue of a trivial subset of the population, its prevalence throughout Southeast Asia as a trading language makes it very much a lingua franca in the Indonesian case (B. Anderson 2006; Mohr 1984; Montolalu and Suryadinata 2007). It should be noted that there had been another possible language regime: the concentration of linguistic power in Javanese. Javanese was a language spoken by roughly half the Indonesian population, including then president Sukarno. It was the language of the "single most creative force in developing the new Indonesia" (B. Anderson 2006: 126). Yet the government rejected this alternative. Why did the government shy away from Javanese and gravitate toward Indonesian?

One explanation suggests that language regime choices are symptoms of ethnic relations, in particular power dynamics. Cultural differences between people can be used in primordial appeals (Geertz 1994). When the opportunity arises, efforts to rally people to primordial attachments can be successful. And when these opportunities involve languages in some capacity, the outcome is a language regime choice. There are, however, two limitations to this type of explanation. First, from a theoretical standpoint, it ignores how group elites mobilize and create ethnic identities through the manipulation of symbols including language (Smith 2000). Ethnicity is malleable, and language repertories can include multiple languages (Laitin 1992: 4–8). Second, from an empirical standpoint, an ethnicity-based argument also fails to explain the events in Indonesia. Javanese was the language of the largest linguistic group. It was also a language of the social elites that had lost some prestige during colonial times (B. Anderson 2006: 196–97). If language regimes are manifestations of ethnic relations, expectations would have been for the Javanese to take advantage of independence and push for a power-concentrating language regime. But this did not happen.

Another explanation often proposed is that language regime choices are the legacies of colonialism. There are two mechanisms that could link colonialism to language regimes. The first is about path-dependence. European colonialists sometimes demarcated people into artificially determined ethnic groups. Based on these demarcations, some languages were recognized, standardized, and developed; other languages, denied. This language regime would remain until the present day (Hirschman 1987; PuruShotam 1998). The second is about substitution. Anticolonialist sentiments evoked mass demands to end the use of the colonial language. This removal, in turn, necessitated an indigenous language to fill the vacuum (Mohr 1984; Montolalu and Suryadinata 2007). Again, there are limitations with a colonial legacy explanation. From a theoretical standpoint, it cannot explain ex ante which of the two mechanisms, path-dependence versus substitution, comes into play. Moreover, in some countries language regimes do change over time. From an empirical standpoint, the second mechanism can account for the choice to replace Dutch—which had been the official language of the colony (Groeneboer 1998)—with an indigenous language. But the substitution mechanism as it stands cannot account for the choice of Indonesian over Javanese.

A third and common explanation is that language regimes are instruments in nation-building. With independence, postcolonial political elites believed that a coherent national identity was necessary for the effective functioning of political institutions (Deutsch 1953; R. Ganguly 2003). In response to this need, governments often used language, a traditional ethnic marker, to give the modern nation "historical authenticity, and thus legitimacy" (D. Brown 2009). On one view, nations form when people interacting in a network can "communicate more effectively, and over a wider range of subjects, with members of one large group than with outsiders" (Deutsch 1953: 97). Here, language regimes are driven less by ethnic composition but more by political leaders in their quest to create a national identity (Gellner 1983; Hobsbawm 1990; Rappa and Wee 2006). While language is certainly an integral component of nation-building (as seen in the Indonesian example), this explanation is insufficient as well. It does not account for the language regime choice itself. Why is one regime chosen at the expense of another for nation-building? The language chosen is too often taken as a given. And when efforts are made to explain the choice, the reasoning is often ex post or functional in character. For instance, one reason commonly given for why the Javanese did not fight for their language and accepted Malay was because they were "farsighted and generous enough" (B. Anderson 2006: 199). This explanation, extremely apolitical, leaves much to be desired. And more important, it is nearly impossible to falsify.

Consistent across all three arguments—ethnic power, colonial legacy, and nation-building—is a failure to fully consider the choices and constraints facing a postcolonial government. Governments do not choose language regimes in a political vacuum. There are strategic calculations in play (Laitin 1992: 33–37). In Indonesia, in the story of Malay/Indonesian trumping Javanese, there were three such calculations.

The first has to do with communicative efficiency. Javanese has its own script; it also has an extensive vocabulary with a large number of loan words from Sanskrit. While some of the other languages are linguistically close to Javanese (e.g., Sundanese), this is not true for the vast majority of the other languages (e.g., Balinese, Minangkabau, and the majority of the Papuan languages). All this would have rendered the language too difficult for nonnative speakers to learn (Drake 1989: 61–62; Mohr 1984: 17). In contrast, a pidgin version of Malay (*pasar*) was used extensively throughout the archipelago (Bertrand 2003: 273). Undoubtedly, there would still be costs to standardize the language and then to reeducate the Indonesian population in the new version. But compared to Javanese, the challenges would be substantially less.

The second calculation has to do with collective equality. Javanese has a strong association with a feudalistic society, in which there is strict adherence to social context. Vocabulary and grammar can change depending on the social status of the two individuals in a conversation. There are roughly three levels. To complicate matters even more, Javanese is littered with honorifics and humilifics (see Keeler 1984). Its use would have perpetuated a hierarchy as stratified as Dutch colonialism. In contrast, Indonesian was seen as democratic. To this end, it could "bond the various peoples of Indonesia" and "provide the base from which . . . a common set of values could be promoted" (Bertrand 2003: 274).

The third calculation has to do with the prestige of the Javanese language. Though Javanese had once been part of a rich culture, its status had diminished quite significantly over time. As a counterfactual, had the jurisdiction of the Dutch East India Company been confined to strictly Java in the nineteenth century, the postcolonial Javanese nation-state would probably have chosen Javanese. But as this was not the case, the Dutch policy was to use Javanese to administer just one part (albeit the most important part) of the colony. In other words, the status of Javanese had dropped to that of a mere provincial language by the 1870s (B. Anderson 2006: 196–97).

Given these concerns, power-neutralization through Indonesian was an optimal alternative. Although this choice was made with minimal conflict by the time the Dutch withdrew, it certainly does not translate into a lack of politics. In fact, the "adoption of Bahasa Indonesia was contested when it was first proposed as the language of the young nationalist movement" (Bertrand 2003: 269). As early as the First Youth Congress in 1926, there was recognition that independence would be impossible in the absence of "unity in diversity." There had to be some bond that could bring together a large number of different interests. Language—specifically Indonesian—was seen as this key vehicle. As Surastri Trimurti, labor minister in 1947–1948, noted, "We had a visionary concept of the tremendous need for unity and intuitively felt that [the Indonesian] language was an essential tool to bring about this hope and dream" (Trimurti, interview in Mohr 1984: 37). Two years later at the Second Youth Congress, the importance of language was embedded in the slogan "one nation, one people, one language" (*satu nusa, satu bangsa, satu bahasa*). During World War II, the Japanese promoted Malay because it was believed to be the only language—Dutch notwithstanding—able to facilitate broader interethnic communication in order to maximize wartime mobilization efforts. This lent Malay greater credibility as the language of the greater Indonesian nation. By the time Indonesia declared independence in 1945 and the Dutch withdrew in 1949, the choice of a power-neutralizing language regimes was noncontentious.

Homogenizing Heterogeneity

The advantages of ethnolinguistic homogeneity are well documented. There are several different explanations. James Habyarimana et al. (2009: 5–13) have identified a list of eight commonly cited mechanisms, grouped into three over-arching categories. The first category is about preferences, especially those toward coethnics. Preferences are important when considering the welfare of coethnics, sharing the same values as coethnics, and choosing to work with coethnics. The second category is about the networks that come with ethnicity. These networks behave very much like technology in that they allow coethnics to operate with greater efficiency, evaluate each other more accurately, interact more frequently, and identify each other more quickly. The third category is about the ability to punish coethnics for behaving in a way inconsistent with expected ethnic preferences and network. Although by no means an exhaustive list, these are some of the mechanisms that allow homogeneous countries to perform well on a number of outcomes, including economic growth. If homogeneity is good (i.e., functional), then heterogeneity is not. What this suggests is that as heterogeneity increases, the probability or extent of some bad outcome increases as well. This linear relationship is reflected in Figure 3.1.

This book challenges this proposition. Fundamentally, the linear relationship in Figure 3.1 ignores the ways governments can use institutions to mimic the purported advantages of homogeneity across different settings. In other words, even if a country is not blessed with a homogeneous population, the government still has instruments at its disposal to homogenize the heterogeneity. Governments can use institutions to generate similar preferences across ethnic boundaries. These same institutions can also allow non-co-ethnics to operate in a larger interethnic network and to reciprocate with each other.

One such instrument is language regime. Language regimes delineate which languages can be used when and where. Some distributions of linguistic power are inherently more equal than others, and fairness is important, if not necessary, to build an "imagined community" (B. Anderson 1983) beyond one ethnolinguistic group. Some distributions of linguistic power are also more efficient than others. The ability to communicate across ethnolinguistic boundaries with minimal transaction costs—much like centralized monies and standardized weights—is absolutely essential for the rationalization of the state (Laitin 1988: 290–91). There are theoretical reasons to believe certain language regimes are more effective than others at "standardizing diversity" (Ginsburgh and Weber 2011: 26–27). The status of Indonesian in Indonesia is one such example. Its use cuts across the 712 ethnolinguistic boundaries and facilitates an encompassing panethnic identity.

Language regimes are not exogenous. The Indonesian government did not simply accept the status quo when the Dutch surrendered. There was a decision to make Malay the "one language" in the "one nation, one people, one language."

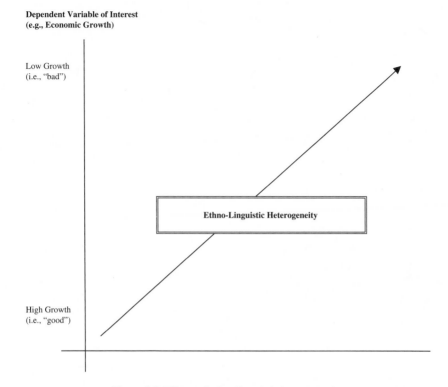

Figure 3.1. Effects of ethnolinguistic heterogeneity.

While it had been a foregone conclusion by 1949, there had been a debate as early as the First and Second Youth Congresses in the 1920s. Here we see evidence that language regimes are endogenous: they are institutional choices. Arguments drawing on ethnolinguistic heterogeneity often fail to account for how governments respond to this very diversity. Governments behave strategically. They prefer state stability to state instability. While state stability is not a sufficient condition for governments to stay in power, it is virtually a necessary condition. Put differently, state instability can threaten the survival of any government.[2]

While the composition of the government can be linguistically heterogeneous, the linguistic group with the most political influence is frequently numerically the largest. Thus, whether linguistic groups bargain within one political party (e.g., Singapore), in a larger preelectoral coalition (e.g., Malaysia), or in the legislature after an election (e.g., Sri Lanka), governments are not neutral actors. They choose language regimes that reflect the preferences of the politically dominant linguistic group. For the politically dominant, the preference is for a regime that concentrates linguistic power exclusively in its one and only language.

This discussion suggests that if the politically dominant linguistic group has a disproportionate amount of power (i.e., size, wealth, or capacity to repress), the actual ability of any other group to extract linguistic concessions from the government is limited at best. Often, under such conditions, these demands fall on deaf ears. In contrast, when a politically nondominant group can effectively organize and threaten to protest en masse, bankrupt the state, or incite violence thereby rendering state stability questionable, the government is constrained. It must consider linguistic concessions.

While the logic here suggests ethnolinguistic heterogeneity matters, it is important to recognize that not all linguistic groups carry the same political clout. For a host of different reasons (e.g., size or concentration, influence in the economy, and presence in the military), the reality is that some groups are politically relevant but others are not. Demographic linguistic heterogeneity is not necessarily congruent with politically relevant linguistic heterogeneity (Cederman, Wimmer, and Min 2010; Posner 2004). Put differently, a country can be demographically diverse without being politically diverse.

Not only is the variation in political relevance cross-sectional, there is also a time series component. The saliency of linguistic cleavages can change over time. Institutions can bring together different linguistic groups under a large panethnic umbrella. Take the evolution of the different regional Thai languages into one standard Thai in the twentieth century. Institutions can also split an existing unit into multiple groups. Consider Yugoslavia. The collapse of communism resuscitated a number of ethnolinguistic group identities that had been frozen during Tito's rule. Over time, these identities can then shift from that of the original ethnie to that of the new ethnie.

Politically relevant linguistic heterogeneity matters for language regime choice, because it constrains governments in three different ways. Governments must make a tradeoff between the three Es: cultural egoism, communicative efficiency, and collective equality. The next subsections discuss the three constraints in detail.

Cultural Egoism

Language is a marker of a distinct culture. For the Javanese, their language was one of "privileged literary" (B. Anderson 2006: 206). There was certainly an element of cultural pride associated with having one's language recognized as one of prestige. It is this same mechanism—cultural egoism—that made it possible for the Dutch to divide-and-conquer the likes of the Balinese and Sundanese temporarily after World War II. At the time, these ethnolinguistic groups were not willing to forfeit claims to their culture. In exchange for political support, the Dutch responded by conceding linguistic recognition.

To deny a group linguistic recognition suggests the culture of the group is somehow inferior. In the long term, to successfully deny a culture its language kills the culture (Fishman 1991). Groups want their languages to be recognized. Linguistic recognition affords its speakers security and a sense of legal entitlement (Shoup 2011: 788). This desire for recognition is driven not always by practicality per se, but sometimes by a matter of principle and rights. It is this egoism that drives minorities such as the Basques, Kurds, and Ukrainians to attach great importance to their "minor" language in the interest of identity maintenance, regardless of whether another language of greater practicality exists. It is a "a form of protest against political domination" (Ericksen 1993: 110).[3]

In this book, cultural egoism is conceptualized in relative terms. There is evidence that people care more about relative than about absolute deprivation (Crosby 1976; Folger 1984; Gurr 1970: chaps. 2–3; Lind, Kanfer, and Early 1990). Each group wants its language recognized. The politically dominant not only wants its language to be recognized, but an egotistical politically dominant also wants its language to be the *only* language recognized. Its preference is for a power-concentrating language regime that would signal a monopolistic ownership of the state by the dominant group.

When a second mother tongue is recognized, another linguistic group can also lay claim to social standing. As more languages are recognized, more groups share in this egoism. At some point, there is a diminishing return: when "too many" languages are recognized, the relative value of each language decreases to a trivial point.

In contrast, when a lingua franca is recognized, cultural egoism is forfeited. Although the politically dominant gains no relative status benefits (i.e., it cannot claim social superiority over some other linguistic groups), this choice can give all speakers some semblance of equality. Recall, as discussed in Chapter 2, very few lingua francas are equally fair for all linguistic groups. With any lingua franca choice, some linguistic group will be inherently advantaged because of the linguistic proximity between their mother tongues and the lingua franca or because of previous exposure to the language. What matters is that with a lingua franca, all groups have forfeited claims to their mother tongues and have become resigned to using what is at best their second preferred language.

The logic is similar for a politically nondominant group. Each linguistic group prefers its own language to be recognized. This recognition, however, is not just from an absolute standpoint. It is not simply about whether there is recognition or no recognition. It is also about how many other languages are recognized. Cultural egoism decreases as more languages are recognized. There is also a relative component.

Consider one scenario. Assume there are x groups. If only one language is recognized, speakers of that one language have more status and an easier life than speakers of the other $x - 1$ languages. This relative position certainly yields some social benefit in addition to having a language recognized. In contrast, consider an alternative scenario: all x languages are recognized but one. Here, speakers of the one denied language are symbolically at the bottom of the social hierarchy; they command less value than everyone else. For them, the lack of recognition is both absolute and relative. Taken together, these scenarios suggest that while a group prefers its own language to be recognized, it has little incentive to encourage the recognition of another language. This discussion leads to the following set of premises:

Premise 1.1: *Cultural egoism decreases as more languages are recognized.*

Premise 1.2: *Cultural egoism is low when a lingua franca is recognized.*

Communicative Efficiency

Language facilitates communication. During colonial times, while Dutch was officially the language of the administration, the continued use of local languages ensured there was a divide (1) between the colonial authorities and the local natives and (2) between the different local natives. In contrast, during World War II, the Japanese—initially seen by Sukarno and the Indonesians as their liberators from the Dutch—promoted the use of Malay to disseminate propaganda and to mobilize the population at large. And on independence, the Indonesian government recognized Indonesian as the official language of the state precisely because it was easy and efficient.

How well language facilitates communication depends on whether the communication is exclusively in one language or spans across multiple languages. This is important because multilingual communication necessitates a cost. Consider the Persian empire. During the reign of Xerxes the Great (486–465 BCE), court official Mordecai had to send out official decrees in 127 different translations (Paulston 2003). This example highlights the potential costs of translations. Imagine every government bill, court ruling, and tax-related paperwork that must be translated and be available in each of the languages. And in the event of discrepancies between two different linguistic versions of the same document, the legal costs to rectify the mistake can be significant (Ginsburgh and Weber 2011: 165).

In addition to translation costs, there are also social costs. Languages bond and identify social networks. These networks allow for efficiency in interactions. But as the number of languages (i.e., social networks) increases, the degree of connectivity of individuals, the norms of reciprocity, and the levels of trust all decrease. This is problematic since a "society characterized by generalized reciprocity is more efficient than a distrustful society" (Putnam 2000: 19).

It would follow that when only one language is recognized, there are minimal costs to communication. This is true regardless whether the one language is that of the politically dominant or a lingua franca.[4] But when multiple languages are recognized (as is the case with power-sharing), there is an efficiency cost. This cost is contingent on the number of languages recognized. As the latter increases per unit, the former increases at an exponential rate. The following premises summarize this discussion:

Premise 2.1: *Efficiency decreases as more languages are recognized.*
Premise 2.2: *Efficiency is high when a lingua franca is recognized.*

Collective Equality

Language is a vehicle through which a community is imagined (B. Anderson 1983). In the Indonesian example, Indonesian brought together a number of ethnolinguistic groups. It built a larger nation that hitherto was merely a scattered collection of islands. The fact that Malay was renamed in 1945 during the nationalist movement as "Indonesian" is testament to the community-encompassing nature of the language. Its choice as the national language emphasized collective equality.

Equality is important. It is a necessary condition for legitimacy (Sadurski 2008: vii). A "legitimate government must treat all those over whom it claims dominion not just with a measure of concern but with *equal* concern" (Dworkin 2006: 97; emphasis original). When people are treated with equality and the government is viewed as legitimate, people identify as a part of a collective community. Legitimacy is desired not just for pride or other abstract purposes but because in its absence—or when it is at a minimum—governments face threats of removal.

Although linguistic recognition is not a sufficient guarantee of legitimacy, withholding recognition (i.e., enforcing inequality) can be costly. Consider the following language regimes. The first is power-concentrating. While these language regimes are efficient, there is a cost to this coercion. These regimes are inherently unequal; there is a bifurcation of "us" versus "them." Consequently, they alienate speakers of all the unrecognized languages. Moreover, there is general intolerance when the politically nondominant group espouses nonstate rhetoric (Connor 1973: 17).

The second is a dual power-sharing regime where two languages are recognized: that of the politically dominant and that of one minority. Compared to the power-concentrating language regime, this regime is more equal. It is also more legitimate. However, it still alienates all the other unrecognized linguistic groups. Finally, the third language regime recognizes every group's language. In contrast to the previous two, this language regime propagates complete equality. In sum, equality increases as the number of groups afforded recognition increases.

Like cultural egoism, collective equality can also involve some relative component. Each linguistic group would like its language to be recognized. These groups, however, can still perceive the government as equal in the absence of any recognition when a lingua franca is recognized. The use of a lingua franca not only neutralizes linguistic power, but it also generates equality in nonrecognition. It is an instrument for building the narrative of a panethnic state. This suggests the following:

Premise 3.1: *Equality increases as more languages are recognized.*
Premise 3.2: *Equality is high when a lingua franca is recognized.*

Hypotheses

As illustrated in Figure 3.2, the fundamental tension is between cultural egoism, communicative efficiency, and collective equality. This is a three-way dilemma. For example, power-concentrating language regimes solidify the politically dominant's ego; they are also efficient. They are, however, far from equal especially in the eyes of the politically nondominant. In contrast, power-sharing language regimes are good for both the linguistic groups' cultural egoism and their collective equality. These benefits, however, come at the cost of communicative

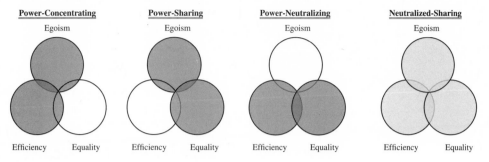

Figure 3.2. Egoism, efficiency, and equality.

efficiency. And finally, while power-neutralizing language regimes are efficient and equal, there is no cultural egoism to be had.

As a hybrid, neutralized-sharing language regimes theoretically confer all three benefits. But these benefits are discounted (hence the lighter-shaded gray). The use of other mother tongues, even when in the presence of a lingua franca, can still introduce inefficiency and inequality. When mother tongues are afforded legal status, it becomes important for speakers of those languages to be bilingual. When this does not happen (i.e., some subpopulation will only learn its mother tongue), communicative efficiency costs emerge. Additionally, when some mother tongues but not others are recognized, this can perpetuate beliefs of inequality. These feelings can decrease as more mother tongues are recognized. But as already established, the recognition of more mother tongues comes with its own set of tradeoffs. Fundamentally, a postcolonial government must find the balance between the competing imperatives of cultural egoism, communicative efficiency, and collective equality.

Under what conditions are linguistic powers concentrated, shared, or neutralized? Language regimes are government responses to politically relevant linguistic heterogeneity levels. When this level is low (i.e., there are few linguistic groups),[5] the government will choose a power-concentrating language regime. There are two major advantages with this choice. First, with respect to cultural egoism, a power-concentrating language regime suggests the superiority of the politically dominant group. Socially, the group is able to secure its linguistic position in the community. Second, with respect to efficiency, the use of the politically dominant language across the state keeps translation costs to a minimum. All official documents are issued and available strictly in that one language. These purported benefits, however, come at a cost to collective equality, especially to those who speak a politically nondominant language. But if there are few linguistic groups of political relevance, such considerations are trivial. This discussion suggests the following hypothesis:

Hypothesis 1.1: *When politically relevant linguistic heterogeneity levels are low, only the politically dominant language will be recognized.*

These calculations, however, change when politically relevant linguistic heterogeneity levels are not low. As the number of groups that are able to threaten state stability grows, it also becomes increasingly difficult for the government to concentrate linguistic power exclusively in the language of the politically dominant. When multiple groups are denied the opportunity to use their own languages, equality costs are no longer just a nuisance. If the costs are sufficiently high, they can outweigh whatever cultural egoism and efficiency benefits the politically dominant would gain with a power-concentrating language regime. Under such conditions, the government must make linguistic concessions.

There are several types of linguistic concessions. One is a power-sharing language regime. Naturally, to the politically dominant, these regimes are less than ideal. Their elite status is not exclusive. Even though their language is recognized, it does not sit alone at the top of the social hierarchy. There is also an efficiency cost. Translations are necessary to make interactions between the different linguistic groups possible. But at the same time, the bruised ego and the efficiency costs are both offset by increasing equality benefits: the power-sharing regime achieves greater consent.

The second type of concession is a power-neutralizing language regime. Again, for the politically dominant, this regime is not the most preferred outcome, all else being equal. The biggest disadvantage with lingua franca recognition is the absence of cultural egoism benefits. The politically dominant is in no position to claim greater social respect, importance, or worth than any of the other linguistic groups. What is given up in cultural egoism, however, is compensated. The use of one language that cuts across ethnic boundaries substantially reduces translations: all official government paperwork needs to be available in only one language. Moreover, the use of a lingua franca breeds a sense of collective equality, which in turn can help with the perceived legitimacy of the government.

There is a third concession. A neutralized-sharing language regime combines the above two in that it recognizes mother tongues *and* a lingua franca. These regimes are akin to Laitin's 3±1 language regimes (1992: 18–19). The tradeoffs for these hybrid regimes are slightly different. On the one hand, unlike the other three pure regimes, these regimes afford cultural egoism, are efficient, and generate equality. On the other hand, however, the efficiency is less than that of a power-neutralizing language regime because a neutralized-sharing regime requires a substantial portion of the population to be bilingual—a desirable but extremely costly outcome. Additionally, the equality is less than that of a power-sharing language regime because inevitably some mother tongues are recognized but others are not.

Which of the concessions is optimal depends on politically relevant linguistic heterogeneity levels. When the level is moderate, the government is better off sharing linguistic power. For the dominant group the cultural egoism is discounted (but only slightly) and efficiency costs increase but also only marginally. This leads to the following hypothesis:

Hypothesis 1.2: *When politically relevant linguistic heterogeneity levels are moderate, language regimes will be power-sharing.*

However, when there are too many politically relevant linguistic groups to accommodate, the costs of a power-sharing language regime are simply too onerous. Calculations change: cultural egoism benefits wither toward zero and efficiency costs explode to the maximum—all for the sake of equality. Under such conditions, the government is better off recognizing a lingua franca, either exclusively or in conjunction with mother tongues. Although the dominant group is still denied any substantive cultural egoism, the adoption of a lingua franca in this scenario facilitates both communicative efficiency and collective equality. The following hypothesis summarizes this discussion:

Hypothesis 1.3: *When politically relevant linguistic heterogeneity levels are high, a lingua franca will be recognized.*

Several comments merit elaboration. First, while the utility of a power-concentration for the politically dominant group decreases as the number of groups increases, it is nonetheless always the largest of the four regimes. This is consistent with the assumption that the dominant would always intensely prefer to have linguistic powers concentrated. The only reason we do not always observe this language regime is because of the latent or manifest power of other politically relevant linguistic groups. Specifically, when there is a threat of state instability, the government is constrained to extend linguistic concessions. When this threat is absent or weak, we observe no concessions (i.e., power-concentrating). This is Hypothesis 1.1.

Second, when power-concentrating language regimes are not an option, power-sharing language regimes are rational alternatives. However, this is only the case when the number of politically relevant linguistic groups is moderate—as argued in Hypothesis 1.2. Moreover, the optimal power-sharing arrangement depends on the number of such groups as well. As the number of groups increases, the number of citizens who are proficient in any of the recognized languages will decrease.

Third, the utility of recognizing a lingua franca is a flat line (value of 0) across all possible values of k (number of politically relevant linguistic groups). Recall that by definition the use of a lingua franca neutralizes linguistic power. All k groups—the politically dominant and the politically dominant—must forfeit cultural egoism; but in exchange, there is communicative efficiency and collective equality. At some point, the utility of recognizing a lingua franca is greater than that of a power-sharing language regime. This finding is consistent with Hypothesis 1.3: at some point, the recognition of too many languages is neither efficient nor practical. This is the case in Indonesia and India.

One notable difference between the Indonesias and the Indias is that not all language regimes that recognize a lingua franca are the same. Some language regimes, like Indonesia's, employ the lingua franca exclusively. Others are hybrids; they supplement the lingua franca with mother tongues (e.g., India). In sum, language regimes not only differ in their *type*, but also in their *degree* of linguistic neutralization. Drawing on the same logic posited above, the expectation is that governments must balance between cultural egoism, communicative efficiency, and collective equality. As the number of politically relevant minority groups increases, the politically dominant linguistic group faces pressures to forfeit ego benefits in exchange for efficiency and equality. As this constraint increases, the emphasis on a lingua franca as an outcome also increases. This suggests the following corollary:

Corollary 1: *As politically relevant linguistic heterogeneity levels increase, the degree of linguistic neutralization increases.*

Discussion

The position of this book is that language regimes matter. To focus strictly on linguistic heterogeneity as a demographic concept fails to account for how governments respond to diversity. While homogeneity may induce some normatively "functional" outcome, governments of heterogeneous countries do have institutional tools at their disposal to effectively standardize this diversity. One such tool is language regimes. Whether—and how—language regimes aid in homogenizing this heterogeneity depends on the precise distribution of linguistic power. Some language regimes are better for generating cultural egoism; some, communicative efficiency; and still others, collective equality.

Which language regime type gets chosen depends on politically relevant linguistic heterogeneity levels. When this level is low, suggesting the nondominant groups are of minimal threat, the government has an incentive to concentrate linguistic power in the dominant group's language. But when heterogeneity levels are not low, the government must make linguistic concessions. One type takes the form of recognizing other mother tongues in some semblance of a power-sharing language regime. At high levels of heterogeneity, however, another type of concession of great importance is the recognition of a lingua franca. Whether exclusively (power-neutralizing) or as a hybrid (neutralized-sharing), lingua franca recognition can be optimal as it is both efficient and equal. The next chapter tests this argument.

Appendix

The sequence of events is simple. As illustrated in Figure 3.3, nature draws the number of linguistic groups in a country $\{k \in Z : 1 \leq k < \infty\}$ and the political relevance of each group $\{\Omega_k \in \mathfrak{R} : -\infty < \Omega_k \leq 0\}$. Of these k groups, there are $k-1$ linguistic minorities. The government D proposes a set number of languages to be recognized $\{n \in Z : 0 \leq n \leq k\}$, where $n = 0$ suggests the recognition of a lingua franca and $n = k$ indicates every linguistic group's language is recognized. Next, each minority linguistic group $d(i)$ moves simultaneously and chooses whether to accept or reject D's proposal. Acceptance yields a language regime; rejection, state instability and possibly civil war. Note that all $k-1$ minority linguistic groups must accept for language regime to be the outcome.

The utility functions for D and $d(i)$ are as follows. Recall that D's utility is composed of three elements: egoism (which is relative to how many other languages are recognized), efficiency (increases exponentially with each language recognized), and equality. Also, both D and $d(i)$ incur a constant utility of 0 when the language regime is power-neutralizing.

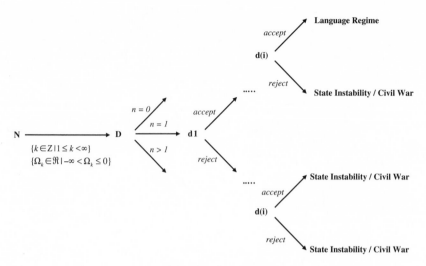

Figure 3.3. Game tree.

$$U_D \ (language \ regime) \quad = \begin{cases} \left(1 - \dfrac{n-1}{k+1-n}\right)\left(\left(\dfrac{1}{n}\right)^2 - \left(\dfrac{k-n}{k}\right)^2\right) & if \ \ n > 0 \\[2mm] 0 & if \ \ n = 0 \end{cases}$$

$$U_D \ (\sim language \ regime) \quad = \Omega_D \in (-\infty, \ 0]$$

$$U_{d(i)} \ (accept \mid n) \quad = \begin{cases} \left(1 - \dfrac{1}{k+2-n}\right)\left(\dfrac{1}{n}\right)^2 & if \ \ n > 0 \ and \ recognized \\[2mm] \left(-\dfrac{1}{k+2-n}\right)\left(\dfrac{1}{n}\right)^2 & if \ \ n > 0 \ and \sim recognized \\[2mm] 0 & if \ \ n = 0 \end{cases}$$

$$U_{d(i)} \ (reject \mid n) \quad = \Omega_{d(i)} \in (-\infty, \ 0]$$

Hypothesis 1: Power-Concentrating Language Regime

Consider $\Omega_{d(i)} < -\dfrac{1}{k+1} \forall d(i)$. Using backward induction, let us start with $d(i)$:

Step 1.1: $n > 0$ and recognized

$U_{d(i)}(accept \mid n > 0)$ $\geq$ $U_{d(i)}(reject \mid n > 0)$

$$\left(1 - \frac{1}{k+2-n}\right)\left(\frac{1}{n}\right)^2 \qquad \geq \qquad -\frac{1}{k+1}.$$

Step 1.2: $n > 0$ and not recognized

$U_{d(i)}(accept \mid n > 0)$ $\geq$ $U_{d(i)}(reject \mid n > 0)$

$$\left(-\frac{1}{k+2-n}\right)\left(\frac{1}{n}\right)^2 \qquad \geq \qquad -\frac{1}{k+1}.$$

Step 1.3: $n = 0$

$U_{d(i)}(accept \mid n = 0)$ $\geq$ $U_{d(i)}(reject \mid n = 0)$

$$0 \qquad \geq \qquad -\frac{1}{k+1}.$$

When $\Omega_{d(i)} < -\frac{1}{k+1}$, $d(i)$ will always accept. Moving up the tree, now let us focus on D:

Step 2.1: $n = 1$ versus $n > 1$

$U_D(n = 1)$ $\gtreqless$ $U_D(n > 1)$

$$1 - \left(\frac{k-1}{k}\right)^2 \qquad \geq \qquad \left(1 - \frac{n-1}{k+1-n}\right)\left(\left(\frac{1}{n}\right)^2 - \left(\frac{k-n}{k}\right)^2\right).$$

Step 2.2: $n = 1$ versus $n = 0$

$U_D(n = 1)$ $\gtreqless$ $U_D(n = 0)$

$$1 - \left(\frac{k-1}{k}\right)^2 \qquad \geq \qquad 0.$$

Claim 1: *When $\Omega_{d(i)} < -\frac{1}{k+1} \; \forall d(i)$, D offers $n = 1$.*

Proof: By Induction[6]
Set $k = 3$

$U_D\,(n=1\,|\,k=3)$ $\gtreqless$ $U_D\,(n>1\,|\,k=3)$

$$\left(1-\frac{n-1}{k+1-n}\right)\left(\left(\frac{1}{n}\right)^2-\left(\frac{k-n}{k}\right)^2\right) \quad\gtreqless\quad \left(1-\frac{n-1}{k+1-n}\right)\left(\left(\frac{1}{n}\right)^2-\left(\frac{k-n}{k}\right)^2\right)$$

$$\frac{5}{9} \qquad\qquad > \quad \left(1-\frac{n-1}{3+1-n}\right)\left(\left(\frac{1}{n}\right)^2-\left(\frac{3-n}{3}\right)^2\right).$$

$U_D\,(n=1\,|\,k=3)$ $\gtreqless$ $U_D\,(n=0\,|\,k=3)$

$$\left(1-\frac{n-1}{k+1-n}\right)\left(\left(\frac{1}{n}\right)^2-\left(\frac{k-n}{k}\right)^2\right) \quad\gtreqless\quad 0$$

$$\frac{5}{9} \qquad\qquad > \quad 0.$$

Set $k=4$

$U_D\,(n=1\,|\,k=4)$ $\gtreqless$ $U_D\,(n>1\,|\,k=4)$

$$\left(1-\frac{n-1}{k+1-n}\right)\left(\left(\frac{1}{n}\right)^2-\left(\frac{k-n}{k}\right)^2\right) \quad\gtreqless\quad \left(1-\frac{n-1}{k+1-n}\right)\left(\left(\frac{1}{n}\right)^2-\left(\frac{k-n}{k}\right)^2\right)$$

$$\frac{7}{16} \qquad\qquad \geq \quad \left(1-\frac{n-1}{4+1-n}\right)\left(\left(\frac{1}{n}\right)^2-\left(\frac{4-n}{4}\right)^2\right).$$

$U_D\,(n=1\,|\,k=4)$ $\gtreqless$ $U_D\,(n=0\,|\,k=4)$

$$\left(1-\frac{n-1}{k+1-n}\right)\left(\left(\frac{1}{n}\right)^2-\left(\frac{k-n}{k}\right)^2\right) \quad\gtreqless\quad 0$$

$$\frac{7}{16} \qquad\qquad > \quad 0.$$

Set $k=5$

$U_D\,(n=1\,|\,k=5)$ $\gtreqless$ $U_D\,(n>1\,|\,k=5)$

$$\left(1-\frac{n-1}{k+1-n}\right)\left(\left(\frac{1}{n}\right)^2-\left(\frac{k-n}{k}\right)^2\right) \quad\gtreqless\quad \left(1-\frac{n-1}{k+1-n}\right)\left(\left(\frac{1}{n}\right)^2-\left(\frac{k-n}{k}\right)^2\right)$$

$$\frac{9}{25} \geq \left(1-\frac{n-1}{5+1-n}\right)\left(\left(\frac{1}{n}\right)^2-\left(\frac{5-n}{5}\right)^2\right).$$

$$U_D\left(n=1\,|\,k=5\right) \gtreqqless U_D\left(n=0\,|\,k=5\right)$$

$$\left(1-\frac{n-1}{k+1-n}\right)\left(\left(\frac{1}{n}\right)^2-\left(\frac{k-n}{k}\right)^2\right) \gtreqqless 0$$

$$\frac{9}{25} > 0.$$

Assume $k=q$ such that:

$$U_D\left(n=1\,|\,k=q\right) \geq U_D\left(n>1\,|\,k=q\right)$$

$$\left(1-\frac{n-1}{k+1-n}\right)\left(\left(\frac{1}{n}\right)^2-\left(\frac{k-n}{k}\right)^2\right) \geq \left(1-\frac{n-1}{k+1-n}\right)\left(\left(\frac{1}{n}\right)^2-\left(\frac{k-n}{k}\right)^2\right)$$

$$1-\left(\frac{q-1}{q}\right)^2 \geq \left(1-\frac{n-1}{q+1-n}\right)\left(\left(\frac{1}{n}\right)^2-\left(\frac{q-n}{q}\right)^2\right).$$

$$U_D\left(n=1\,|\,k=q\right) \geq U_D\left(n=0\,|\,k=q\right)$$

$$\left(1-\frac{n-1}{k+1-n}\right)\left(\left(\frac{1}{n}\right)^2-\left(\frac{k-n}{k}\right)^2\right) \geq 0$$

$$1-\left(\frac{q-1}{q}\right)^2 \geq 0$$

Now let us consider $k=q+1$:

$$U_D\left(n=1\,|\,k=q+1\right) \gtreqqless U_D\left(n>1\,|\,k=q+1\right)$$

$$\left(1-\frac{n-1}{k+1-n}\right)\left(\left(\frac{1}{n}\right)^2-\left(\frac{k-n}{k}\right)^2\right) \gtreqqless \left(1-\frac{n-1}{k+1-n}\right)\left(\left(\frac{1}{n}\right)^2-\left(\frac{k-n}{k}\right)^2\right)$$

$$1 \geq \left(1-\frac{n-1}{q+2-n}\right)\times$$

$$\left(\left(\frac{1}{n}\right)^2-\left(\frac{q+1-n}{q+1}\right)^2\right)+\left(\frac{q}{q+1}\right)^2.$$

$$U_D\,(n=1\,|\,k=q+1) \qquad\qquad \gtreqless\; U_D\,(n=0\,|\,k=q+1)$$

$$\left(1-\frac{n-1}{k+1-n}\right)\!\left(\left(\frac{1}{n}\right)^2-\left(\frac{k-n}{k}\right)^2\right) \;\gtreqless\; 0$$

$$1-\left(\frac{q}{q+1}\right)^2 \qquad\qquad\qquad \geq\; 0$$

$$1 \qquad\qquad\qquad\qquad\qquad \geq\; \left(\frac{q}{q+1}\right)^2.$$

Conclusion: *Claim 1 holds true. When* $\Omega_{d(i)} < -\dfrac{1}{k+1}\,\forall d(i),\ D$ *offers* $n=1.$

Hypothesis 2: Power-Sharing Language Regime

Consider $\Omega_{d(i)} \geq -\dfrac{1}{k+1}$ for some subset of $d(i)$. Using backward induction, let us start with $d(i)$:

Step 1.1: $n>0$ and recognized

$$U_{d(i)}\,(accept\,|\,n>0) \qquad\qquad \geq\; U_{d(i)}\,(reject\,|\,n>0)$$

$$\left(1-\frac{1}{k+2-n}\right)\!\left(\frac{1}{n}\right)^2 \qquad \geq\; -\frac{1}{k+1}.$$

Step 1.2: $n>0$ and not recognized

$$U_{d(i)}\,(accept\,|\,n>0) \qquad\qquad \geq\; U_{d(i)}\,(reject\,|\,n>0)$$

$$\left(-\frac{1}{k+2-n}\right)\!\left(\frac{1}{n}\right)^2 \qquad \ngeq\; -\frac{1}{k+1}.$$

Step 1.3: $n=0$

$$U_{d(i)}\,(accept\,|\,n=0) \qquad\qquad \geq\; U_{d(i)}\,(reject\,|\,n=0)$$

$$0 \qquad\qquad\qquad\qquad \geq\; -\frac{1}{k+1}.$$

When $\Omega_{d(i)} > -\dfrac{1}{k+1}$, $d(i)$ will never accept if $n>0$ and its language is not recognized. Let us now focus on D:

Step 2.1: $n > 1$ $(n < k)$ versus $n = 1$

$U_D (n > 1)$ $\gtrless U_D (n = 1)$

$$\left(1 - \frac{n-1}{k+1-n}\right)\left(\left(\frac{1}{n}\right)^2 - \left(\frac{k-n}{k}\right)^2\right) \gtrless \{\Omega_D \in \mathfrak{R} : -\infty < \Omega_k \leq 0\}.$$

Step 2.2: $n > 1$ $(n < k)$ versus $n = 0$

$U_D (n > 1)$ $\gtrless U_D (n = 0)$

$$\left(1 - \frac{n-1}{k+1-n}\right)\left(\left(\frac{1}{n}\right)^2 - \left(\frac{k-n}{k}\right)^2\right) \gtrless 0.$$

Claim 2: *When* $\Omega_{d(i)} \geq -\dfrac{1}{k+1}$ *for some subset of d(i) and when* $k < 5$, *D offers* $n > 1$.

Proof: By Induction

Set $k = 3$

$U_D (1 < n < k \mid k = 3)$ $\gtrless U_D (n = 1 \mid k = 3)$

$$\left(1 - \frac{n-1}{k+1-n}\right)\left(\left(\frac{1}{n}\right)^2 - \left(\frac{k-n}{k}\right)^2\right) \gtrless \{\Omega_D \in \mathfrak{R} : -\infty < \Omega_k \leq 0\}$$

$$\left(1 - \frac{2-1}{3+1-2}\right)\left(\left(\frac{1}{2}\right)^2 - \left(\frac{3-2}{3}\right)^2\right) \geq \{\Omega_D \in \mathfrak{R} : -\infty < \Omega_k \leq 0\}$$

$$\frac{5}{72} \geq \{\Omega_D \in \mathfrak{R} : -\infty < \Omega_k \leq 0\}.$$

$U_D (1 < n < k \mid k = 3)$ $\gtrless U_D (n = 0 \mid k = 3)$

$$\left(1 - \frac{n-1}{k+1-n}\right)\left(\left(\frac{1}{n}\right)^2 - \left(\frac{k-n}{k}\right)^2\right) \gtrless 0$$

$$\left(1 - \frac{2-1}{3+1-2}\right)\left(\left(\frac{1}{2}\right)^2 - \left(\frac{3-2}{3}\right)^2\right) > 0$$

$$\frac{5}{72} > 0.$$

Set $k=4$

$U_D\,(1<n<4\,|\,k=4)$ $\qquad\qquad$ $\gtreqless\ U_D\,(n=1\,|\,k=4)$

$$\left(1-\frac{n-1}{k+1-n}\right)\!\left(\left(\frac{1}{n}\right)^2-\left(\frac{k-n}{k}\right)^2\right) \quad \gtreqless\ \{\Omega_D\in\Re:-\infty<\Omega_k\le 0\}$$

$$\left(1-\frac{n-1}{4+1-n}\right)\!\left(\left(\frac{1}{n}\right)^2-\left(\frac{4-n}{4}\right)^2\right) \quad \ge\ \{\Omega_D\in\Re:-\infty<\Omega_k\le 0\}$$

$$0 \qquad\qquad\qquad\qquad\qquad >\ \{\Omega_D\in\Re:-\infty<\Omega_k\le 0\}.$$

$U_D\,(1<n<4\,|\,k=4)$ $\qquad\qquad$ $\gtreqless\ U_D\,(n=1\,|\,k=4)$

$$\left(1-\frac{n-1}{k+1-n}\right)\!\left(\left(\frac{1}{n}\right)^2-\left(\frac{k-n}{k}\right)^2\right) \quad \gtreqless\ 0$$

$$\left(1-\frac{n-1}{4+1-n}\right)\!\left(\left(\frac{1}{n}\right)^2-\left(\frac{4-n}{4}\right)^2\right) \quad \ge\ 0$$

$$0 \qquad\qquad\qquad\qquad\qquad =\ 0.$$

Set $k=5$

$U_D\,(1<n<5\,|\,k=5)$ $\qquad\qquad$ $\gtreqless\ U_D\,(n=1\,|\,k=5)$

$$\left(1-\frac{n-1}{k+1-n}\right)\!\left(\left(\frac{1}{n}\right)^2-\left(\frac{k-n}{k}\right)^2\right) \quad \gtreqless\ \{\Omega_D\in\Re:-\infty<\Omega_k\le 0\}$$

$$\left(1-\frac{n-1}{5+1-n}\right)\!\left(\left(\frac{1}{n}\right)^2-\left(\frac{5-n}{5}\right)^2\right) \quad \gtreqless\ \{\Omega_D\in\Re:-\infty<\Omega_k\le 0\}.$$

$U_D\,(1<n<5\,|\,k=5)$ $\qquad\qquad$ $\gtreqless\ U_D\,(n=0\,|\,k=5)$

$$\left(1-\frac{n-1}{k+1-n}\right)\!\left(\left(\frac{1}{n}\right)^2-\left(\frac{k-n}{k}\right)^2\right) \quad \gtreqless\ 0$$

$$\left(1-\frac{n-1}{5+1-n}\right)\!\left(\left(\frac{1}{n}\right)^2-\left(\frac{5-n}{5}\right)^2\right) \quad <\ 0.$$

Assume $k = q$ such that:

$U_D (1 < n < q \mid k = q)$ $\geq$ $U_D (n = 1 \mid k = q)$

$$\left(1 - \frac{n-1}{k+1-n}\right)\left(\left(\frac{1}{n}\right)^2 - \left(\frac{k-n}{k}\right)^2\right) \geq \{\Omega_D \in \Re : -\infty < \Omega_k \leq 0\}$$

$$\left(1 - \frac{n-1}{q+1-n}\right)\left(\left(\frac{1}{n}\right)^2 - \left(\frac{q-n}{q}\right)^2\right) \geq \{\Omega_D \in \Re : -\infty < \Omega_k \leq 0\}.$$

$U_D (1 < n < q \mid k = q)$ $\geq$ $U_D (n = 0 \mid k = q)$

$$\left(1 - \frac{n-1}{k+1-n}\right)\left(\left(\frac{1}{n}\right)^2 - \left(\frac{k-n}{k}\right)^2\right) \geq 0$$

$$\left(1 - \frac{n-1}{q+1-n}\right)\left(\left(\frac{1}{n}\right)^2 - \left(\frac{q-n}{q}\right)^2\right) \geq 0.$$

Now let us consider $k = q + 1$:

$U_D (1 < n < q+1 \mid k = q+1)$ $\geq$ $U_D (n = 1 \mid k = q+1)$

$$\left(1 - \frac{n-1}{k+1-n}\right)\left(\left(\frac{1}{n}\right)^2 - \left(\frac{k-n}{k}\right)^2\right) \geq \{\Omega_D \in \Re : -\infty < \Omega_k \leq 0\}$$

$$\left(1 - \frac{n-1}{(q+1)+1-n}\right)$$

$$\geq \{\Omega_D \in \Re : -\infty < \Omega_k \leq 0\}.$$

$$\left(\left(\frac{1}{n}\right)^2 - \left(\frac{(q+1)-n}{(q+1)}\right)^2\right)$$

$U_D (1 < n < q+1 \mid k = q+1)$ $\geq$ $U_D (n = 0 \mid k = q+1)$

$$\left(1 - \frac{n-1}{k+1-n}\right)\left(\left(\frac{1}{n}\right)^2 - \left(\frac{k-n}{k}\right)^2\right) \geq 0$$

$$\left(1 - \frac{n-1}{(q+1)+1-n}\right)$$
$$\left(\left(\frac{1}{n}\right)^2 - \left(\frac{(q+1)-n}{(q+1)}\right)^2\right)$$
$$< \quad 0.$$

Conclusion: *Claim 2 holds true. When* $\Omega_{d(i)} \geq -\frac{1}{k+1}$ *for some subset of* $d(i)$ *and when* $k < 5$, *D offers* $n > 1$.

Hypothesis 3: Power-Neutralizing Language Regime

Consider $\Omega_{d(i)} \geq -\frac{1}{k+1} \forall d(i)$. Using backward induction, let us start with $d(i)$:

Step 1.1: $n > 0$ and recognized

$U_{d(i)} (accept \mid n > 0)$ $\qquad\qquad \geq \quad U_{d(i)} (reject \mid n > 0)$

$$\left(1 - \frac{1}{k+2-n}\right)\left(\frac{1}{n}\right)^2 \qquad \geq \quad -\frac{1}{k+1}.$$

Step 1.2: $n > 0$ and not recognized

$U_{d(i)} (accept \mid n > 0)$ $\qquad\qquad \geq \quad U_{d(i)} (reject \mid n > 0)$

$$\left(-\frac{1}{k+2-n}\right)\left(\frac{1}{n}\right)^2 \qquad \ngeq \quad -\frac{1}{k+1}.$$

Step 1.3: $n = 0$

$U_{d(i)} (accept \mid n = 0)$ $\qquad\qquad \geq \quad U_{d(i)} (reject \mid n = 0)$

$$0 \qquad\qquad\qquad\qquad \geq \quad -\frac{1}{k+1}.$$

When $\Omega_{d(i)} > -\frac{1}{k+1} \forall m(i)$, $d(i)$ will never accept if $n > 0$ and its language is not recognized. Given this condition, this suggests $n = k$. Moving up the tree, now let us focus on D:

Step 2.1: $n=0$ versus $n=1$

$U_D(n=0)$ $\gtreqless U_D(n=1)$

0 $\geq \{\Omega_D \in \mathfrak{R} : -\infty < \Omega_k \leq 0\}.$

Step 2.2: $n=0$ versus $n>1$ $(n=k)$

$U_D(n=0)$ $\gtreqless U_D(n>1)$

0 $\geq \dfrac{2-k}{k^2}.$

Claim 3: *When* $\Omega_{d(i)} > -\dfrac{1}{k+1} \forall m(i),$ *D offers* $n=0.$

Proof: By Induction
Set $k=3$

$U_D(n=0 \,|\, k=3)$ $\gtreqless U_D(n=1 \,|\, k=3)$

0 $\geq \{\Omega_D \in \mathfrak{R} : -\infty < \Omega_k \leq 0\}.$

$U_D(n=0 \,|\, k=3)$ $\gtreqless U_D(1 < n=3 \,|\, k=3)$

0 $\gtreqless \left(1 - \dfrac{n-1}{k+1-n}\right)\left(\left(\dfrac{1}{n}\right)^2 - \left(\dfrac{k-n}{k}\right)^2\right)$

0 $\gtreqless \left(1 - \dfrac{k-1}{k+1-k}\right)\left(\left(\dfrac{1}{k}\right)^2 - \left(\dfrac{k-k}{k}\right)^2\right)$

0 $> -\dfrac{1}{9}.$

Set $k=4$

$U_D(n=0 \,|\, k=4)$ $\gtreqless U_D(n=1 \,|\, k=4)$

0 $\geq \{\Omega_D \in \mathfrak{R} : -\infty < \Omega_k \leq 0\}.$

$U_D(n=0 \,|\, k=4)$ $\gtreqless U_D(1 < n=4 \,|\, k=4)$

0
$$\gtrless \left(1-\frac{k-1}{k+1-k}\right)\left(\left(\frac{1}{k}\right)^2-\left(\frac{k-k}{k}\right)^2\right)$$

0
$$> -\frac{1}{8}.$$

Set $k=5$

$U_D\,(n=0\,|\,k=5)$
$$\gtrless U_D\,(n=1\,|\,k=5)$$

0
$$\geq \{\Omega_D\in\Re:-\infty<\Omega_k\leq0\}.$$

$U_D\,(n=0\,|\,k=5)$
$$\gtrless U_D\,(1<n=5\,|\,k=5)$$

0
$$\gtrless \left(1-\frac{k-1}{k+1-k}\right)\left(\left(\frac{1}{k}\right)^2-\left(\frac{k-k}{k}\right)^2\right)$$

0
$$> -\frac{3}{25}.$$

Assume $k=q$ such that:

$U_D\,(n=0\,|\,k=q)$
$$\geq U_D\,(n=1\,|\,k=q)$$

0
$$\geq \{\Omega_D\in\Re:-\infty<\Omega_k\leq0\}$$

0
$$\geq \{\Omega_D\in\Re:-\infty<\Omega_k\leq0\}.$$

$U_D\,(n=0\,|\,k=q)$
$$\geq U_D\,(1<n=q\,|\,k=q)$$

0
$$\geq \left(1-\frac{n-1}{k+1-n}\right)\left(\left(\frac{1}{n}\right)^2-\left(\frac{k-n}{k}\right)^2\right)$$

0
$$\geq \left(1-\frac{q-1}{q+1-q}\right)\left(\left(\frac{1}{q}\right)^2-\left(\frac{q-q}{q}\right)^2\right)$$

0
$$\geq \frac{2-q}{q^2}.$$

Now let us consider $k=q+1$:

$U_D\,(n=0\,|\,k=q+1)$
$$\gtrless U_D\,(n=1\,|\,k=q+1)$$

0
$$\geq \{\Omega_D\in\Re:-\infty<\Omega_k\leq0\}.$$

$U_D\ (n=0\,|\,k=q+1)$

$\gtreqless\ U_D\ (n=1\,|\,k=q+1)$

0

$\geq\ \left(1-\dfrac{n-1}{k+1-n}\right)\left(\left(\dfrac{1}{n}\right)^2-\left(\dfrac{k-n}{k}\right)^2\right)$

0

$\geq\ \left(1-\dfrac{(q+1)-1}{(q+1)+1-(q+1)}\right)\times$

$$\left(\left(\dfrac{1}{q+1}\right)^2-\left(\dfrac{(q+1)-(q+1)}{q+1}\right)^2\right)$$

0

$\geq\ -\dfrac{q-1}{(q+1)^2}.$

Conclusion: *Claim 3 holds true. When* $\Omega_{d(i)} \geq -\dfrac{1}{k+1}\ \forall m(i),,\ D$ *offers* $n=0$.

CHAPTER 4

Language Regime Choice: Evidence

The previous chapter suggested possible relationships between politically relevant linguistic heterogeneity levels and language regime choice. Governments respond to threats from linguistic groups. When politically relevant linguistic heterogeneity levels are low, the optimal choice for the government is one that power-concentrates in the dominant group language. Such language regimes offer substantial egoism and efficiency benefits to just one group while leaving the excluded population with little recourse. But when politically relevant linguistic heterogeneity levels are either moderate or high, a prudent government will make linguistic concessions. These concessions can take one of the following forms: power-sharing, power-neutralizing, or a hybrid of the two.

The advantage (and conversely, disadvantage) of each language regime type is unique. Power-sharing bestows collective equality, but it comes at a hefty price with respect to cultural egoism and communicative efficiency. This price only increases as the number of other groups requiring appeasement increases. In contrast, with power-neutralizing language regimes, all linguistic groups forfeit substantive claims to cultural egoism. In exchange, however, these regimes are efficient: they facilitate interethnic communication. They are also egalitarian: they present an image of a panethnic state collectively shared by all, as opposed to being dominated simply by just one group. Power-neutralizing language regimes are optimal when politically relevant linguistic heterogeneity levels are high. Alternatively, neutralized-sharing language regimes have the advantage of being able to deliver all three Es: cultural egoism, communicative efficiency, and collective equality. However, unlike the other three, because these regimes are hybrids, the benefits are attenuated. The recognition of additional mother tongues in conjunction with a lingua franca can still introduce inefficiency and inequality.

This chapter empirically examines the above arguments by employing two different tests. One is a large N statistical analysis. The purpose of this test is first to evaluate the face validity of the argument and to then assess the generalizability of the findings. The other test is a controlled comparison of four causal-process observations: two countries (Malaysia and Singapore) over two periods. By process-tracing in each observation, the objective is to establish whether the purported causal mechanism is indeed in play. Specifically, are governments choosing language regimes in response to minority constraints? The results offer strong evidence confirming the link between politically relevant linguistic heterogeneity levels and language regime choice—both the likelihood of recognition and the level of recognition. The chapter concludes by discussing the implications of this argument.

Language Regime Choice in Asia

To ensure the Indonesian story from the previous chapter is not an anomaly and to test the claim that politically relevant linguistic heterogeneity levels affect language regime choice, I begin with a large N statistical test. The sample for this test includes all Asian countries 1945–2005. The unit of analysis is *country-year.*

Research Design

Language Regime: The dependent variable of interest is language regime. Here, language regime is measured using two different coding schemes. As discussed in Chapter 2, the first measure is quadrachotomous. A language regime is considered "power-concentrating" if one—and only one—mother tongue is employed in the education curriculum. If multiple mother tongues—but no lingua francas—are recognized, then the regime is rendered "power-sharing." Among language regimes that do recognize a lingua franca, if the lingua franca is recognized exclusively, the regime is coded as power-neutralizing. Otherwise, the language regime is deemed neutralized-sharing. The values assigned to each corresponding language regime are shown in Table 4.1.

Complementing the quadrachotomous measure is a continuous one: the degree of power-neutralization in the education system. The advantage of this alternative measure is that it gets at not just whether a lingua franca is recognized, but also to what extent. The results using the quadrachotomous measure only show whether the level of politically relevant linguistic heterogeneity matters for the recognition of a lingua franca. In contrast, the use of a continuous measure allows

Table 4.1: Operationalizing Language Regimes

Language regime type	Assigned value
Power-Concentrating	
Recognition of one mother tongue	0
Power-Sharing	
Recognition of multiple mother tongues	1
Power-Neutralizing	
Exclusive recognition of a lingua franca	2
Neutralized-Sharing Hybrid	
Recognition of lingua franca and mother tongues	3

us to observe the variance across the 3 ± 1 types (Laitin 1992: 18–19) against the backdrop of a language regime that has neutralized completely. As a reminder, this variable is bounded from a minimum of 0 (no recognition of a lingua franca whatsoever) to a maximum of 1 (complete recognition of a lingua franca).

Politically Relevant Linguistic Heterogeneity: The primary independent variable is the level of politically relevant linguistic heterogeneity. Constructing this measure requires decisions on three concepts. The first concept is "politically relevant." Just because a group exists as a social-demographic construct does not necessarily imply it has the clout or resources to matter politically. To address this concern, I use data from Cederman, Wimmer, and Min (2010). The corresponding dataset (ETH Ethnic Power Relations)[1] identifies all politically relevant ethnic groups not just across a global sample but also over time (1946–2009). A group is considered "politically relevant" if "at least one political organization claims to represent it in national politics or if its members are subjected to state-led political discrimination" (Cederman, Wimmer, and Min 2010: 99).

After identifying all politically relevant groups, the second concept requiring attention is "linguistic." Not all ethnic groups identified in the ETH Ethnic Power Relations database are linguistic in nature. In the United States, African Americans are identified as a politically relevant ethnic group. Yet neither the position of the political organization representing this group nor the source of the political discrimination is over language per se. As another example, consider the United Kingdom and specifically Northern Ireland. The two politically relevant groups there are the (Irish) Catholics and the (British) Protestants. Although there is a shallow linguistic cleavage (the Irish language is still used by a minority of Irish Catholics), the primary cleavage is that between the descendants of

Irish natives and of British settlers. For an ethnic group to be considered a linguistic group, the group must speak an "ethnic" language identified in either the *Ethnologue* (Lewis 2009) or the *L'aménagement linguistique dans le monde* (Leclerc 2010) databases. In each country, the ethnic group identified as having the most political relevance according to the ETH Ethnic Power Relations database is considered here as the politically dominant. And correspondingly, its mother tongue is the politically dominant language.

With "politically relevant" and "linguistic" operationalized, the last concept of interest is "heterogeneity." Heterogeneity is conceptualized in two different manners. The first is a simple raw count of the number of politically relevant linguistic groups. Under this rubric, the three most heterogeneous countries in 2005 are China (49), Russia (37), and India (17).[2] Given the nonnormal distribution of this count measure (i.e., in contrast to China, Russia, and India, 90 percent of the countries have ten groups or fewer), I take the log transformation of this variable.

The problem with using a raw count is that it assumes all groups have equal weight in political relevance. Given this potential validity concern, I also employ an alternative measure. The Herfindahl-Hirschman concentration index measures the likelihood that two individuals chosen at random will be from different politically relevant linguistic groups $\left(1 - \sum_i^k s_i^2\right)$. The index ranges from 0 to 1, with the former indicating complete homogeneity and the latter, complete heterogeneity. The three most politically linguistically heterogeneous countries in 2005 are Nepal (0.7584), China (0.6654), and Afghanistan (0.6562).

Control Variables: Inevitably, other variables matter as well for language regime choice. The first is regime type. Democracies provide institutionalized channels for voicing preferences. They are also generally associated with higher levels of civil liberties (Poe and Tate 1994; Poe, Tate, and Keith 1999). Taken together, the ex ante expectation is that democracies—especially those with proportional electoral rules—are less likely to choose power-concentrating language regimes and more likely to opt for ones that share. However, as it stands, a priori, there is no theoretical reason to believe either democracies or authoritarian regimes are more likely to favor lingua franca recognition. By construction, lingua franca recognition—whether exclusively or in combination—involves forfeiting linguistic power. No government, regardless of the institutional constraints present, prefers forfeiting power above keeping power. Regime type is measured using POLITY (Marshall and Jaggers 2008). A country's democracy (DEMOC) and authoritarian (AUTOC) score is based on the competitiveness of political participation, the openness and competitiveness of executive recruitment, and the level of constraints on the chief executive. Consistent with the literature, the two scales have been combined into one single index, which ranges from −10 (most authoritarian) to 10 (most democratic).

The second control variable is wealth. Wealth can matter through at least two different mechanisms. One is that poorer countries may simply face greater challenges with allocating the necessary resources to recognize multiple languages. Recognition is costly (Laitin 1988; Pool 1991). The other mechanism has to do with conflict moderation. With poverty, there is "pressure on the upper strata to treat the lower classes beyond the pale of human society" (Lipset 1959: 83). But when wealth levels are high, "tolerance norms" (84) increase and cleavages become less salient. The prior expectation therefore is that when wealth levels are low, the likelihood of a power-concentrating language regime is high; and the likelihood of a power-sharing language regime, low.

These two mechanisms, however, differ on their expectations with respect to lingua franca recognition. If the story is about physical capital, then low levels of wealth should have a positive effect. The rationale is that power-neutralizing language regimes, like power-concentrating ones, require fewer translations and are thus cheaper. If the story is, however, about conflict, then the effects are less clear. On the one hand, if the use of a lingua franca is a *symptom* of existing tension, then power-neutralizing language regimes should be most prevalent at low levels of wealth. On the other hand, if the use of a lingua franca is a *solution* to existing tensions, then linguistic neutralization should happen more frequently at higher levels of wealth. Wealth is measured as GDP per capita, rescaled by the US$1,000 unit. The data source is the IMF's Direction of Trade (DOT) statistics.

Colonialism is also important. Four types are of particular interest. The first is a British legacy. British colonialism—especially when compared to other forms of colonialism (namely, French)—has been linked to higher-quality governments (La Porta et al. 1999; Von Hayek 1960), stronger economies (Przeworski et al. 2000), and multilingual education curriculums (Albaugh 2009; B. White 1996). In the sense that former British colonies are more likely to be democratic and wealthier and to recognize minority languages, the expectation is that a British legacy would have a negative effect on the likelihood of a power-concentrating language regime but a positive one on those that share—with or without a lingua franca.

The second colonial legacy of interest is that of continental Europeans (Dutch, French, Portuguese, and Spanish). In contrast to the British, these colonial authorities were less likely to establish developmental institutions. Instead, they were more likely to be extractive and to administer using the colonial language. Given this legacy, the expectation would be that continental European colonies are less likely to power share but more likely to power neutralize.

The third colonial legacy is a Russian one. The collapse of the Soviet Union was a critical moment when a number of countries could break free from Moscow's influence. There were, however, still a number of considerations for continuing to recognize the Russian language. First, there was a sizable Russian minority in many of these countries. This was often the result of mass migration during the Soviet era. Second, despite its association as a colonial language, Russian is a lingua franca among these countries. To continue recognizing this language could prove economically advantageous in the future. Given this discussion, the expectation is that countries formerly in the Soviet Union are not likely to choose a power-concentrating language regime, but instead are more likely to opt for neutralized-sharing where a titular language (e.g., Kazakh), other mother tongues, and Russian are all recognized.

The last colonial legacy of interest is that of the nonlegacy. Some countries were never colonized by a western force; they did not have the practices and policies of another country imposed upon them for a prolonged period of time. The implication is that in these countries there is no colonial lingua franca on the menu of options. Thus, the expectation is that countries without a colonial legacy are less likely to choose language regimes that recognize a lingua franca.[3] All four colonial variables are coded as dichotomous. The data source for colonial legacy is from Hadenius and Teorell (2005).[4] The absence of a (western) colonial legacy is the reference category.[5]

The last control variable of interest is the federal/unitary status of the country. Federalism separates power between different levels of governments and is often characterized by a "bicameral legislature with a strong federal chamber to represent the constituent regions" (Lijphart 1999: 187). In India, these constituent regions have largely matched linguistic boundaries. Additionally, such federal arrangements bestow upon each regional government the authority to decide the official language of the state. Such powers not only protect the majority language within each state, but they may also confer recognition on other "large" minorities within each state that would otherwise not have gotten a voice at the national Union level. All this has been absolutely instrumental in defusing ethnic violence (Stuligross and Varshney 2002). Whether federalism is the cause of minority language recognition or an indication of the political strength of minority groups to extract concessions from the government is not the precise point. Instead, what is of interest is the ex ante theoretical expectation that federalism is highly

Table 4.2: Expected Effects of Control Variables

Control variable	Concentrating	Sharing	Neutralizing	Hybrid
Regime type	−	+	Ø	Ø
GDP/capita (1000)	−	+	−/+	−/+
Colonialism: British	−	+	Ø	+
Colonialism: Continental	Ø	−	+	Ø
Colonialism: Russian	−	+	−	+
Colonialism: none	Ø	Ø	−	−
Federalism	−	+	Ø	+

correlated with power-sharing and neutralized-sharing language regimes. The data source is the Institutions and Elections Project (Regan and Clark 2010). For this book, the variable *federal* is assigned a value of 1 if there are autonomous federative entities (e.g., states and provinces).

In summary, the expected effects of each control variable on language regime choice are shown in Table 4.2. It is critical to note that absent from this list is the lagged dependent variable. Language regimes are political institutions. The choice to neutralize linguistic power—and to what extent in this period—is heavily shaped by the choice in the previous period. Put differently, language regimes change infrequently. Consequently, to include a lagged dependent variable may unduly influence the estimates (Achen 2000).

Empirical Evidence

In all, there are eight models. To streamline the substantive focus and minimize clutter, I relegate all technical discussions and tables to the Appendix at the end of this chapter. The results are robust: language regime choice is very much shaped by the level of politically relevant linguistic heterogeneity. As illustrated in Figure 4.1, when politically relevant linguistic heterogeneity levels are low, there is a high likelihood of power-concentrating language regimes (black shade). This is consistent with Hypothesis 1.1 from the previous chapter. The government has every incentive to recognize exclusively the language of the dominant group when it faces weak political constraints. Doing so yields sizable benefits. There are benefits with respect to cultural egoism. There are also benefits with respect to communicative efficiency: everyone should be able to interact in the same language, thereby rendering translations unnecessary. These

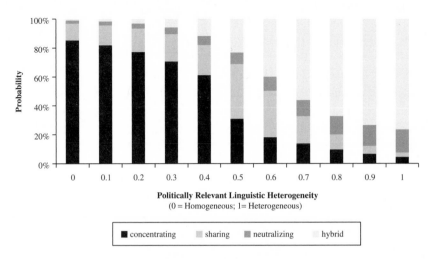

Figure 4.1. Likelihood of language regime choice.

combined benefits ensure that the government will consider any accrued inequality costs trivial.

The results also indicate that as the level of politically relevant linguistic heterogeneity increases, the likelihood of a language regime being power-sharing, power-neutralizing, or neutralized-sharing increases as well. When many other significant groups dilute the political relevance of the dominant group, linguistic concessions must be made. There are three possible concessions. One is the use of multiple mother tongues, another is the recognition of a lingua franca, and the third is a hybrid of the two.

In theory, which of these concessions is optimal depends on politically relevant linguistic heterogeneity levels. As postulated by Hypothesis 1.2, a power-sharing language regime is attractive at moderate levels of heterogeneity, but at high levels, it can be unattractive. In this scenario, it is very costly. The costs of inefficiency can be quite astounding with marginal returns to egoism and equality. Under such conditions, the optimal language regime is either power-neutralizing or neutralized-sharing. The recognition of a lingua franca produces both efficiency and equality. Put differently, when the level of politically relevant linguistic heterogeneity increases from a minimum of 0 to a maximum of 1, the likelihood of a power-neutralizing language regime increases from 2 to 16 percent (lighter of the two gray shades in Figure 4.1). The same shift also increases the probability of a neutralized-sharing language regime from 1 to 77 percent (white shade in Figure 4.1).

There is, however, a caveat. In spite of Figure 4.1, the difference in the likelihood of a power-neutralizing regime versus a neutralized-sharing hybrid is' not statistically significant. This is consistent with Hypothesis 1.3: at high levels of heterogeneity, a priori, we cannot differentiate between the two types of concessions. All we can predict is that a lingua franca will be recognized. Its use can both facilitate communicative efficiency and generate collective equality.

It is possible that there is a measurement concern. It is likely that the blunt quadrachotomous operationalization is suppressing any meaningful variation in the degree of power-neutralization. For instance, a regime that recognizes a lingua franca for just one year but is otherwise dominated by one mother tongue is coded as the same as one that recognizes a politically dominant language for one year but uses the lingua franca as the primary medium. To assess this concern, I employ an alternative measure of language regime. To this end, I focus on how much of the education curriculum is carried out in a lingua franca. Recall that this measure is continuous where a maximum value of 1 suggests the curriculum is completely dominated by a lingua franca and no mother tongue is used.

The results suggest there is evidence supporting Corollary 1: as the level of politically relevant linguistic heterogeneity increases, the extent of lingua franca recognition also increases. This finding is robust whether heterogeneity is measured as a count of the number of groups or as a concentration index. For instance, as the number of linguistic groups increases, the proportion of the education curriculum carried out through a lingua franca also increases. A one standard deviation increase in the number of linguistic minority groups (from three groups to seven) can increase the use of a lingua franca by 45 percent.

Alternatively, as an illustration, see Figure 4.2. At one end of the x-axis is a Herfindahl-Hirschman concentration index of 0 (complete homogeneity). Here, the degree of power-neutralization is expected to have an average value of 0 with a mathematical (but not theoretically possible) minimum of -0.09. But at the other end of the x-axis (complete heterogeneity), the expected value increases to an average of 0.29 with a possible maximum of 0.36. Put simply, Figure 4.2 suggests that politically relevant linguistic heterogeneity levels can drive a government's choice to neutralize linguistic powers. As the former increases, the latter increases as well.

All in all, the results confirm that language regime choice is indeed shaped by the level of politically relevant linguistic heterogeneity. Those same results also suggest other variables may be in play as well. The first alternative explanation is regime type. Recall, the ex ante expectation was that democracies are (1) less likely to concentrate and (2) more likely to share. There are at least two pos-

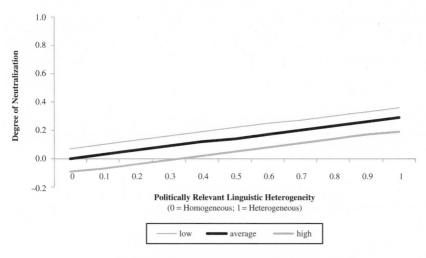

Figure 4.2. Level of power-neutralization.

sible mechanisms. Democracies are generally associated with human rights and minority protections. Moreover, electoral constraints make democratic governments more likely to trade policies for votes. Yet, there is no evidence that democracies are less likely to concentrate or more likely to share linguistic power. It is possible that the effects of regime type warrant a proviso: under winner-takes-all democratic systems, one might expect "a tyranny of the majority." Often the majority is not a majority at all, but rather a dominant plurality. For democratic politicians under such conditions, the incentive is to choose a power-concentrating language regime. As expected, democracies are just as likely as nondemocracies to avoid power-neutralizing language regimes when possible.

Wealth, measured as GDP per capita, is another variable expected to affect language regime choice. The effects, however, are only evident when it comes to choosing either power-neutralizing or neutralized-sharing language regimes. In agreement with Lipset's findings (1959: 83–84), as wealth increases, the likelihood of a language regime where linguistic power is completely neutralized increases. The story can also be told from the perspective of the minorities. Specifically, high levels of wealth can be the product of extensive minority assimilation. When minorities are assimilated, there is linguistic standardization. Here, standardization breeds efficiency, and efficiency in turn breeds growth. If the use of any language other than a lingua franca (i.e., minority language) simply increases transaction costs, there is little desire for minority groups to demand recognition or for governments to extend any recognition (see Grin 2003: chap. 10).

Colonial legacy is important. Recall, there are four types of legacies of theoretical interest. The first is British. Compared to other European colonies, British colonies are associated with better quality governments (La Porta et al. 1999; Von Hayek 1960), more robust economies (Przeworski et al. 2000), and more minority-friendly education curriculums (Albaugh 2009; B. White 1996). This in turn should matter for language regime choice. The results are somewhat weak. British colonies are indeed more likely to recognize a lingua franca. However, there are two caveats. First, if a British colony did not recognize the English language, the likelihoods of power-concentrating ($\beta = -3.81$; SE $= 0.94$) and power-sharing ($\beta = -3.79$; SE $= 0.90$) are substantively the same. Second, if a British colony did recognize English, the likelihood of a power-neutralizing language regime is statistically much larger than the likelihood of a neutralized-sharing regime. Taken together, these findings suggest that British ex-colonies, although willing to recognize a lingua franca, were not necessarily minority friendly.

The results also suggest that colonies of continental Europe were most likely to recognize a power-neutralizing language regime in the colonial language, followed by one that was either power-concentrating or a neutralized-sharing hybrid. The least likely language regime was one that strictly power-shared. The post-Soviet republics, as expected, were most likely to choose neutralized-sharing language regimes. This was the case in the likes of Kazakhstan. In those that did not recognize Russian (e.g., Azerbaijan), the language regime was strictly power-concentrating (e.g., Azerbaijan).

The last colonial legacy of interest is the nonlegacy. The argument is as follows: countries without a nineteenth- and twentieth-century European colonial legacy by definition do not have a colonial language to inherit on independence. This is critical, as colonialism is the most common source (although certainly not the only source) for a lingua franca. Under such conditions, the likelihood of lingua franca recognition and the level of linguistic neutralization are both low. The result for noncolonialism is highly significant and robust. A country with a colonial legacy—any legacy—is 16 percent more likely than a country without a colonial legacy to choose a power-neutralizing language regime. Additionally, among those that do recognize a lingua franca, the degree of linguistic neutralization is 15 percent greater in the former than in the latter.

The last control variable is federalism. By design, federalism is a power-sharing institution. Each level of government has a distinct and often territorially based jurisdiction. Whether federalism is a reason for minority language recognition or is an indication of the political relevance of minority groups, the ex ante expectation is that federal countries are less likely to choose power-concentrating language regimes and more likely to choose power-sharing. They are also more likely to adopt neutralized-sharing. There are no priors about the effects of federalism on either the likelihood of a power-neutralizing language regime or the level of linguistic neutralization. The results reveal that federalism has no effect on whether a country power-concentrates, power-shares, or neutralizing-shares. Theoretically, this may be the result of a tradeoff between descriptive representation and substantive representation. Just because a minority group is given an institutionalized political voice does not imply that minority-favorable policies (e.g., minority language recognition) will immediately follow. Put differently, "descriptive representation is neither absolutely necessary nor entirely sufficient for substantive representation to occur" (Reingold 2008: 128). But if a lingua franca is recognized, it is statistically not likely to be the exclusive language of recognition. This suggests that when countries with federal institutions make efforts to recognize a lingua franca to generate some sense of equality, they will match that choice with the recognition of multiple mother tongues. An example of this is India.

Language Regime Choice in Southeast Asia

The previous analysis demonstrated that politically relevant linguistic heterogeneity levels affect language regime choice. The hypothesized causal mechanism is the constraints facing a government balancing between cultural egoism, communicative efficiency, and collective equality. To examine whether these mechanisms are indeed operating, I process-trace through a controlled comparison of Malaysia (1957–) and Singapore (1959–). Before turning to the two cases, I first discuss how I identify the units of analysis: *country-period*. I then explain how I operationalize and measure the two variables of interest: language regime and politically relevant linguistic heterogeneity.

Research Design

As we have seen in Chapter 2, Malaysia and Singapore lend themselves to a most similar systems design (Przeworski and Teune 1970; Seawright and Gerring 2008: 304–5). By comparing between two (or more) cases that are different on the key explanatory variable and the outcome of interest—but are effectively similar on all the alternative explanations, these designs offer substantial leverage to better understand the primary variable of interest vis-à-vis all other possible variables.

Both countries have been governed by hegemonic parties; started econom-ically at comparable levels of development (low); and share a British colonial experience. Additionally, for two years (1963–1965), Singapore was a part of the larger Malaysian Federation. Not only are these two cases appropriate for cross-unit comparison, the fact that there were language regime changes in both Ma-laysia and Singapore allows for diachronic analysis. In each country, the language regime choice before and after a critical juncture (1969–1971 in Malaysia; 1963–1965 in Singapore) offers two more observations subject to a most similar design. Altogether, the two periods in the two countries provide for four causal-process observations (D. Collier, Brady, and Seawright 2004). This will allow for a sys-tematic qualitative test of the relationship between politically relevant linguistic heterogeneity levels and language regime choices.

Period: A period in this mode of analysis is delineated between two critical junc-tures. Critical junctures—triggered by crises (R. Collier and D. Collier 1991: 29–31)—are characterized by macro changes to the political system. These changes often, but not always, coincide with a regime change; and conversely, these changes rarely coincide with a mere change in the head of state or head of govern-ment. For example, in Malaysia, the second period covers the rule of multiple prime ministers. In contrast, in Singapore, the same prime minister straddled two periods. A period begins with the introduction of new institutions. With these new institutions, the processes for voicing preferences and how conflict is resolved subsequently change. Examples of such critical junctures include transi-tions between colonialism and independence, and between democracy and au-thoritarianism.

Critical junctures are vital to the analysis because language regimes, as po-litical institutions, can be products of path dependence (see Thelen 2004: 23–31). Once a country sets down one trajectory, there is some sort of stickiness. Change is possible (i.e., path dependence is not synonymous with irreversibil-ity), but generally only during transitional moments (Mahoney 2000). Even then, there is still a strong preference to reinforce the status quo because of high sunk costs. The prospective costs of change include, but are not limited to, re-educating a large portion of the population in a new language; developing new textbooks and training educators; and standardizing vocabulary and grammar. Failure to pay these costs can render a large segment of the population margin-alized and disenfranchised (Ginsburgh and Weber 2011: chap. 6). Yet, despite these costs, changes still do happen. Here, I focus on two such periods in each of the two cases.

<u>Language Regime</u>: The dependent variable of interest is language regime. Consistent with the large N coding scheme, language regime is coded by examining the education curriculum. There are, however, two significant departures from the previous test as discussed in Chapter 2. First, the focus here is on primary, secondary, *and* tertiary education. Since university curriculums are politically and technocratically much more difficult to establish and later reform (K. Y. Lee 2000: 174–77; see also Brimble and Doner 2007), any observed change—whether expansion or contraction—will allow for an even clearer understanding of how the government sees the distribution of linguistic power (see Albaugh 2009, 2014; Kaplan and Baldauf 1997: 4–14).

The second difference is that attention is given here not only to the formal laws governing mediums of instruction but also to the de facto conditions. Just because all languages are legally recognized does not imply practical equality. To measure which language, if any, is first among equals, the focus will also include languages as subjects. If language x is an obligatory subject of instruction in a school where the medium of instruction is language y, but the opposite is not true, this would suggest language x has higher status than language y.

The broad conceptualization of each language regime type remains unchanged. The language regime in the first period in both Malaysia and Singapore was neutralized-sharing: English was afforded recognition alongside Chinese, Malay, and Tamil. Despite similarities in the first period, language regimes would subsequently diverge in the second period. In Malaysia, linguistic power shifted toward de facto power-concentrating in the Malay language. Although Chinese- and Tamil-medium schools continued to operate, Malay was a mandatory subject in those curriculums. In contrast, in Singapore, the language regime shifted from a neutralized-sharing to one that was effectively power-neutralizing in the English language.

<u>Politically Relevant Linguistic Heterogeneity</u>: To measure the independent variable again requires operationalization of three concepts: political relevance, linguistic group, and heterogeneity. Let us start with linguistic group identity. In both Malaysia and Singapore, ethnic classifications have largely matched linguistic classifications. For instance, the Chinese speak "Chinese" (i.e., Mandarin), the "Indians" speak Tamil, and the Malays speak "Malay." Admittedly, this statement is a broad generalization, as each racial group is an aggregation of a number of linguistic communities. For instance, the Chinese race encompasses speakers of Cantonese, Hainanese, Hakka, Hokkien, Mandarin, and Teochew; the Indian race, speakers of Bengali, Hindi, Tamil, and Urdu; and the Malay race, speakers of Boyanese, Bugis, Javanese, Minankabau, and Peninsular Malay (Chua 2005).

Table 4.3: Language Regime Choice in Malaysia and Singapore

	Malaysia 1957 (Alliance Party era)	Malaysia 1971 (National Front era)	Singapore 1959 (Pre-merger era)	Singapore 1965 (Post-merger era)
Outcomes of interest				
Language regime choice	Neutralized-Sharing	Power-Concentrating	Neutralized-Sharing	Power-Neutralizing
	Malay, Minority, English	*Malay Dominant*	*English, Minority, Malay*	*English*
Possible explanations				
Cultural diversity	High	High	High	High
Political structure	UMNO-led Coalition	UMNO-led Coalition	PAP	PAP
Party leadership	British-Educated	British-Educated	British-Educated	British-Educated
Party ideology	Anti-Communist	Anti-Communist	Anti-Communist	Anti-Communist
Wealth (GDP/capita)	Low (427.64)	Low (667.264)	Low (434.00)	Low (1005.55)
Colonial legacy	British (1957)	British (1957)	British (1959)	British (1959)
Size: area/population	Big/Large	Big/Large	Small/Small	Small/Small
Primary explanation				
Minority group strength	Strong	Weak	Strong	Weak
State strength	Weak	Strong	Weak	Weak
Politically relevant				
Linguistic heterogeneity	High	Low	High	High

For this book, the identity of a linguistic group is based on the country's census. The census in the first Malaysia period (1957–1971) identified four races: Chinese, Indian, Malay, and a generic other. However, beginning in the second period (post-1971), Malay was reclassified as Bumiputera ("sons of the soil")[6] so as to include indigenous persons as well. The story is similar but slightly different in Singapore. In the first period (1959–1965), the census demarcated four groups: Chinese, Eurasian,[7] Indian, and Malay. But by the start of the second period (post-1965), the Eurasian category had been dropped. In its place was the generic "other."

Just because a group is identified in the census does not suggest it is politically relevant. Not all groups are equally significant. Moreover, the relevance of a group can change over time. To measure political relevance, I focus on (1) the strength of the linguistic group *relative* to (2) the strength of the state. Thus, a group can be politically relevant through two different, although not mutually exclusive, channels. The first is that the linguistic group is strong from an absolute standpoint. Strength is defined by the presence of a coherent institutionalized organization: clear leadership, a large membership base, and available financial resources. The second channel is through a weak state. The strength of the state is determined by the simultaneous interplay of several different constraints—"systemic vulnerability" (Doner, Ritchie, and Slater 2005: 328). One such constraint is scarce resource endowments. The ability of a government to repress or buy off an opposition with pork partly depends on the size of the available coffers. Another constraint is severe security threats. The source of these threats can be either international or domestic, if not both (see Slater 2010: 5).

With political relevance and linguistic groups identified, it is now possible to operationalize politically relevant linguistic heterogeneity. Heterogeneity is measured as a dichotomy. It is coded as "high" if there are multiple politically relevant linguistic groups. Put differently, is there more than one linguistic group forcing concessions from the government? If the answer is yes, then politically relevant linguistic heterogeneity is considered high. Otherwise, the variable is coded as "low." Table 4.3 summarizes the values for the variables of interest across all four causal-process observations.

Malaysia: The Alliance Party Era (1957–1969)

The Malaysian story begins in 1945. With the Japanese surrender, the British advocated for the creation of a Malayan Union. Under this arrangement, eleven of its colonies would be unified under one central administration. Descendants of non-Malay immigrants (i.e., Chinese and Indians) would be given automatic citizenship. In 1946, the United Malay National Organization (UMNO) emerged to represent Malay interests and to resist this proposal. Widespread opposition led the British to replace the Union with the Malayan[8] Federation in 1948. Under this new arrangement, the sultans retained their symbolic positions (Simandjuntak 1969: 14). Aside from the matter of the Malayan Union and the citizenship of non-Malays, the UMNO was cooperative with the colonial authorities. In fact, the party's moderate (non-anti-imperialist and noncommunist) position elevated its importance when the negotiations eventually shifted to independence.

Although the colonial authorities looked favorably on the UMNO, the party leaders knew that independence—which the British were willing to grant—was only possible if London was convinced racial differences could be abated. Put differently, negotiations would be suspended as soon as evidence of tensions surfaced. Despite Malay having been long recognized as the language of the indigenous population (Shaw 1976: 92), this was no trivial matter. Under such constraints and preferences for complete decolonization, the UMNO was forced to invite two minority groups to the table.

Numerically, the Chinese accounted for approximately 30 percent of the country's population. Their presence was most notable in the urban centers, including the capital Kuala Lumpur, Johor, Penang, Perak, and Selangor. Financially, the Chinese were disproportionally wealthy: the average Chinese income was 2.4 times greater than that of the average Malay (T. H. Silcock in Abdul Samad 1998: 65). Some of these resources came from abroad, but many were domestically generated. The source of this inequality dated back to colonial times. The Malays and the Chinese had pursued very different economic activities; these activities in turn would have long-term ramifications. Aside from some civil service jobs, the Malays were predominantly confined to the agrarian sector (73 percent). Only 7 percent of the Malays were engaged in commerce and industry in comparison with 68 percent of the Chinese (Rasiah 1997). The Chinese had gone from the basic wholesale and retail trade to controlling and owning commercial businesses. Moreover, living in urban centers meant they could take advantage of educational opportunities to learn English. This qualified them for skilled labor and clerical occupations in the British administration and in private firms.

To further aggravate a tense relationship, the Chinese community was ideologically split. On the right, representing the noncommunists, was the Malaysian Chinese Association (MCA); and on the left, the Malaysian Communist Party (MCP). Both parties were highly organized with large recruitment bases and solid international support. Between the two alternatives, for the UMNO it was clear that the MCP was the worse of the two evils. The MCP was responsible for the "spasmodic outbreaks of urban attacks, area curfews north and south of the capital, . . . the enemy infiltrating all levels of society, including the Chinese triads (secret societies) and drug trade" (Abdul Samad 1998: 134).

Given these conditions, the UMNO reached out to the MCA in 1952. The proposed informal coalition would contest the twelve seats in the Kuala Lumpur municipal council elections. The agreement was that the two parties would avoid competing over the same seats. In heavily Malay-populated districts, the MCA would not field a candidate; instead, it would urge its Chinese supporters in that district to vote for the UMNO candidate. The opposite would happen in the Chinese-concentrated precincts. The results were transformative: the UMNO-MCA coalition won nine of the twelve seats, dealing a crushing blow to the larger anti-imperialist Malay parties and the MCP (Rahman Putra 1986: 35, 51).

Given the 1952 success, the UMNO subsequently reached out to the Indian community, represented by the Malaysian Indian Congress (MIC). While a smaller population, the largely Tamil-speaking Indian minority was still a politically relevant linguistic group. As far as the colonial government in London was concerned, the appeasement and incorporation of the Tamil community was just as important as that of the Chinese (Shaw 1976: 93–95; Simandjuntak 1969: 85–86). Moreover, given the weakness of the Malayan state, the UMNO could not afford to alienate any potentially cooperative group. Recall, political relevance is conceptualized in relative terms. Security was a concern; crises were frequent. As Dr. Mahathir bin Muhammad (hereafter "Mahathir"), the fourth and longest-serving prime minister, noted,

> when the British returned, the Sino-Malay relationship was anything but cordial, and when the Communists (mostly Chinese) tried to set up a Government for each of the Malay states, bloody Sino-Malay clashes were precipitated. These clashes would have developed into a racial war, but for the arrival and imposition of the British Military Administration backed by the full weight of the British Armed Forces. The communists were frustrated in their attempt to take over Malaya. (bin Muhammad 1970: 7)

For the 1955 Legislative Council election, the UMNO-MCA-MIC coalition ran under the formal banner of the "Alliance Party." The Alliance Party won all but one of the fifty-two seats. The one seat went to the Pan-Malaysian Islamic Party

(PAS). Given this dramatic success, the three members of the Alliance Party moved forward with negotiations for independence.

What were the implications of this critical juncture for the postcolonial language regime? The expectation would be that the UMNO, constrained by its two junior partners in the Alliance Party, could not choose a power-concentrating language regime. Instead, it must make substantial linguistic concessions to the Chinese and Tamils. In this case, the concession was a neutralized-sharing language regime. These concessions would come to be known as the Merdeka Agreement, a contract that included multiple provisions. This agreement would prove to be not only an instrument for easing racial tensions—and therefore securing Malayan independence—but also a vehicle to guarantee Alliance control in the new government.

One of the arrangements in the Agreement was the recognition of Malay as an official language of the state (Burhanudeen 2006). Although the MCA and the MIC lobbied hard for Chinese and Tamil recognition, both parties "refrained from pushing this issue" because of the larger—and shared—desire to end colonialism (H. Lee 2007: 128). As noted by Tunku Abdul Rahman (hereafter "Tunku"), UMNO leader and first prime minister, "the matter was not suitable to discuss at the moment as it would cause a split in the unity of the people to fight for independence" (MCA 2010). By backing the Alliance Party, however, the MCA and the MIC did lose some popularity with their own linguistic communities. The UMNO therefore "owed [MCA and MIC] support" (Shaw 1976: 120–21).

This support resulted in two linguistic concessions. First, English was recognized, temporarily, as an official language: "for a period of ten years after Independence Day [1967], and thereafter until Parliament otherwise provides, the English language may be used in both houses of Parliament, in the legislative assembly of every state, and for all other official purposes" (Legislative Council Debates, July 10, 1957). Second, Tunku also promised that the "Alliance government would never abolish vernacular languages, culture, and educational facilities" (MCA 2010). This promise had some credibility. During this time, the MCP-led insurgency against the British known as the "Emergency" was in full force. The British, "afraid of pushing the Chinese into the arms of the communists, agreed to the Chinese demands to look into their educational needs" (H. Lee 2007: 125). The result was the Fenn-Wu Committee, which recommended the continuation of Chinese and Tamil in the education curriculum.[9]

Although the Merdeka Agreement ultimately ensured independence, Tunku found himself challenged by multiple competing demands throughout his entire tenure as prime minister. On the one hand, there were the demographically dominant

Malays and their interests in concentrating linguistic power in their own language. On the other hand, his Chinese and Tamil partners required some linguistic concession, whether through the recognition of their mother tongues, English, or both.

The 1957 Education Ordinance (preceded by the 1956 Razak Report) reflected a compromise. The Ordinance established two types of education curriculums, both publicly funded by the Ministry of Education. In one curriculum (the national schools), Malay was to be the medium of instruction. English was to be an obligatory subject. Chinese and Tamil were to be taught if there was demand—"sufficient demand" defined as at least fifteen students whose parents wanted their children to learn the relevant language. This distribution of linguistic power could be found at both the primary and secondary levels of schooling. In contrast, in the other curriculum (the national-type schools), the main medium of instruction at the primary level included the two minority languages (Chinese and Tamil) and English. In these schools, regardless of the principal language of instruction, both English and Malay were to be compulsory subjects (Š. Ganguly 2003; Shaw 1976: 92). At the secondary level, however, English would be the only medium of instruction.

Chinese concerns over language-in-education heightened following the 1960 Talib Report and the 1961 Education Act. Although there was continued support for the provision of primary education in Chinese and Tamil, the Act was seen as a "knife hanging over Chinese education" (MCA 2010). The emphasis on the Malay curriculum, especially in reading, writing, and arithmetic, was construed as setting the groundwork for a Malay-only educational system. Even more contentious was Clause 21(2) in the Education Act, which read: "Where at any time the Minister is satisfied that a National-type primary school may be converted into a National primary school, he may be order [*sic*] direct that the school shall become a National Primary school" (1961 Education Ordinance). The authority of the education minister to make this conversion would prove contentious over the next three decades.

As movement for Chinese education picked up steam, this challenge alarmed some of the Malays. One response was the establishment of the National Language Action Front (NLAF). The NLAF unequivocally demanded that Malay become the sole official language after 1967—ten years after Independence Day (Š. Ganguly 2003: 248). In response, Tunku passed the 1967 National Language Act. The Act designated Malay as the sole official language. There were, however, two caveats. First, it allowed for the continued use and teaching of other languages. Second, while English was no longer an official language, there was still a de facto policy whereby all government bodies and formal institutions (e.g., universities) had to maintain every official document not only in Malay but also in English (Hashim 2003).

Much to the chagrin of the NLAF, Tunku, as the leader of the UMNO, had initially been forced to forfeit Malay cultural egoism for collective equality. The Merdeka Agreement was undoubtedly essential for Malaysia's transition to independence. It was the product of a majority-group-led government constrained by its two coalition partners. For Tunku, this constraint meant "defend[ing] . . . the friendship of the Chinese" as it was "the only guarantee for the happiness, peace, and prosperity of the country" (Rahman Putra 1978: 91). What would have happened if this "friendship"—constraint—had been absent? As it turns out, there is a natural counterfactual.

Malaysia: The National Front Era (1971–)

Both Donald Horowitz (1985) and Arend Lijphart (1977) cite Malaysia's Alliance Party era as an example of successful democratic coalition building. However, it was also during this period that Malaysia witnessed the emergence of the aforementioned NLAF and other Chinese parties to challenge the MCA (to be discussed below). These developments suggest that between 1957 and 1969, what Tunku called "friendship" was arguably muted racial discontent. Mahathir, for instance, wrote that the "UMNO came into being because of the Malay fear of losing out to the Chinese. The honeymoon period immediately before and after Independence lessened this fear, but it was never really absent" (bin Muhammad 1970: 10).

The tensions would explode following the 1969 election. The election was vicious. On the one hand, the PAS—the only non-Alliance party to secure any seat in the 1955 elections—pursued aggressive outflanking and accused the UMNO of having given in to Chinese demands. Many saw these concessions as a "betrayal" of the Malay vision and charged Tunku for "having sold the Malays down the drain" (H. Lee 2007: 131; also see K. Y. Lee 2000: 263–65). On the other hand, a Chinese opposition party, the Democratic Action Party (DAP), had emerged in 1965 claiming that the MCA had sold out the Chinese to the Malays. The DAP was interested in a "Malaysian Malaysia" where the three mother tongues would be treated equally (Means 1991; Rahman Putra 1978: 96).

Although the Alliance Party won the May 10 election, there were several notable setbacks. These included a significantly reduced margin of victory for the Alliance Party and the MCA's sweeping electoral defeat at the hands of the DAP in the Chinese districts. On May 12, thousands of Chinese marched through Kuala Lumpur parading in triumph at the DAP's electoral victories. In response the UMNO decided to host its own victory counterprocession. On May 13, as UMNO members gathered for the parade, there were reports of Malays being attacked as they were headed to the UMNO gathering. When news spread about the death of a Malay army officer, allegedly at the hands of Chinese hooligans, the parading Malays swiftly sought revenge by killing two Chinese passersby. The riots subsequently began. The chaos would spread throughout the capital and the greater Selangor area within forty-five minutes (Shaw 1976: 206).

The sultan of Malaysia (Yang di-Pertuan Agong) responded by declaring a state of emergency, suspending Parliament, and ordering an immediate curfew throughout Selangor. A few days later, he established the National Operations Council (NOC) headed by Deputy Prime Minister Tun Abdul Razak (hereafter "Razak"). With Parliament suspended, the sultan gave the NOC de facto executive and legislative control for the next eighteen months. As director of operations, Razak had almost unlimited executive power. It was not a coincidence that during this time, Tunku resigned, first as head of the government and then as president of the party (Abdul Samad 1998; Rahman Putra 1978).

When Parliament reopened in 1971, Razak, as the second prime minister, had an opportunity to change the language regime. The temporary status of English as an official language had already expired. Moreover, the political landscape had changed quite drastically. The previous coalition (Alliance Party) had been characterized by a horizontal relationship: UMNO and its two junior partners were largely collegial. However, a clear hierarchy defined the new post-1969 coalition. While the MCA and MIC would remain partners, the UMNO now dominated the National Front, a grand coalition with as many as thirteen parties. This change reflected the circumstances from which each coalition emerged. The Alliance Party had been "born out of necessity of the three major races to work together to fulfill the prerequisite set by the British for negotiating independence" (Abdul Samad 1998: 118). The National Front was created for very different reasons: it "came to life as the savior of a nation on the brink of collapse" (118). With the National Front, UMNO power increased significantly, "rais[ing] the specter of no interethnic bargaining mechanisms being in place in the new government" (Means 1991: 7).

Another big difference in the political landscape was the change in which groups counted among the linguistic minorities. This was especially true for the

Chinese. A series of events made it very clear that by this point the MCA was of minimal relevance. Several opposition parties had emerged to challenge the dominance of the MCA in the Chinese community. Many of these parties, most notably the DAP, fought for greater parity in linguistic rights between the Chinese and the Malays, not only in schools but also in official state matters. This was in stark contrast to the MCA, which continued to support Malay as the sole official language. Despite its previous status as the largest partner in the Alliance Party and supposedly *the* Chinese party, MCA's disappointing 1969 electoral performance highlighted the discontent of the Chinese community.

The intense fractionalization among the Chinese would prove again and again to be a source of political frustration for the MCA. Since the MCA leaders were "relatively powerless in shaping policy, they were often subject to competition from aspiring middle-level leaders who could easily generate a following at the grass-roots levels by articulating some of the accumulated grievances of the Chinese community" (Means 1991: 176). Moreover, the inclusion of five other Chinese-representing parties[10] in the National Front highlighted that the Chinese were no longer sufficiently organized. The MCA was relegated to a marginal symbolic position.

Aside from internal fractionalization, there were also external factors that diminished the political relevance of the Chinese community. Tunku had believed in the electoral importance of the Chinese. He saw their inclusion in the decision-making process as absolutely necessary for state survival. In contrast, some Malay leaders felt it was imperative to curb what they regarded as increasing displays of Chinese and Indian chauvinism. It was, however, not possible to execute any policy in this vein as long as Tunku was in power. To many Malays, Tunku simply "sold out the country to the Chinese" (K. Y. Lee 2000: 265). Whether Tunku overestimated the political relevance of the Chinese, and if he did, why, are subject to debate. However, the fact remains that once Razak become prime minister, the Chinese community lost an important—if not the most important—political ally.

Given the general—but not complete—weakening of the MCA and the MIC, the expectation for language policy would have been a shift away from any emphasis on English (Hypothesis 1.3). We do see evidence of this shift despite MCA making noise. The likelihood of a Malay power-concentrating language regime increased. There is no doubt Razak would have chosen a Malay-only language regime if possible. But as the Chinese and Indian communities were still of *some* relevance, the ultimate language regime chosen was power-concentrating with some concessions. Note that while there were concessions, they were trivial compared to those of pre-1969.

These concessions took place within the larger framework for the New Economic Policy (NEP). The NEP was the government's strategy for simultaneously addressing two objectives: eradicating general poverty and restructuring a society that had become closely aligned with ethnicity. Under the NEP, the government would not expropriate Chinese assets. It would, however, redirect the benefits of rapid economic growth disproportionately to the Malays. Examples of this included (1) a Malay preference in government employment; (2) aggressive government interventions in major (state and private) enterprises; and (3) a law that required all banks—even those privately owned—to earmark a significant portion of their business loans (about 20 percent) to Malays (Esman 1987).

In addition to the aforementioned economic policies, there was also a linguistic component. All English-medium public schools were to be converted into Malay-language schools. Recall that, as mandated by the 1957 Education Ordinance, the Ministry of Education established two types of publicly funded education curriculums. The national schools operated exclusively in the Malay medium. In contrast, the national-type schools used a number of different mediums, including English. Under the NEP, those operating in English faced gradual extinction.

Malay became the medium of instruction in the first grade (standard 1). By 1975, conversion at the primary level was completed so that English-medium primary schools no longer existed (Burhanudeen 2006). Chinese and Tamil primary schools, although limited in numbers, were allowed to stay open (Š. Ganguly 2003; H. Lee 2007). The Malay language, however, was a compulsory subject starting in the first year. Students who wished to continue their studies from these schools (about 30 percent in 1983) were required to attend a one-year Malay-medium transition school before proceeding to the secondary level (Kaplan and Baldauf 2003: 115).

While the education system remained multilingual, the phasing out of English deeply concerned the Chinese and Indians. In response, in 1975 the MCA submitted a Memorandum on Education to the government proposing that Chinese as a medium be extended to the secondary level. The proposal was rejected (MCA 2010). The UMNO-led government continued with the conversion of English-medium schools at the secondary level in 1976. The phasing out was completed in 1978 (Burhanudeen 2006).

The scope of the NEP and the increasing dominance of the Malay language were also evident at the tertiary level. Between 1971 and 1980 enrollment quadrupled. This was no small feat. In 1968 admission to the University of Malaya, the only university at the time, was based strictly on objective competitive criteria. Under these conditions, the majority (67 percent) of the student population were non-Malay. However, by the late 1970s with affirmative action, 75 percent of the students were Malay (Esman 1987; H. Lee 2007). Moreover, to support increasing enrollment, there was an expansion in opportunities. In the 1970s, the government established the National University of Malaysia, the country's first Malay-medium university (Š. Ganguly 2003).

Not surprisingly, these changes faced strong opposition from the Chinese and Indians. Their demands for greater levels of power-sharing were viewed by the Malays as a direct challenge. The Malays argued they had the legal right to establish one national language as stipulated in Article 152 of the constitution. This right was reflected in the revised 1971 National Language Act, whereby English was stripped of its status as an official language. Malay became the unequivocal sole official language of Malaysia. To "put a lid on the passionate debate on language policies" (H. Lee 2007: 132), the UMNO-led government passed an amendment to the 1948 Sedition Act. This change made it an offense to "question" the status of Malay as the sole official language. In effect, this policy prohibited the MCA and MIC (and any other citizen) from (1) questioning the special status of the Malay language or (2) advocating a multilingual language policy (132–33).

Although Razak's unexpected death left a power vacuum in the UMNO leadership, the language regime would remain unchanged. Prime ministers Hussein Onn (1976–1981) and Mahathir (1981–2003) continued what Razak started. Since 1969, the intensity and frequency of accommodationist rhetoric about the need to cooperate with the Chinese and Indians has significantly decreased. Rather, the majority of attention since the Emergency has been directed at the larger national economic plans. The foci were to promote development broadly and decrease the inequality gap between the Chinese and the Malays specifically.[11]

Singapore: The Pre-Merger Era (1959–1963)

The Singapore story starts out very similar to Malaysia's. With the defeat of the Japanese, the British returned, with the first elections set for 1959. The election, however, was to take place within a framework of limited independence, also known as "three quarters independence" (K. Y. Lee 1998: chap. 15). In anticipation of this election, a group of men, led by Lee Kuan Yew, formed the People's

Action Party (PAP). While Lee Kuan Yew and the majority of the founding members were ethnically Chinese, the more common and salient denominator of the party's cadres was their English education. Many of them had not only attended English-medium schools in Singapore (or Malaysia) but had pursued their higher education in Britain. During this time, group identification was based on "the language of one's primary socialization, or one's 'native speech' " (E. Tan 2007: 79). With this classification, Lee Kuan Yew and other PAP leaders saw themselves as more English than Chinese.[12] Aside from English, there was another factor that distinguished this group of men. Although left-leaning in their ideologies, they were fundamentally noncommunist (K. Y. Lee 2000: 24; Rajakumar 2001: 99–101).

From the outset, this group of English-speaking men (a numerical minority to the Chinese) knew they needed the cooperation of other linguistic groups if electoral victory and complete independence were to be had. The largest and most important group was the Chinese communists, who, led by the charismatic Lim Chin Siong, constituted over 50 percent of the island's population by liberal estimates.[13] Furthermore, the group had access to financial resources. There were several independently wealthy communist sympathizers, both domestically and abroad, who offered monetary support.

The ability of Lim Chin Siong to mobilize the masses at will was no laughing matter. The communists protested en masse and incited violence frequently. There were two notable events. In 1955, workers from the Hock Lee Amalgamated Bus Company, urged on by Lim Chin Siong, went on a strike to protest against the poor working conditions, long working hours, and low pay. These strikes crippled the island's entire transportation system. When the police attempted to break up the 2,000-person demonstration, riots broke out (K. Y. Lee 1998: 201–3). Similarly, in the following year, the government deregistered, dissolved, and banned three procommunist organizations. One of these was the Singapore Chinese Middle School Students Union. In protest, students camped out at two different schools and demonstrated for two weeks. When the government ultimatum for the schools to be vacated went unanswered, riots again broke out across the island. The riots lasted for five days (204).

Despite the many differences—linguistic and ideological—between Lee Kuan Yew and Lim Chin Siong, the former was fully aware that he needed the political support of the latter. Without the cooperation of the Chinese, complete independence would be impossible. As a result, the PAP heavily courted the Chinese. In 1955, the two groups campaigned for the first time under the same banner. In contrast to Malaysia's Alliance Party, which was one coalition of multiple parties, the PAP was one party of multiple factions, one English (led by Lee Kuan Yew) and one Chinese (led by Lim Chin Siong). Despite this coalition, the relationship was hostile. All evidence suggests each faction viewed the other with suspicion and "expected trouble" (K. Y. Lee 1998: 328). For instance, Lee Kuan Yew recounted that from the beginning, the communist Chinese were an absolute "albatross around [our] necks" (373). In fact, he wasted little time before expressing his dislike for the junior partner once the PAP won the 1959 election. In his first speech as prime minister, Lee Kuan Yew warned, "if we fail, brute force returns" (319).

During this period, the institutional organization of the Chinese faction was impressive and the strength of the state relatively weak, making the political relevance of the Chinese absolutely high. Despite coopting the Chinese into a ruling party, the English faction and its leaders recognized the arrangement was precarious at best. In response, they made concessions, linguistically and politically, to other minority linguistic groups: Malays and Tamil-speaking Indians.

What were the implications of these constraints on language regime choice? In line with Hypothesis 1.3, the English faction opted for a neutralized-sharing language regime whereby Chinese, English, Malay, and Tamil were all recognized as official languages of the state. As Lee Kuan Yew decided, "Whether or not it was practical, the only politically defendable policy was trilingualism, with Malay as the lingua franca and the future national language of Malaya, English as the language of international commerce and science, Mandarin as the mother tongue of the Chinese, and Tamil, Hindi, or Punjabi for the Indians" (K. Y. Lee 1998: 216). It is interesting to note that despite the status of English as the colonial language, Malay was designated the lingua franca. Efforts to promote Malay in Singapore included the development of an Institute of Malayan Culture for popularizing and synthesizing Malayan culture (*Sunday Times*, August 23, 1959) and the promotion of a Malay language awareness week (*Sunday Times*, March 25, 1959).

The development of the education curriculum reflected this trilingualism. Given the fragmented system inherited from the British, the English faction believed it was "political[ly] imperative [and urgent] to create an indigenous and integrated national school system united by a common language policy" (E. Tan 2007: 79). All four languages were subsequently recognized as mediums of instruction across both the primary and secondary curriculums. This, however, necessitated standardization—with the English curriculum serving as the standard bearer.

The Chinese curriculum was restructured, much to the chagrin of the Chinese community. Two changes proved exceptionally contentious. First, the curriculum was reduced from a total of twelve[14] to ten years to match that of the English schools (Fong 1979). Second, a new measure was enacted requiring all junior middle school students to pass their exams in order to move on to senior middle school (K. C. Lee 1988: 68). The Malay and Tamil curriculums were also restructured (Gopinathan 1974: 29–31). The primary emphasis was on standardizing the primary curriculums and making them available at large. Historically, the British policy was to support only primary secular morning classes for the Malay community. The Malay community bore the costs for the afternoon Qur'an instruction. In contrast, the British supported Tamil-medium education in full. However, as many Indians did not complete their primary studies (for a host of different reasons), Tamil secondary education was never developed (Burhanudeen 2006). There were also talks of developing Malay and Tamil secondary schools. Across all four curriculums, English and Malay were required subjects (Kaplan and Baldauf 2003: 128–29).

The "inevitable showdown" (K. Y. Lee 1998: 355) between the English and Chinese factions of PAP happened in 1961. On the eve of the election, Lee Kuan Yew publicly demanded the resignation of Lim Chin Siong and other Chinese faction leaders from the party. The charge was their commitment to "overthrow the leadership and capture the party to use it for their purposes . . . . What is clear is that [they] are prepared to go to any lengths—even to destroying the party with which they are ostensibly associated" (371). When the PAP lost the by-election in Anson, Lee Kuan Yew became "preoccupied with the coming battle" as he realized the Chinese faction had "demonstrated once again that they had penetrated the higher ranks of the trade unions and the party so effectively that they could split the PAP vote at short notice, switching popular support to [a candidate] known to be unstable and undependable" (371). In response, he purged the party to ensure that each remaining PAP assemblyman (and party member) was loyal to his cause.

Those purged from the PAP (mostly members of the Chinese faction) subsequently formed a party called the Socialist Front (Barisan Socialis). It proved to be highly organized. In 1961 alone, there were 116 strikes: 84 of them came after the split (K. Y. Lee 1998: 389). The Socialist Front was also overwhelmingly popular. In the 51 districts previously controlled by PAP, it was now the preferred party in 35 (according to a forced head count conducted by the PAP leadership). Goh Keng Swee, the deputy prime minister, recalled, "what surprised us was the ease and speed with which [the communists] broke up all our organizations and left us with nothing within a matter of two weeks" (S. Tan 2007: 100).

Capitalizing on this momentum, the Socialist Front called for a motion of confidence. The PAP won a bare majority, 26 of the 51 votes. Many individuals, including the parliamentary secretary for the Home Affairs Ministry, voted against the motion not because of anti-PAP positions, but because they believed the Socialist Front was bound to win in the long run (K. Y. Lee 1998: 377). All this served as a reminder of why the English faction had coopted the Chinese faction into the PAP in the first place.

Since cooperation with the Chinese was no longer a viable alternative, PAP stepped up its rhetoric for merger with Malaya. Absolutely convinced merger was the only way to ensure the PAP's survival, Lee Kuan Yew explained in a public broadcast,

> Everyone knows the reasons why the Federation is important to Singa-pore. It is the hinterland which produces the rubber and tin that keeps our shop-window economy going. It is the base that made Singapore the cap-ital city. Without this economic base, Singapore would not survive. With-out merger, without a reunification of our two governments and integration of our two economies, our economic position will slowly and steadily get worse. Your livelihood will get worse. Instead of there being one unified economic development for Malaya, there will be two. The Federation, instead of cooperating with Singapore, will compete against Singapore for industrial capital and industrial expansion. In this competition, both will suffer. (1998: 397)

To promote the merger, the concessions proposed to the Alliance Party and Malaya were exceptional. Electorally, the PAP promised the Alliance Party that it would not extend its political influence beyond Singapore and into the rest of Malaysia. Instead, the agreement was that PAP would focus only on the elections within Singapore (K. Y. Lee 1998).[15] And with respect to linguistic concessions, the notion of Malay-medium secondary schools went from rheto-ric to reality. In October 1961, Education Minister Yong Nyuk Lin opened the first school (Sang Nila Utama) and welcomed 447 students and 18 teachers (Gopinathan 1974).

Although it was "the only politically defendable policy," this neutralized-sharing language regime served two purposes. First, it avoided antagonizing the Chinese. To the Chinese parents, Chinese schools had been seen as a necessary vehicle for classical Chinese scholarship. But these schools had also been a tradi-tional breeding ground for communism. With declining enrollment rates, the preservation of a Chinese curriculum became especially important for Lim Chin

Siong and his colleagues. Had Lee Kuan Yew and the English faction concentrated linguistic powers in English, this policy would have allowed the Chinese faction the opportunity to brand them as "enemy and destroyer of Chinese culture" (K. Y. Lee 1998: 409).

Second, this proposed language regime demonstrated to the Alliance Party that Singapore's inclusion in the Malaysian Federation would have minimal repercussions with respect to ethnicity. After 1961, the PAP aggressively advocated for, and desperately needed, a merger because it was believed to be the only solution to avoid a communist takeover. This language regime, by emphasizing Malay as a lingua franca, signaled a credible commitment to Malaysian nation-building.

Singapore: The Post-Merger Era (1965–)

In 1963, Singapore secured its independence from the British with a merger into the Malaysian Federation. It had begun lobbying for merger as early 1959. However, because of its sizable Chinese population—many presumed to be of the communist persuasion—the UMNO-led Alliance Party had originally not been interested. But by 1961 the British convinced Tunku that the only way to control the communist insurgency in Singapore was to incorporate the island. And so in 1963, Singapore—along with Sabah and Sarawak, two other less Chinese-populated British colonies—merged into the Federation. Although both parties had agreed to the terms of the merger, matters changed quite drastically once Singapore was part of the Federation (K. Y. Lee 1998: 570–80; Rahman Putra 1978: 41–42).

Despite a gentlemen's agreement that neither side would compete in the other's home electoral domain, both parties were guilty of violating the terms. The Alliance Party endorsed an opposition party in Singapore's general election. Likewise, the PAP fielded four candidates in Malaysia's federal election. Then, in 1964 the PAP proposed to Tunku to allow it to replace the MCA in the Alliance Party as the organization representing Chinese interests. This proposal was vehemently rejected by both the UMNO and MCA (MCA 2010; Rahman Putra 1978). As the non-Malay opposition parties grew restless with what was perceived as the Alliance Party's increasing Malay hegemony, the leaders met in Singapore to discuss the formation of an alternative united front.

The result was the creation of the Malaysian Solidarity Convention (MSC), which demanded a "Malaysian Malaysia against communalism" (K. C. Lee 1988:

78). Tensions would only continue to escalate, culminating in the 1965 "separation." The exact details of the separation are still debated. One version is a story of expulsion driven by racial considerations. When Tunku returned from a trip to London on August 8, 1965, he faced a mass demonstration led by UMNO youths carrying signs that read "Lee Kuan Yew Malaysia Enemy 1" and "We suffer under the PAP Government." In response, the top officials of the Alliance Party held emergency consultations, agreed upon Singapore's expulsion, and then informed the Singapore ministers of the decision. It was not easy for the PAP to accept as it "tried to convince the Tunku of other possible alternatives, perhaps even a looser arrangement—a confederation" (Fong 1979: 166–67). Tunku, however, was absolutely convinced that expulsion was necessary to "avoid the possible repercussion and prevent bad blood as between the different races" (Rahman Putra 1978: 69).

In contrast, another version provides an account of secessionism fueled by economic disagreements. The PAP had long worked to develop a common market. However, continued frustrations over Singapore's expected—and highly disproportional—contributions toward the national treasury eventually forced Goh Keng Swee, the Singapore finance minister and deputy prime minister, to present to Razak, the acting prime minister while Tunku was in London, a proposal outlining Singapore's secession (S. Tan 2007: 114–23). Razak responded with little trepidation (Kwok 1999: 56). Three rounds of negotiations later, on August 9, 1965, Lee Kuan Yew announced Singapore's sovereignty and his reassumed role as the prime minister of the new nation (K. C. Lee 1988: 80; K. Y. Lee 1998: 648–63; also see Young 1994).

The separation in 1965 marked the first time Singapore was left to govern its own affairs completely. During this time, politically relevant linguistic heterogeneity levels were still high. Although the same key individuals occupied the PAP apparatus, the bargaining stage had changed. Previously, the major political cleavage had been between the English and Chinese factions within the PAP and then interparty between the PAP and the Socialist Front. In these circumstances the PAP had proposed Malay as the lingua franca. But in the post-merger period, with Singapore-Malaysia tensions still high, the key cleavage within Singapore and in intergovernmental relations was now between the Chinese and Malays. Demographically, the Chinese were roughly 70 percent of the island's population; the Malays, 20 percent.

This shift in cleavage was reflected in changes in census classifications. Bear in mind that before 1965, group identification was based on one's "native speech."

However, in 1966, "mother tongue" was redefined to mean strictly the "symbolic language of the group of one's paternal ancestry" (E. Tan 2007: 79). With this new definition, Lee Kuan Yew became "Chinese" overnight. Changing also overnight was the shift of Malay from lingua franca to minority language and of English to lingua franca.

Unlike the first period when the Chinese were institutionally organized (and had therefore increased the political relevance of other minority groups), in the second period whatever political relevance existed was because of the weakness of the state. Recall that political relevance is relative: it is measured with respect to the strength of the state.

During this post-merger period, the Singapore state was extremely weak. There were economic difficulties: a lack of foreign reserves, not enough land to grow rice, an absence of natural resources, and high unemployment. Further contributing to the stress was the impending withdrawal of British troops. British military spending accounted for a large portion of Singapore's GDP; the military base was also an important source of employment (K. Y. Lee 2000: 69–73). Dr. Albert Winsemius, a Dutch economist who led the UN team to examine Singapore's potential industrialization, was right to express concern: "Singapore is walking on a razor's edge" (quoted in K. Y. Lee 2000: 66).

In addition to the economy, there were also security threats. With the withdrawal of the British, two threats became especially pronounced. The first was Indonesia. Since the early 1960s, Indonesia and Malaysia had been engaged in a low intensity conflict (*Konfrontasi*). The war was the result of Indonesia's opposition to the creation of the Malaysian Federation. For Indonesia's President Sukarno, the idea of a Malaysian Federation was simply a contemporary version of British imperialism. And since Singapore had been a part of that larger plan, it still felt some of the enduring effects even after the expulsion. Most notably, the lack of trade between Singapore and Indonesia only added to the heightened economic woes (K. C. Lee 1988: 83; K. Y. Lee 2000: 66).

The other threat was Malaysia. Tensions between Singapore and Malaysia continued: "the pressures following separation were relentless [and] there was never a dull moment in [Singapore's] relations with Malaysia" (K. Y. Lee 2000: 261; also see S. Tan 2007: 127–33). One such moment had to do with the recruitment into the armed forces and law enforcement services. Escalating racial tensions between the Chinese and the Malays, which included riots spilling over from Malaysia, raised questions about Malay allegiance to the new Singapore. Moreover, since Singapore was a predominantly Chinese state in between two

Muslim-majority countries, the PAP was concerned that Malays could not be trusted to protect Singaporean interests in the event of a domestic racial riot or external aggression by a Muslim state (Li 1989). In response, the PAP decided to deny Malay recruitment into the otherwise mandatory military service on the island (Kassim 1974: 45; K. Y. Lee 2000: 27).[16]

Government rhetoric consistently reflected this vulnerability. For instance, Foreign Affairs Minister S. Rajaratnam remarked, "when we talk of survival, it is not with a view of rallying support for a tottering government . . . . We are not thinking about the next elections. We are thinking of how Singapore can survive" (Chan and ul Haq 1987: 210–11). Although politically relevant linguistic heterogeneity levels in Singapore were nowhere as extreme as those of Indonesia, the sense of state vulnerability was very similar. This precarious situation—this "deep sense of crisis that prevailed" (K. Y. Lee 2000: 109)—would increase the (relative) political relevance of each minority group. Theoretically, as postulated in Corollary 1, the expectation would have been for the PAP to neutralize linguistic powers completely.

From a de jure standpoint, the four languages—Chinese, English, Malay, and Tamil—remained official languages of the state. They also remained mediums of instruction. As for the Malay language, the rhetoric from the government was that there was "no language issue" over the continued status of Malay as the national language (*Sunday Times*, November 22, 1966). From a de jure standpoint, government action matched the rhetoric. Little was done to change the status quo.

Any pretense toward maintaining the previous status of the Malay language, however, was short-lived. The language regime shifted to power-neutralization through the English language. With changes to the definition of "mother tongue" for the census, the major linguistic cleavage was now between the Chinese and the Malays. Malay was no longer considered the lingua franca; in its place was now English. By 1979, the Education Ministry passed the Goh Report, a "key document in marking the PAP's clear ideological shift towards meritocracy" (Kwok 1999: 62). The Goh Report emphasized economic efficiency in manpower, technical, and vocational training (Doshi and Coclanis 1999: 38–39) over cultural egoism and collective equality. In fact, it did little to assuage Malay perceptions of the PAP as a "Chinese-based party whose multiracial ideology was little more than rhetoric" (Rahim 1998: 73). Malay grievances such as the lack of facilities in Malay-medium schools, the lack of high school certificate classes in the Malay stream, and the proposed closing down of the Malay Studies Department at Nanyang University (Kassim 1974: 73) all fell on deaf ears. Between

1983 and 1987, all non-English schools (not just Malay but Chinese and Tamil as well) were closed. Ever since then, the national school system has been characterized by English as the first—if not the exclusive—language of instruction (Š. Ganguly 2003; Kaplan and Baldauf 2003; Gopinathan 1998), rendering the language regime power-neutralizing.[17]

Discussion

The story of Malaysia and Singapore in each of the two periods highlights the limitations of existing arguments for explaining language regime choice. One explanation focuses on ethnic relations. Specifically, language regimes are reflections of how groups interact with each other. When there are cultural differences, minority-unfriendly linguistic arrangements (i.e., power-concentrating) emerge when one group draws on primordial appeals and has the opportunity to impose its will over another. But such arguments are inadequate in these cases. The linguistic group identities have been the same in the two countries cross-nationally and over time. Even if the Chinese and Malays genuinely do not like each other as claimed by Mahathir, this static account does not match up to the dynamism of language regimes. Moreover, if minority-friendly linguistic arrangements happen when no group can dominate, what explains whether language regimes are power-sharing, power-neutralizing, or a hybrid of the two?

Arguments that focus on colonial legacies suggest that the British, when compared to other European colonizers, were more likely to leave quality governments, better economies, and multilingual education systems. This seems to have been the case in both Malaysia and Singapore in their first periods. In fact, the British took great care to ensure that the transfer of power was to a noncommunist government (the UMNO-led Alliance Party and the PAP). But this colonial explanation, a static and exogenous one, cannot explain why the UMNO-led National Front pursued power-concentration while the PAP shifted to even greater degrees of linguistic neutralization.

Finally, arguments about nation-building and its corresponding priorities correctly highlight that language regimes play an important role in helping the government shape the future of new states. But these accounts take language regimes as strictly instrumental. There is little explanation for why a particular distribution of linguistic power is considered more appropriate for nation-building than another; and when there is an explanation it is often ex post or functional in character.

The argument here offers an alternative and distinct explanation. When linguistic minorities are a minimal constraint on the dominant group, as was the case in post-1971 Malaysia, the government (i.e., the UMNO-led National Front) has few incentives to distribute linguistic power beyond the electorally dominant majority. In Malaysia, Malay dominance has meant the concentration of linguistic power in one language. In contrast, when minorities constrain electoral freedom, linguistic concessions become necessary. Power-neutralizing and neutralized-sharing language regimes are both viable alternatives as evident in the choices made in 1957–1969 Malaysia and in both periods in Singapore (before 1963 and after 1965).

Conclusion

With the preliminary findings from the large N analysis and the underlying mechanisms shown to be plausible in Malaysia and Singapore, there is reason to believe these arguments may be generalizable beyond Indonesia and Southeast Asia. In Indonesia, the choice of a power-neutralizing language regime was a strategic response to extreme linguistic diversity. The use of a lingua franca forced the Javanese to forgo satisfaction with their cultural egoism but in exchange fostered communicative efficiency and collective equality. These in turn proved instrumental in building the Indonesian state.

Drawing on the Indonesian case, the previous chapter laid out a theoretical argument positing a relationship between politically relevant linguistic heterogeneity levels and language regime choice. Specifically, when levels are low, the optimal language regime is power-concentrating. It feeds the politically dominant's egoism through its monopoly of cultural recognition; it is also efficient in communication. But when these levels are higher, the government is constrained to make linguistic concessions. These concessions can be power-sharing, power-neutralizing, or a hybrid of the two. The likelihood and the level of linguistic neutralization both increase as the level of heterogeneity increases. The evidence provided in this chapter—both qualitatively and quantitatively—lends support to this argument.

If politically relevant linguistic heterogeneity level affects language regime choice, what are the economic implications of this choice? In other words, does the distribution of linguistic power matter in some way for economic growth? The simple answer is an unequivocal yes—although the effect is indirect. The next chapter lays out the theoretical foundation, detailing the two different mechanisms through which language regimes matter: breeding social capital and attracting foreign capital.

Appendix

The primary set of results can be found in Table 4.4. The first two models measure language regime using the quadrachotomous coding scheme. To help with interpretation, the first set of numbers in the first column (Model 1) are the probabilities of a power-concentrating language regime Pr ($Y=0$); the second set of numbers again in the same column, the likelihood of a power-sharing language regime Pr ($Y=1$); and the third set of numbers still in the same column, the likelihood of a power-neutralizing language regime Pr ($Y=2$). Note that the reference category is the probability of a neutralized-sharing language regime Pr ($Y=3$). What this means is that a positive coefficient in the first set of numbers suggests a greater likelihood of a language regime being power-concentrating than one that is a neutralized-sharing language regime. In contrast, a negative coefficient indicates a greater likelihood of neutralized-sharing. The interpretation for the numbers in the second and third sets of numbers in the same column is similar. The reported standard errors are clustered by country.

The independent variable of interest here is politically relevant linguistic heterogeneity. In Model 1, heterogeneity is measured using a (logged) count variable for the number of linguistic groups; and in Model 2, heterogeneity is operationalized using the Herfindahl-Hirschman concentration index. The positive coefficients in each column tell the same story. First and foremost, consistent with Hypothesis 1.1, linguistic power is concentrated when heterogeneity is low. Second, as heterogeneity increases, the government is constrained to make linguistic concessions. While there is evidence validating Hypothesis 1.1, the results from these two models lend weak support to Hypothesis 1.2. At higher levels of politically relevant linguistic heterogeneity, there is no statistical difference between the likelihoods of power-concentrating and power-sharing—but there is one between power-sharing and neutralized-sharing. Moreover, consistent with Hypothesis 1.3, at high levels, power-neutralizing and neutralized-sharing are statistically the same.

The next two models (3 and 4) replicate the above models but use a continuous measure of power-neutralization. The findings are robust. Specifically, as the level of politically relevant linguistic heterogeneity increases, the extent of lingua franca recognition increases as well. In other words, consistent with Corollary 1,

Table 4.4: Language Regime Choice

| | Quadrachotomous | | Continuous | |
	Model 1	Model 2	Model 3	Model 4
DV: *Power-Concentrating* (=0)				
Heterogeneity variables				
(log) # Groups	**−1.67 (0.95)***			
Concentration index		**−10.7 (3.96)‡**		
Control variables				
Regime type	−0.05 (0.06)	−0.01 (0.05)		
GDP/capita (1000)	0.20 (0.14)	0.22 (0.13)		
Colonialism: British	−3.75 (1.82)†	−3.81 (0.94)‡		
Colonialism: continental	−2.37 (1.52)	−2.40 (1.94)		
Colonialism: Russian	−4.95 (1.70)‡	−6.48 (1.47)‡		
Federalism	−0.75 (0.62)	−1.33 (1.04)		
DV: *Power-Sharing* (=1)				
Heterogeneity variables				
(log) # Groups	**−0.11 (0.46)**			
Concentration Index		**−7.93 (4.00)†**		
Control variables				
Regime type	0.03 (0.06)	0.06 (0.05)		
GDP/capita (1000)	0.19 (0.13)	0.17 (0.13)		
Colonialism: British	−3.04 (1.52)†	−3.79 (0.90)‡		
Colonialism: continental	−3.05 (1.75)*	−2.98 (1.60)*		
Colonialism: Russian	−3.10 (1.53)†	−4.24 (1.27)‡		
Federalism	−0.44 (0.59)	−0.26 (0.93)		
DV: *Power-Neutralizing* (=2)				
Heterogeneity variables				
(log) # Groups	**0.48 (0.61)**			
Concentration index		**−3.00 (4.52)**		

Control variables

	Model 1	Model 2	Model 3	Model 4
Regime type	0.04 (0.08)	0.05 (0.08)		
GDP/capita (1000)	0.34 (0.12)‡	0.25 (0.12)†		
Colonialism: British	14.5 (1.86)‡	13.8 (1.20)‡		
Colonialism: continental	16.9 (1.49)‡	16.2 (1.35)‡		
Colonialism: Russian	−3.83 (1.74)†	−4.86 (1.06)‡		
Federalism	−19.6 (2.74)‡	−17.8 (0.93)‡		

DV: *Degree of Neutralization*

Heterogeneity variables

	Model 1	Model 2	Model 3	Model 4
(log) # Groups			0.05 (0.02)†	
Concentration index				0.29 (0.08)‡

Control variables

	Model 1	Model 2	Model 3	Model 4
Power-Sharing regime			−0.13 (0.04)‡	−0.10 (0.03)‡
Regime type			0.00 (0.00)	0.00 (0.00)
GDP/capita (1000)			0.00 (0.00)	0.00 (0.00)
Colonialism: British			0.07 (0.04)*	0.03 (0.04)
Colonialism: continental			0.17 (0.09)*	0.15 (0.08)*
Colonialism: Russian			0.18 (0.05)‡	0.16 (0.05)‡
Federalism			−0.04 (0.04)	−0.01 (0.04)

	Model 1	Model 2	Model 3	Model 4
N	1951(48)	1948 (47)	1951(48)	1948 (47)
(Pseudo) R^2	0.3317	0.3782	0.2099	0.2851
Log Pseudo-Likelihood	−1435.79	−1344.71		

Note:
Standard errors clustered by country. *$p \leq 0.100$, †$p \leq 0.050$, ‡$p \leq 0.010$.
Constants not reported.
Base category in Models 1 and 2 = 3 (Neutralized-Sharing)

as linguistic heterogeneity increases, the optimal extent of linguistic neutralization also increases.

Robustness Checks

I run several additional models to check the stability of these findings. The results are presented in Table 4.5. The first two models replicate the results of Model 1 but using alternative measures. Model 5 uses a different measure of democracy. If the recognition of either minority languages and/or lingua francas is a policy concession by the government, then it is possible that the only mechanism of importance is that of multiple parties existing to contest elections. There is possibly a concern that the 21-point POLITY measure is not only an aggregation of two different scales, but that each scale is also an index of four (for democracy) or five (for autocracy) components. The use of an indexed scale runs the risk of aggregating conceptually noncomparable components. Alternatively, I use the dichotomous measure of democracy as first introduced by Przeworski et al. (2000) and since updated by Cheibub, Gandhi, and Vreeland (2009). A regime is considered a democracy (value of 1) when there are multiple parties contesting for executive and legislative elections and there has been turnover; otherwise, the regime is considered a dictatorship (value of 0).

Model 6 relaxes the definition of a "federation" and focuses on simply where there is an autonomous region. Autonomous regions need not be the same as states or provinces. They can also exist in unitary states. But because they are self-governing, it is possible that they have the same authority to govern over language matters as their subnational counterparts in a federation. The data source for this variable is the Database of Political Institutions (Beck et al. 2001; Keefer 2012).

The results in Table 4.5 suggest the use of either one of the alternative measures does not substantively change the results. Of greatest interest for this book, when politically relevant linguistic heterogeneity levels are low, language regimes are most likely to be power-concentrating. But as this level increases, we see linguistic concessions. In Model 6, when the levels are moderate, these concessions take on the form of power-sharing; and when the levels are high, these concessions involve a lingua franca recognition. There is no statistical difference whether the lingua franca recognition is exclusive or in conjunction with a mother tongue—consistent with Hypothesis 1.3. In Model 6, we see a similar trend that as heterogeneity increases, the need for the government to make a

Table 4.5: Sensitivity Test

	Dichotomous democracy	Autonomous region	Lagged DV	Region effects
	Model 5	Model 6	Model 7	Model 8
DV: Power-Concentrating (=0)				
Heterogeneity variables				
Concentration index	−9.27 (3.27)‡	−11.3 (4.56)†	−12.7 (4.02)‡	−12.1 (5.10)†
Control variables				
Regime type	−0.22 (0.69)	−0.08 (0.05)	−0.07 (0.11)	−0.19 (0.11)*
GDP/capita (1000)	0.06 (0.06)	0.17 (0.11)	0.16 (0.13)	0.21 (0.23)
Colonialism: British	−3.35 (1.10)‡	−3.83 (1.24)‡	−3.86 (1.98)*	
Colonialism: continental	−2.53 (1.75)	−3.19 (2.58)	−7.24 (2.05)‡	
Colonialism: Russian	−5.60 (1.41)‡	−6.17 (1.93)‡	−2.40 (1.44)*	
Region: East				4.84 (3.27)
Region: South				5.31(2.86)*
Region: West				7.97 (1.92)‡
Region: Central				−0.83 (2.84)
Federalism	−0.51 (0.84)	−3.27 (1.42)†	2.22 (1.44)	2.51 (1.26)†
(lag) dependent variable			−22.3 (2.10)‡	−19.7 (2.23)‡
DV: Power-Sharing (=1)				
Heterogeneity variables				
Concentration index	−6.75 (3.27)†	−6.97 (4.31)	−12.9 (3.65)‡	−8.64 (3.65)†
Control variables				
Regime type	0.18 (0.64)	0.08 (0.05)	0.11 (0.10)	0.01 (0.08)
GDP/capita (1000)	0.02 (0.06)	0.15 (0.11)	−0.06 (0.11)	0.08 (0.22)
Colonialism: British	−3.35 (1.14)‡	−3.05 (1.14)‡	−4.20 (2.07)†	
Colonialism: continental	−2.85 (1.55)*	−2.43 (1.87)	−8.21 (2.10)‡	
Colonialism: Russian	−3.67 (1.33)‡	−4.73 (1.52)‡	−2.16 (1.43)	
Region: East				7.74 (2.73)‡
Region: South				3.55 (2.63)

	(1)	(2)	(3)	(4)
Region: West				10.20 (1.76)‡
Region: Central				3.01 (2.55)
Federalism	0.31 (0.87)	2.32 (1.21)*	1.97 (1.40)	1.81 (0.89)†
(lag) dependent variable			−11.1 (0.69)‡	−9.15 (2.16)‡
DV: Power-Neutralizing (=2)				
Heterogeneity variables				
Concentration index	**−0.55 (3.62)**	**−1.76 (4.77)**	**−1.63 (2.89)**	**14.87 (10.21)**
Control variables				
Regime type	−0.07 (0.42)	0.01 (0.06)	−0.13 (0.09)	−0.27 (0.07)‡
GDP/capita (1000)	0.09 (0.06)	0.20 (0.11)*	0.31 (0.13)†	0.78 (0.36)†
Colonialism: British	13.63 (1.15)‡	13.49 (1.25)‡	14.10 (2.30)‡	
Colonialism: continental	15.36 (1.01)‡	15.80 (1.12)‡	15.64 (2.27)‡	
Colonialism: Russian	−4.23 (0.94)‡	−4.75 (1.50)‡	−6.55 (2.33)‡	
Region: East				−12.4 (4.43)‡
Region: South				−18.7 (1.75)‡
Region: West				−44.2 (29.2)
Region: Central				−21.2 (1.67)‡
Federalism	−16.5 (0.81)‡	0.64 (1.95)	−16.1 (0.86)‡	−21.8 (2.30)‡
(lag) dependent variable			−7.84 (0.24)‡	−8.16 (0.90)‡
N	1917 (47)	1871 (45)	1926 (47)	1926 (47)
(Pseudo) R^2	0.2963	0.4467	0.9613	0.9648
Log Pseudo-Likelihood	−1489.28	−1118.45	−82.07	−74.70

Note:
Standard errors clustered by country. $*p \le 0.100$, $†p \le 0.050$, and $‡p \le 0.010$.
Constants not reported.
Base category in Models 1 and 2 = 3 (Neutralized-Sharing)

linguistic concession increases. However, it is important to note that the coefficient for power-sharing in Model 6 is no longer statistically significant ($\beta = -6.97$; $SE = 4.31$).

The third model includes a lagged dependent variable. As a reminder, the lagged dependent variable had been excluded in all the models thus far to ensure it was not biasing any of the other estimates. The results in Model 7 indicate the inclusion of a lagged dependent variable does not change the effects of politically relevant linguistic heterogeneity levels. While the coefficient magnitude is larger, the directions remain unchanged. When politically relevant linguistic minorities are far and few, the optimal language regime is power-concentrating; and at high levels of politically relevant linguistic heterogeneity, the optimal language regime is one that recognizes a lingua franca.

The fourth and final test uses regional effects. It is possible that countries within the same region are subject to similar diffusion effects or share similar historical developments that may include more than just colonialism. For instance, the fact that the countries in South Asia were also British colonies means that English was a lingua franca in each one of them. The politics over the English language in India did not go unnoticed in neighboring countries. The same logic applies for countries in Central Asia with the status of the Russian language. In East Asia, many of the countries were at some point historically under Chinese rule and then later under Japanese control. And finally, in West Asia, the dominance of Islam has elevated the status of Arabic. To control for any possible spatial diffusion effects and historical developments, I include five regional dummies: East, Southeast, South, West, and Central. Data considerations come from the *CIA World Factbook* and M. Brown and Š. Ganguly (2003). Southeast Asia is the reference category.

The results in Model 8 highlight that even when controlling for regional effects, politically relevant linguistic heterogeneity matters. As the number of linguistic constraints increases, the government increases the degree of lingua franca concession. Here, we see that regime type also matters. The results suggest that democracies are less likely to choose a power-concentrating ($\beta = -0.19$; $SE = 0.11$) or power-neutralizing ($\beta = -0.27$; $SE = 0.07$) language regime. This suggests that when governments are electorally constrained, they are indeed more likely to acknowledge minority languages, whether alongside the politically dominant language or in conjunction with a lingua franca.

PART III

Economic Effects of Language Regimes

CHAPTER 5

Economic Effects of Language Regimes: Theory

Language regimes delineate which languages can be used when and where, but what are the economic implications—if any—of these choices? This chapter suggests that language regimes matter for economic growth, but that the posited effects are indirect. Language regimes are instrumental because they can build communities—even those "imagined" (B. Anderson 1983). When language regimes are able to unify a population through collectively recognized group equality or coordinated efficiency, they strengthen state capacity and enable the government to promote other growth policies with greater success.

Of the four language regime types, I argue that power-neutralizing language regimes have the largest positive effect. There are two explanations. First, when language regimes equalize the distribution of linguistic power, this creates a sense of fairness. This equality is essential for generating "social capital"—the "features of social organization, such as trust, norms, and networks, that can improve the efficiency of society facilitating coordinated action" (Putnam 1993: 167). Power-sharing, power-neutralizing, and neutralized-sharing language regimes all can develop such communities with high trust levels and dense social networks.

The second explanation has to do with efficiency. Language regimes are efficient when few languages are recognized. When there is little demand for translation between languages, transaction costs are kept to a minimum.[1] Such linguistic arrangements can make a country attractive to foreign direct investment (FDI). These arrangements include the use of one mother tongue (i.e., power-concentrating) and the recognition of a lingua franca (i.e., power-neutralizing and neutralized-sharing).

In this third part of the book, I hypothesize and test that power-neutralizing language regimes are optimal for both generating social capital, namely trust, and attracting foreign capital, specifically FDI. If capital—physical and/or human—is necessary for growth (exogenous models: Solow 1956; endogenous models:

Barro 1991; Grossman and Helpman 1994; Romer 1986, 1994), this would suggest that a country endowed with quality labor and access to foreign capital has the capacity to drive economic growth.

Here, I should note that the suggested mechanisms are not exclusive to power-neutralizing language regimes. They can be found in any language regime that recognizes a lingua franca. Thus a neutralized-sharing language regime (i.e., 3 ± 1) should theoretically also have the predicted positive effects of generating social capital and attracting foreign capital. This discussion suggests that *any* lingua franca recognition is better than *none*.

However, there is also reason to believe that when there is lingua franca recognition, *more* recognition is better than *less*. The presence of other mother tongues, even when in conjunction with a lingua franca, can still introduce inequality and inefficiency. In a neutralized-sharing language regime, the recognition of some mother tongues but not others can perpetuate perceptions of inequality. Also, in these regimes, the addition of other languages requires bilingualism. There is an inherent risk that some subset of the population never learns the lingua franca. When this is the case, translations between lingua franca and mother tongues become necessary. As the subset that does not speak the lingua franca increases, communicative efficiency accordingly decreases.

This chapter begins with an illustrative case: the Indonesian story. The analysis now shifts to the economic implications of having neutralized linguistic power by adopting a lingua franca. The Indonesian example enables us to explore the limitations of existing explanations for economic growth. Inspired by this case, I then lay out a theoretical framework by focusing first on social capital and then on foreign capital. The last section brings the two mechanisms together in discussing the broader economic effects of language regimes.

An Illustrative Case: Indonesia

When Indonesia opted for a power-neutralizing language regime upon independence, the educational arrangements were pluralistic. Initially during Sukarno's rule (1949–1968), a number of indigenous languages—as few as seven (Mohr 1984: 9) and as many as ten (Kaplan and Baldauf 2003: 101)—were permitted as mediums of instruction in grades one, two, and three. And then in the fourth grade, there was a shift to Indonesian.[2] During this period, Chinese was also permitted and used in the Chinese schools (Handoko 2008). This linguistic arrangement is, however, now a story of the distant past. Ever since Suharto assumed power (1968), the language regime in Indonesia has been unequivocally power-neutralizing. While local languages and other "locally designed matter" may now be taught, Indonesian is still the only language of the national curriculum and in the public schools (Bjork 2003: 184).

Today, Indonesia boasts the fifteenth largest economy in the world, with a GDP of US$1.121 trillion (CIA World Factbook).[3] This number dwarfs those in the wake of the Dutch withdrawal. For instance, Kristian Gleditsch (2002) in the Direction of Trade (DOT) Dataset estimates Indonesia's GDP in 1949 at $14.078 million—0.0013 percent of what it is today! As noted in Chapter 1, Indonesia's economic growth has been very robust. In the 1990s, the Indonesian economy showed annual growth rates of about 7.1 percent. Moreover, poverty levels—defined as people "lacking such basic necessities as clean water, food, and shelter" (World Bank 1993: 4)—dropped from 58 percent in 1960 to 17 percent in 1990 (33). Simply put, in three decades, Indonesia achieved what few other postcolonial countries could: increased growth *and* decreased inequality simultaneously (World Bank 1993: 4).[4]

In 1997–1998, there were severe setbacks with the East Asian Financial Crisis. The crisis had its origins in neighboring Thailand when the government there, faced with growing foreign debt, floated its currency (*baht*). Although the economic landscape in Indonesia had been quite drastically different from that of Thailand, the political landscape made the country fertile ground. Aside from family members, Suharto's coalition of cronies during the New Order had included ethnic Chinese business groups with a disproportional control of the country's mobile capital, domestic firms with links to the military, and an emerging class of indigenous entrepreneurs whose assets were largely fixed (Pepinsky 2009). The competing preferences of each group over how to handle the emerging crisis meant Suharto was the only political veto player in Indonesia (MacIntyre 2001).

When the Central Bank widened the rupiah trading band from 8 to 12 percent on July 11, this shook investor confidence. Faced with a sudden demand to trade in the rupiah for U.S. dollars, the monetary authorities floated the rupiah completely. This only heightened the economic woes. Suharto responded strongly by (1) tightening liquidity and driving up interest rates on the monetary front and (2) cutting expenditures and introducing a new luxury tax on the fiscal front. Although the rupiah would stabilize in September, stability was short lived. In October, Suharto turned to the International Monetary Fund (IMF) for help. Despite agreeing to the IMF terms of spend less and save more, Suharto, as the singular veto player in Indonesia, swung "widely" between aggressive austerity measures and equally assertive expansionary macroeconomic policies (MacIntyre 2001: 84). Such vacillations drove massive capital flight by his ethnic Chinese cronies, divided the military, and ultimately led to his own downfall (Pepinsky 2009).

In 1998, the exchange rate for the rupiah fell by more than 50 percent; over 128 banks were closed; and the GDP contracted by more than 13 percent (MacIntyre 2001; Pepinsky 2009). Despite these numbers, it was only a matter of time before the economy would recover. Its sustained success and projected potential would garner the attention of the Group of Seven (G7) finance ministers with the creation of the G20 in 1999. The G20 is a group of finance ministers and central bank governors from the nineteen largest economies and that of the EU. In addition to inclusion in the G20, there has been no shortage of acclaim. This is evident in the number of acronyms coined by various global financial institutions to refer to high-potential economies. These groups include EAGLEs (Emerging and Growth Leading Economies)[5] by Banco Bilbao Vizcaya Argentaria; 3G (Global Growth Generators)[6] with Citigroup; CIVETS[7] with the Economist Intelligence Unit and Hong Kong and Shanghai Banking Corporation; F-10[8] with the Frontier Strategy Group; MIKT[9] and N-11[10] with Goldman Sachs; and BRIC+2[11] by the World Bank. In fact, with respect to the last acronym, some have proposed adding Indonesia (and possibly deleting Russia) in the coveted BRIC grouping of fast-growing economies (Farzad 2010). Even with the recent global financial crisis, the Indonesian economy simply "continues to surprise" (Thee 2010). What explains Indonesia's "miraculous" (World Bank 1993) growth?

One explanation suggests the importance of regime type. Economies are stronger when countries are democratic (Barro 1990; Dick 1974; Findlay 1990; Grier and Tullock 1989; Olson 1993; Pourgerami 1991; Przeworski and Limongi 1993). In democracies, barriers into and out of office are low; the costs of political participation are also low (Baum and Lake 2003). Electoral constraints and responsiveness ensure there is accountability. Consequently, we observe more social spending (D. S. Brown and Hunter 1999; Lake and Baum 2001) and more investments in human capital formation (D. S. Brown and Hunter 2004; Stasavage 2005)—all important elements of growth. Also, in democracies, civil liberties are generally better protected (Poe and Tate 1994; Poe, Tate, and Keith 1999). There is freedom of speech and assembly. There is also freedom of the press. The free dissemination of information is important for investments and growth.

The Indonesian story, however, does not fit any democratic development account. In this case, democratization came after significant growth and rises in

GDP per capita. While Indonesia is today the world's third largest democracy, this was not the case before 1998. For five years following independence, there was some semblance of parliamentary democracy. But shortly thereafter, Sukarno, playing the role of the puppet master, suspended democracy, and ushered in an era of authoritarian rule (Guided Democracy).

Guided Democracy would end in 1965–1968 when six high-ranking generals were abducted and killed—allegedly by the communists (PKI). Led by General Suharto, the Indonesian army launched a counterattack, mobilizing and targeting PKI members and sympathizers. Since many of the PKI members were of Chinese descent, security efforts shifted from an ideological dimension to one that was ethnic and quickly spread throughout the archipelago. These massacres not only resulted in a bloodbath, but also rendered Sukarno politically sterile. On March 11, 1966, Sukarno signed a letter that gave Suharto the right to use any means necessary to restore order. With this authority, Suharto banned the PKI, strengthened the army's political organization Golkar (Organization of Functional Groups), and purged the People's Consultative Assembly of pro-Sukarno members. The Assembly subsequently stripped Sukarno of any powers in 1967 and then formally endorsed Suharto as president in 1968.

Suharto would follow an even more authoritarian path than Sukarno. The New Order was characterized by extreme levels of repression and centralization of power. Golkar closely monitored nongovernmental organizations, business associations, and media personnel. The surviving Chinese were further subjugated, including the forced changing of their family names to those more Indonesian sounding. Separatist movements in Aceh, Irian Jaya, and Timor-Leste were all handled brutally. It was not until the dramatic collapse of the Suharto regime that Indonesia would begin its transition to democracy. In sum, democracy cannot be the explanation for Indonesia's growth. On the contrary, growth occurred under Suharto's dictatorship.

A second explanation focuses on initial endowments and developmental levels. There are multiple reasons why low levels of wealth can impede growth. First, poverty exacerbates conflict. When the gap between the haves and have-nots becomes all too salient, this generates discontent (Lipset 1959: 83–84). Whether this discontent manifests in the form of a high frequency of protests or high intensity civil war, such conflict is not conducive to any substantive long-term investment. Alternatively, poverty is not a cause but a symptom of weak institutions. When European settlers died at high rates (Acemoglu, Johnson, and Robinson 2000), there were few incentives to establish any set of developmental institutions. Instead, colonial institutions existed for strictly extractive purposes (Engerman and Sokoloff 1994). When institutions such as an independent judiciary and property rights are absent, growth levels are inevitably low.

In Indonesia, independence came with an empty coffer. In 1950, per capita income was a pitiful US$177 (Gleditsch 2002). Yhe corresponding figure in neighboring Philippines was twice that of Indonesia; in neighboring Malaysia, three times; and in the Netherlands, tenfold. The poverty was so extreme that Sukarno described the period as a "struggle for survival." Specifically, he recounted:

> Our economy, government administration, transportation systems, communications media, methods of production were all damaged . . . . [T]ypical of my whole country Challenges overwhelmed us on all sides. With industry completely undeveloped, with insufficient foodstuffs and insufficient confidence, with a people scarred by feudalism, colonialism and Fascism, most of whom couldn't read or write—we still had to pick ourselves up and make order out of chaos. We very nearly sank. (quoted in Adams 1966: 264)

In addition to the chaos, the high levels of ethnolinguistic heterogeneity across an archipelago that hitherto had not existed as a single entity only made matters worse. There had been no centralized institutional structure under the Dutch; whatever existed had been destroyed. Simply put, all the conditions were ripe to ensure some sort of a poverty trap. Yet this would not be the case: Indonesia broke out from the traps of a low-level equilibrium.

A third possible explanation for development looks at either colonial legacies or neocolonial relations. Extracting resources and proselytizing the locals were big reasons for colonialism. Yet despite similar objectives, the Europeans pursued different strategies in their colonies. The British are noted for having adopted more liberal policies than other European colonizers. They were more likely to establish new administrative structures that mirrored those at home, recruit civil-service employees locally, and establish institutions that were better equipped to handle the market economy (La Porta et al. 1999; Von Hayek 1960). Additionally, they were more likely to recognize multiple indigenous languages (Albaugh 2014). This was all in stark contrast to the French who pursued very restrictive policies in administration and education. The argument that typically follows is that when countries became independent, those with a British colonial legacy were better equipped institutionally, from the government structure to the legal system, from the market to the classrooms. These institutions would translate into an advantage for facilitating growth.[12]

As it turns out, Dutch policies in Indonesia were largely similar to those of the other continental European colonial authorities. From an institutional standpoint, there was little resemblance to the British colonies. In fact, the Dutch went to great lengths to segregate whatever Dutch institutions existed from the indigenous ones. Moreover, as a part of divide and conquer, the Dutch ensured there was decentralization across the archipelago. If colonial legacies matter, the fact that Indonesia was a Dutch colony should have ensured the country's economic demise. But this clearly has not been the case.

What follows suggests one alternative and neglected explanation for Indonesia's economic growth. Indonesia lacked democracy, favorable initial endowments of resources or climate, and British colonial legacies, but its postcolonial language regime proved highly instrumental for economic growth, specifically, its recognition of a lingua franca. The economic effects of language regimes, however, manifest through two indirect channels. The first was the development of social capital. The use of Indonesian has facilitated a sense of a larger community: it has created a panethnic Indonesian state.[13] For instance, a bureaucrat in the Ministry of Education noted in a 2008 interview that, "My family is from Sulawesi [a large island in the middle of the Indonesian archipelago], but I will always be an Indonesian first. My ties to Sulawesi are familial, but to Indonesia, they are national . . . things like language."[14] When people, like this bureaucrat, identify as being a part of a larger Indonesian community,[15] this can suggest people are more likely to trust each other. This sense of a collective community, while neither a necessary nor a sufficient condition for social capital, is hard to ignore. Put differently, trust is difficult to come by in the absence of a community.

How extensive is this sense of a larger Indonesian community? The Asian Barometer Survey includes three questions about social capital. Specifically, the Survey asks about *generalized trust* ("Generally, do you think most people can be trusted or do you think that you can't be too careful dealing with people?"); *altruism among other people* ("Do you think that people generally try to be helpful or do you think that they mostly look out for themselves?"); and *altruism of the respondent* ("If you saw somebody on the street looking lost, would you stop to help?").[16]

The percentage of respondents who answered positively to each of these three questions is illustrated in Figure 5.1. Each pair of bars corresponds to one Asian Barometer Survey question. Within each pair, there is one bar for Indonesia

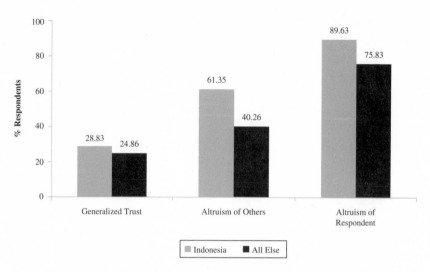

Figure 5.1. Social capital in Indonesia. Asian Barometer survey.

(shaded gray) and one for all other surveyed countries in the sample (shaded black).

It is evident from Figure 5.1 that across all three measures, social capital levels are higher in Indonesia. In fact when compared to non-Indonesians, Indonesians are 16.0 percent more likely to trust other people, 52.4 percent more likely to believe in the altruism of others, and 18.2 percent more likely to help others. These numbers are even more telling when broken down by the respondent's ethnolinguistic affiliation.

The World Values Survey asks the same question about generalized trust (but not altruism). It also asks about the respondent's mother tongue: "What language do you normally speak at home?" The results (see Figure 5.2) indicate that while there is variance, Indonesians—regardless of which of the 712 languages is spoken at home—are deaf to linguistic differences when it comes to trusting other people. Almost half the respondents answered in the affirmative. Moreover, the numbers are largely similar between those speaking Indonesian (lingua franca) at home and those speaking Javanese (the politically dominant language).

Recall that in Indonesia, the new language regime choice was driven largely by the "visionary concept of the tremendous need for unity" and the belief that Indonesian was "an essential tool to bring about this hope and dream" (Trimurti, interviewed in Mohr 1984: 37). This choice to neutralize linguistic power across the 712 languages has clearly played a significant role in generating social capi-

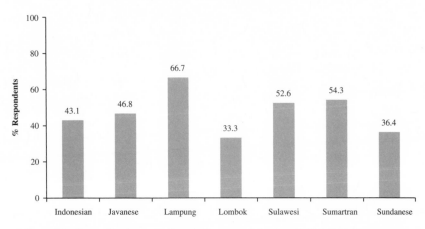

Figure 5.2. Generalized trust by linguistic groups in Indonesia. World Values survey.

tal. And if social capital is an important prerequisite for economic growth (Knack and Keefer 1997; Ostrom 1990; Putnam 1993), this suggests the choice to recognize a lingua franca can have positive economic implications.

The argument being suggested here is that the relevant effects of power-neutralization on social capital were *direct*, and therefore that the effects of language regime on economic growth were *indirect*, mediated by social capital. The argument is about the importance of certain language regimes being present so that the basics of a political community—a state—can even exist. Of course, an appropriate social capital-enhancing and therefore growth-conducive language regime is not sufficient for an economic "take-off" or sustained growth. Other policies matter. Suharto's macroeconomic policies, arguably, are responsible for much of Indonesia's economic growth. Upon assuming office, Suharto reversed many of his predecessor's import-substitution policies. Suharto's policies included reducing government subsidies, stabilizing the exchange rate, sending signals to foreign investors of a hospitable investment environment, and developing large-scale infrastructure projects. These policies were definitely important. And although there may be debate surrounding the magnitude of their effects, the claim is that these policies would have yielded much less in the absence of the successful manufacture[17] of an Indonesian community—the product of a power-neutralizing language regime.

I hypothesize that in addition to unifying members of the Indonesian community, the recognition of a lingua franca broadly—a power-neutralizing language regime specifically—can also affect economic growth indirectly through a second mechanism of interest. By coordinating around one language, the new regime has allowed for efficient communication within education, public and private institutions, and the media. This efficiency in turn can be attractive to foreign investors. A manager of a Chinese company, when asked about her company's motives for investing in Indonesia, highlighted the importance of efficiency. "We like investing in Indonesia. . . . People speak one language." This attitude was reflected in several other interviews with managers from Australia, the EU, South Korea, and Taiwan.

When firms invest abroad, there is some probability that the language of the firm and that of the host country may not be the same. When the languages are the same, this can make the host country very attractive for efficiency reasons. For instance, a Malaysian company was drawn to Indonesia because "Indonesian and Malay are the same." But when the languages do not match up, translations are rendered necessary. These translations can be costly in both time and money. Additionally, the likelihood of translation errors or general misunderstanding is high. Any factor that can cut costs can prove instrumental—as evidenced by the Chinese quote. So when the country is able to provide a workforce that speaks the same singular language, even if that language is not the language of the investing firm, this reduces transaction costs substantially.

This discussion would suggest countries with one language cutting across the entire population, such as Indonesia, are preferred receivers of foreign capital. Figure 5.3 plots foreign direct investment (FDI) levels in Indonesia against the average investment levels for the other countries in Southeast Asia. With the exception of a small period in the wake of the 1997 East Asian Financial Crisis, FDI levels has been higher in Indonesia than the average elsewhere.

Figure 5.3 is consistent with what the manager of the Chinese company said. Language regime choice can attract (or repel) foreign capital. For countries like Indonesia, FDI is important for multiple reasons. Aside from the influx of capital, it also creates jobs, facilitates technology transfers, and encourages knowledge spillovers (Borensztein, De Gregorio, and Lee 1998; De Mello 1999). Given the cards dealt at independence (712 languages across 13,000 islands), the fact that Indonesia was able to use a lingua franca to ensure efficiency is no trivial matter.

Again, a caveat is in order. The claim is not that this choice of a power-neutralizing language regime was *the* most important factor for attracting FDI. Realistically, the size of the economy, its geographical proximity to Australia and other Asian countries, and other economic-related considerations are all more important. Instead, the argument is that, ceteris paribus, foreign firms, when choos-

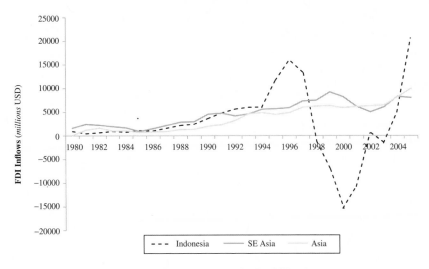

Figure 5.3. FDI in Indonesia. World Bank.

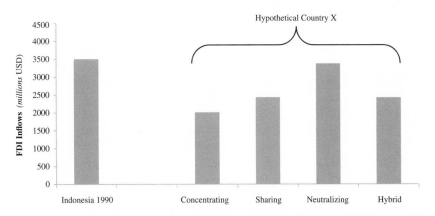

Figure 5.4. Counterfactual FDI in Indonesia.
Expected values generated using Table 7.1, Model 1.

ing where to invest, prefer destinations where linguistically derived transaction costs are minimal. As an illustration, consider the counterfactual. Specifically, what would Indonesia's FDI levels look like today if the language regime had not been power-neutralizing?

Figure 5.4 plots the actual FDI inflows for Indonesia in 1990 (US$3,532 million). To the right are four more bars. These are the expected FDI inflows for a

hypothetical country (Country X) that mirrors Indonesia on all dimensions except for the language regime. Note how much less FDI Country X would have
attracted if the language regime had been power-concentrating ($2,013 million).
While investments would have increased with either power-sharing or neutralized-
sharing, the language regime associated with the most inflows is one that exclusively recognizes a lingua franca. In sum, when language regimes facilitate
efficiency—as in the case of Indonesia—this can have a positive effect on FDI.

Mechanism 1: Social Capital

The first mechanism hypothesized to link language regimes to economic growth
is social capital. Social capital is the set of resources that include "authority relations, relations of trust, and consensual allocations of rights" (Coleman 1990:
300–301). These resources (e.g., trust, norms, networks) can help structure interactions between individuals, thereby making society function at greater efficiency
(Putnam 1993: 167). Yet despite its importance, for multiple reasons, social capital is a fuzzy concept. It "spans too many units of analysis; inadequately engages
with questions of power and inequality; uses tautological reasoning; fails to accommodate the fact that harmful consequences can flow from cooperation and
trust; shoehorns distinctive social concepts into economic ('neo-liberal') theory;
and is unclear with regard to whether it is a cause or effect, a stock or a flow, a
'structural' or cognitive/behavioral phenomenon" (Woolcock 2010: 482). Sometimes social capital loses almost all meaning and scientific utility—especially as
typically defined. Yet, as an "essentially contested concept," it still retains importance (482).

To minimize, and more important, to avoid conceptual stretching (D. Collier
and Levitsky 1997; Sartori 1970), the focus here is primarily on trust. Trust—
whether between individuals, across communities, or in general—is arguably
one of the most important conceptualizations of social capital (L. Anderson 2010;
Coleman 1990; Kawachi, Subramanian, and Kim 2010; Putnam 1993). It is what
"permits obligations to be repaid, which in turn facilitates social interactions that
would otherwise not be possible" (Whiteley 2000: 448). Trust also "promotes
norms which abjure self-interest and reinforces the idea that individuals should
act in the interests of the group in order to solve collective action problems" (448).
At the individual and national levels, "many things that are normatively desirable
seem connected to social trust" (Rothstein and Uslaner 2005: 42).

Trust is important for economic growth. In fact, in the absence of any sort of trust, the development of a vibrant economy is difficult if not impossible (Knack and Keefer 1997; Ostrom 1990; Putnam 1993). When trust levels are high, it "reduce[s] transaction costs in the market economy, minimizes the deadweight burdens of enforcing and policing agreements, and holds down the diseconomies of fraud and theft" (Whiteley 2000: 443). It is not a coincidence that almost "every commercial transaction has within itself an element of trust, certainly any transaction conducted over a period of time" (Arrow 1972: 357; cited in Knack and Keefer 1997: 1252). Moreover, with trust, innovation and investment in physical and human capital is more likely (Knack and Keefer 1997: 1253). Simply put, trust is "productive, making possible the achievement of certain ends that would not be attainable in its absence" (Putnam 1993: 167).

Given the importance of trust, it is natural to then ask about its genesis. Sources range from associations to families, from schools to the media (Levi 1996; Newton 1999; Putnam 1993). What is consistent across these different origins is some semblance of a "community." Put differently, whether the community is a necessary condition or a symptom of something larger, trust cannot exist in the absence of a community. If communities can be "imagined" (B. Anderson 1983), then this suggests language regimes can be instrumental in the development and maintenance of trust.

Language regimes matter for trust, especially for interethnic trust. Language regimes distribute linguistic power. This precise distribution is important as some distributions are more equal than others. Consider two examples. Chinese speakers are minorities in both Malaysia and Vietnam. In Malaysia, the language regime is de jure power-sharing: Chinese is a medium of instruction. In contrast, in Vietnam, the language regime is de jure power-concentrating: Vietnamese is the only acceptable language of the curriculum. From a Chinese perspective, the two linguistic arrangements are not comparable. One is fairer than the other. In other words, a speaker of a minority language is more likely to view a power-sharing language regime as fairer (i.e., more equal) than one that concentrates linguistic power in the politically dominant language. This perception of equality in turn matters for the quality of the larger community, specifically, whether the community is collective or divided. When communities are collective, there is a general cohesion, which parlays into growth (Whiteley 2000).

Given the above discussion, theoretical expectations would suggest that certain language regimes are better suited for generating social capital than others. Of the four language regimes, power-concentrating ones arguably fare the worst at fostering any sense of trust, norms, and networks, especially *among* speakers of the excluded languages and *between* those excluded and those not. By definition, power-concentrating language regimes are characterized by the exclusive use of the politically dominant language. These regimes, such as that of Thailand, "can cause injustice," "repress minorities," and "reinforce other social structures of oppression and disadvantage" (Mowbray 2012: 17). For speakers of a nonrecognized language (e.g., Chinese, Khmer, or Vietnamese), there is inequality in opportunity to use one's mother tongue. Government services and education curriculums are available in only that one language. There is also inequality in linguistic proficiency. Speakers whose languages are not recognized may have a more difficult time learning the mother tongue of the politically dominant. And finally, there is a symbolic inequality: there is an image of the state monopolized by a subset of the population. Such arrangements may be welcomed by those in the politically dominant group. However, for those excluded, this is bound to be divisive, generate resentment, and possibly decrease social capital.

The following hypothesis reflects these arguments:

Hypothesis 2.1(a): *Power-concentrating language regimes have a negative effect on social capital.*

Hypothesis 2.1(b): *Power-concentrating language regimes have a positive effect on social capital for the politically dominant.*

In contrast, power-sharing language regimes recognize multiple mother tongues. In theory, this recognition ensures greater equality between speakers of the different languages. There is equality in proficiency—or at least in the opportunity to be proficient. Linguistic barriers to forums, markets, and status are lower. Both the politically dominant and those not so can engage publicly in their own languages. This is especially important for the latter group. When the freedoms for assembly, movement, and speech are not hindered by linguistic limitations, politically nondominant groups can, in principle, voice their grievances more effectively with the state in particular and with the society at large. There is also greater equality in symbolism. Here, grievances of chauvinism on the part of the politically dominant are muted. Linguistic recognition is more than just about a particular vehicle of communication. It is about acknowledging a group's identity and granting it legitimacy (see Horowitz 1985: 220). In theory, speakers of different languages are equal. When authorities follow protocol and display respect, people are more likely to accept and be satisfied with the outcomes, regardless of the outcomes in and of themselves (Casper, Tyler, and Fisher 1988;

Huo et al. 1996; Tyler et al. 1997). Psychologists have on multiple occasions found that people place greater emphasis on procedures than on outcomes (De Cremer et al. 2004; Koper et al. 1993; Thibaut and Walker 1975; Tyler et al. 1997). For example, when minorities can use their own language in judicial proceedings, they are more likely to express confidence in the justice system. Even if the ultimate verdict is not in their favor, they are more likely to view the institution as legitimate when they believe the case has been tried fairly by a jury of their peers (Liu and Baird 2012). In sum, when people feel respected, such as having the right to use their own language in public, they are more likely to identify as members of the collective community. The following hypothesis summarizes this argument:

Hypothesis 2.2: *Power-sharing language regimes have a positive effect on social capital.*

The effects of a power-neutralizing language regime on social capital are similar to their power-sharing counterparts. In this instance, the lingua franca becomes an effective instrument to generate equality. No group can easily claim greater cultural egoism from having its culture recognized than any other. The use of a third party language also removes any semblance of a zero sum game. In the Indonesian story, for example, the use of Indonesian played a critical role in keeping tensions between the Javanese and the non-Javanese at a minimum. Recall, one concern with the use of Javanese was that it would have merely perpetuated a new form of hierarchy no different from Dutch colonialism (Mohr 1984: 27).

Employing a lingua franca means no group is absolutely disadvantaged. First, from a linguistic standpoint, even though speakers of one language may struggle with learning a non-mother-tongue language (i.e., the lingua franca), this challenge is not theirs alone. Even the speakers of the most demographically prevalent language face the same set of difficulties with the use of a lingua franca. Second, from a symbolic standpoint, the use of a third party language can reduce and perhaps remove minority narratives of a society dominated by one group. The lingua franca cultivates an image of a larger and truly panethnic state. The community is genuinely collective as opposed to being controlled and represented by the symbols of just one group. In Indonesia, the recognition of a lingua franca has been an important catalyst for the building of a larger Indonesian community. Bureaucrats hailing from the island of Sulawesi, for instance, consider themselves "Indonesian" first and foremost. In the World Values Survey, 51 percent of the respondents in Indonesia said they "strongly agreed" with the statement "I see myself as a citizen of the Indonesian nation." Another 48 percent answered "agreed." Of almost 2,000 respondents, only four said they "strongly disagreed."

Other survey numbers from the Asian Barometer and World Value Surveys suggest social capital levels are high in Indonesia. Not only are trust levels high, they are also consistent across the different linguistic groups, with 67 percent of Lampung speakers (in south Sumatra, a major island in the west) indicating they generally trust other people. The following hypothesis summarizes this argument:

> **Hypothesis 2.3:** *Power-neutralizing language regimes have a positive effect on social capital.*

The effects of a neutralized-sharing language regime merit some discussion. On the one hand, since these language regimes recognize mother tongues and a lingua franca, there is reason to expect a positive effect. On the other hand, however, there is no guarantee that all linguistic groups have their mother tongues recognized. In fact, it is possible that the only mother tongue recognized is that of the politically dominant. When this happens, it is possible that the symbolic inequality can have a dampening effect. This suggests that while the effects may still be positive, the magnitude is less than that of either power-sharing or power-neutralizing.

> **Hypothesis 2.4:** *Neutralized-sharing language regimes have a positive effect on social capital.*
> **Corollary 2:** *The positive effects of neutralized-sharing language regimes are less than either power-sharing or power-neutralizing.*

Mechanism 2: Foreign Capital

In addition to social capital, there is a second mechanism of interest. FDI is desirable for a number reasons. Aside from being another source of capital, foreign investors can provide opportunities for employment, offer employee training, and bring with them innovative ideas and the knowhow of new technology (Borensztein, De Gregorio, and Lee 1998; De Mello 1999; Feldstein 2000). It is because of these purported advantages that governments adopt a multitude of strategies to attract foreign investors, from tax incentives and subsidies (Aitken and Harrison

1999) to institutional organization memberships (Blomstrom and Kokko 2003). Another vehicle for encouraging investment from abroad is the quality of the workforce (Globerman and Shapiro 2002; Mody and Srinivasan 1998). Quality can be especially important as a country loses its cheap labor advantage. This was the case in Thailand in the 1990s: when China and other lower wage producing countries began to emerge, the government responded by increasing the supply of trained personnel (Brimble and Doner 2007: 1022).[18]

One way to signal workforce quality is with linguistic repertoire. In the FDI literature, one explanation for bilateral investment flows focuses on whether the two countries share a common language (Bandelj 2002; Bénassy-Quéré, Coupet, and Mayer 2007; Leblang 2010). The logic is that the greater the cultural distance between the two countries, the greater the barriers to carrying out the transactions. In these works, cultural distance is conceptualized as being static, specifically, whether the sending and receiving states share the same official language. But a state trying to attract FDI need not share the same official language as the sending state; all that is necessary is for the former to have a workforce proficient in the latter's official language (Kim et al. 2015; also see Lien, Chang, and Selmier 2011). To this end, the focus should be on the languages in the classrooms.

Language regimes matter for foreign capital. They can enhance efficiency. Like common exchange rate pegs (Froot and Stein 1991), dual tax treaties (De Mooij and Ederveen 2001), preferential trade agreements (Büthe and Milner 2008; Makki and Somwaru 2004; Tomz, Goldstein, and Rivers 2007), and common international organization memberships (Blomstrom and Kokko 2003), language regimes are institutional solutions for reducing transaction costs. By keeping these costs minimal, governments can send a signal to foreign firms of an investor-friendly environment. It is not a coincidence that the aforementioned Chinese company in Indonesia emphasized efficiency. Another Chinese-speaking manager, after complaining about paperwork volume and the bureaucracy process, said as an afterthought, "At least it's all in one language. Even when it's time to give bribes, it's done in that language [Indonesian]." As foreign capital flows into a country, this can have positive implications for economic growth.

Given the above discussion, theoretical expectations would suggest that certain language regimes are better suited for attracting FDI than others. While power-concentrating language regimes are unequal, they are highly efficient: the population in general speaks the same language. Even if the language of the foreign firm is different from that of the politically dominant or the majority, the fact that there is one language standardizing the population means reduced translation volume. When the barriers to transaction are minimal, the expectation is that foreign capital levels will be high. The following hypothesis reflects this argument:

Hypothesis 3.1: *Power-concentrating language regimes have a positive effect on foreign capital.*

On the other hand, while power-sharing language regimes are equal in nature, they may be extremely inefficient. Of the four language regimes, power-sharing has the highest barriers to transaction. The presence of numerous recognized languages amounts to an abundance of translations. The recognition of each additional language increases the number of necessary translations at an exponential rate. These translations, in aggregate, are inefficient; and this inefficiency can deter potential foreign capital. The following hypothesis summarizes this argument:

Hypothesis 3.2: *Power-sharing language regimes have a negative effect on foreign capital.*

Finally, language regimes that recognize a lingua franca—both power-neutralizing and neutralized-sharing language regimes—are efficient. The logic parallels that of power-concentrating language regimes: because the population at large speaks the same language (except in this case, a lingua franca), this facilitates ease in business operations. Foreign firms can communicate with the domestic work force with relative ease. The following hypotheses reflect this discussion:

Hypothesis 3.3: *Power-neutralizing language regimes have a positive effect on foreign capital.*
Hypothesis 3.4: *Neutralized-sharing language regimes have a positive effect on foreign capital.*

Not only do lingua francas coordinate the linguistic repertoire across a population at large, lingua franca recognition can have another advantage that power-concentrating language regimes lack. If the lingua franca happens to be the politically dominant language in the sending state (e.g., Portuguese in Timor-Leste versus Portuguese in Portugal), this drastically reduces transaction costs. Even if companies do not originate from a country where the lingua franca is a mother tongue, communication barriers can still be relatively minimal. For instance, the firm may have already invested in the translation costs for another country. One example of this would be a Japanese company investing in Brunei (translation to Malay) and then investing in Indonesia. The following corollary reflects this discussion:

Corollary 3: *The positive effects of a power-concentrating language regime are less than either power-neutralizing or neutralized-sharing.*

Implications for Economic Growth

The discussion above generates additional predictions about the indirect effects of lingua franca recognition on economic growth. Like power-sharing language regimes, both power-neutralizing and neutralized-sharing can generate trust. When individuals perceive a language regime as being fair, this can aid in the development of trust and norms, both important for "improv[ing] the efficiency of society by facilitating coordinated action" (Putnam 1993: 167). And like power-concentrating language regimes, both power-neutralizing and neutralized-sharing language regimes can attract FDI—in fact, maybe even more. The prevalence of one language across a larger population can reduce the barriers for any transacting firm. When considering the two mechanisms together, this leads to another hypothesis:

Hypothesis 4.1: *The recognition of a lingua franca has a positive, indirect effect on economic growth.*

Not all language regimes that recognize a lingua franca, however, are the same. Some, like Indonesia's, are characterized by the exclusive use of a lingua franca; others, like India's, recognize a lingua franca in addition to a set of mother tongues. While *any* lingua franca recognition is better for economic growth than *none*, I also argue that *more* recognition is better than *less*. When other languages are recognized in conjunction with a lingua franca, this can potentially introduce some semblance of inequality akin to those in power-concentrating and moments of inefficiency like those found in power-sharing. This would suggest that the magnitude of economic effects of power-neutralizing language regimes is larger than those of neutralized-sharing:

Hypothesis 4.2: *The indirect economic effects are larger for power-neutralizing language regimes than for neutralized-sharing.*

The next two chapters test these hypotheses. Chapter 6 focuses on social capital. It begins with a review of three alternative explanations to account for social capital levels. The empirical tests then follow. The first is a large N analysis employing several different surveys. The second test uses process-tracing to identify the effects of language regime in the second periods of Malaysia and Singapore on generalized trust levels today. The structure of Chapter 7 on foreign capital mirrors that of the previous chapter. It also concludes with a detailed analysis and discussion of the implications of social capital and foreign capital—individually and in aggregate—for economic growth.

CHAPTER 6

Mechanism 1: Social Capital

The previous chapters highlighted the institutionalized properties of language regimes. First, language regimes distribute linguistic power (see Knight 1992). They delineate which languages can be used when and where, suggesting speakers of certain languages can lay claim to greater respect (Horowitz 1985: 220). This recognition in turn is shared across some imagined community (B. Anderson 1983). Second, language regimes encourage efficiency (see North 1990). These rules constrain and structure human behavior. Within a relevant polity, people expect the same languages to be spoken by everyone, every day, and everywhere.

As institutions, language regimes matter for economic performance. The mechanism of interest explored in this chapter is social capital, primarily generalized trust and secondarily altruism. When language regimes distribute linguistic power equally, this creates a sense of a collective community that is shared by all. Power-sharing, power-neutralizing, and neutralized-sharing language regimes are inherently equal in their linguistic distribution, although the precise character of this equality is slightly different. At one end, power-sharing language regimes generate equality by adopting other mother tongues; at the other end, power-neutralizing language regimes perpetuate a sense of fairness by using a lingua franca; and in the middle are the neutralized-sharing hybrids which are a combination of the two.

In contrast, power-concentrating language regimes, by recognizing only the politically dominant language, perpetuate inequality on multiple dimensions. This inequality can cause resentment among those denied their language rights, thereby impeding any collective panethnic community. This sense of community is critical for generating social capital (e.g., trust), which over time and in aggregate parlays into high economic growth.

This chapter begins with a review of several alternative explanations for social capital levels, and examines whether there is prima facie evidence for my theoretical claims regarding language regimes. The results, robust across model specifications and alternative samples, confirm that language regimes matter for social capital. The third section is a pair of process-tracings (post-1971 Malaysia and post-1965 Singapore). A comparison of the ways language regime changes following a critical juncture have affected social capital levels today helps elucidate causal mechanisms. The final section discusses the implications of these findings.

Rival Hypotheses

Although important, it is possible that language regimes are neither a necessary nor a sufficient condition for social capital generation. There may be alternative explanations to account for the varying levels of generalized trust between groups and across countries. This section explores three competing hypotheses and considers each in turn: ethnic heterogeneity, regime type, and wealth.

Ethnic Heterogeneity

The predominant view in the political behavior literature is that heterogeneity has a negative effect on social capital (Alesina and La Ferrara 2005; C. Anderson and Paskeviciute 2006; Costa and Kahn 2003; Delhey and Newton 2005; Knack and Keefer 1997; Putnam 2007; Rice and Steele 2001). Social identity theory (Tajfel 1982; Tajfel and Turner 1979) tells us that it is human nature for people to group others around them into either an "us" or a "them" category. This bifurcation of in-group versus out-group can be especially important when it affects security matters. Out-groups may be deemed a threat when they are culturally distinct (Gambetta and Hamill 2005); when there are extreme levels of inequality (Costa and Kahn 2003); and when their presence (e.g., size) or public visibility increases (Oliver and Wong 2003; Quillian 1995, 1996). Whether these threats are real or perceived is not of relevance here. Instead, the focus is on the consequences of these threats. Members of an in-group are inclined to respond by negatively stereotyping those in out-groups (Caddick 2010; Deschamps 2010; Tajfel and Turner 1985). Specifically:

> Residents of ethnically diverse communities are less likely to trust people in their neighborhoods, the clerks where they shop, the people they work with, and even (quite remarkably) people of their own ethnic group. . . .

Residents of more diverse communities are more likely to be personally isolated; they claim fewer friends and confidants, spend less time socializing with friends and relatives, and have less sense of community with their friends. (Saguaro Seminar 2001: 5)

There is, however, a contrasting viewpoint that champions ethnic heterogeneity as being good for social capital formation. The argument is that heterogeneity can build communities by developing tolerance and understanding of group differences. When different ethnic groups interact increasingly and repeatedly, this can generate intergroup trust and parlay into higher levels of generalized trust (Oliver and Wong 2003). There is evidence that individuals in heterogeneous neighborhoods are more trusting than their counterparts in homogeneous ones (Marschall and Stolle 2004). In homogeneous communities, the lack of contact or direct knowledge of people from different backgrounds can reinforce existing stereotypes (Bobo 1988).

Here, we are at a theoretical impasse. Additionally, there are three concerns with ethnic heterogeneity as an explanation for social capital levels. First, from a conceptual standpoint, on a broad understanding, ethnicity is a composite indicator. It can include any combination of the following: language, religion, race, kinship, laws, customs, dress, crafts, music, architecture, and food (M. Brown 1993: 4). Thus, to identify an ethnic group objectively (not to mention accurately) is no small feat (Chandra 2006; Chandra and Wilkinson 2008). If group boundaries cannot be correctly identified ex ante, then the intergroup interactions of concern are also subject to the same concerns.

Second, from a theoretical standpoint, to focus only on heterogeneity ignores the importance of institutions. Governments have institutional tools, such as language regimes, at their disposal to shape and mediate the social effects of heterogeneity. To overlook institutions would suggest some countries are simply destined to have low trust levels. Last, from an empirical standpoint, not all ethnic groups are politically relevant (Cederman, Wimmer, and Min 2010; Posner 2004). To focus on all ethnic groups inevitably includes a large number of irrelevant cases which in turn can muddy the empirical results (Mahoney and Goertz 2004).

Regime Type

Regime type can matter for social capital. The general supposition in political science has been that trust levels are higher in democracies. There are two mutually enforcing explanations for this claim. First, democracies are by definition a set of institutions that purport to be governments "of the people, by the people, for the people." When a government takes into consideration the preferences of its constituents, people are more likely to develop confidence in their government. This confidence in turn facilitates some sense of community, and it is this community that matters for building generalized trust (Brehm and Rahn 1997; Cleary and Stokes 2006: chap. 1; Hardin 2002; Levi 1996; Offe 1999). Second, democracies are generally characterized as having more civil liberties: freedom of assembly, speech, and the media. The exchange of information under such conditions can increase awareness and facilitate broad community development. And again, where such communities exist, there is generalized trust.

Empirical evidence suggests that democracies and social capital are highly and positively correlated (Inglehart 1990; Muller and Seligson 1994; Putnam 1993). There are, however, two concerns. First, democracies are characterized by "one person, one vote." While fair with respect to procedures, this system is not necessarily fair with respect to outcomes. Descriptive representation does not always translate into substantive representation (Reingold 2008: 128). Critical mass is neither necessary nor sufficient to guarantee a preferred policy; and vice versa. With democracy, the prospects of a tyranny of the majority—*any* majority—have long been a concern (Madison, *Federalist* 10; also see Mill 1859/1989: 7–8; Tocqueville 1835/2002: pt. 2, chaps. 7–8). When members of a minority feel their preferences are not being taken into account, this can affect their confidence in government institutions and the larger community. It would seem, then, that democracy—especially those with electoral rules that favor a majority—can have a negative effect on social capital.

Second, institutional confidence is not a phenomenon exclusive to democracies. Authoritarian governments have just as much incentive as their democratic counterparts to cultivate these attitudes (Jamal and Nooruddin 2010). Moreover, these regimes vary in their institutional designs (Gandhi 2008; Geddes 1999; Slater 2003; Wright 2008). When citizens believe their preferences are being protected by some set of institutions (e.g., legislative elections), it is likely that they will express confidence in the government. There is no theoretical basis to believe government satisfaction is lacking en masse across this heterogeneous grouping of authoritarian regimes. While some authoritarian governments like Zaire's Mobutu Sese Seko are predatory (Evans 1989), others, like South Korea's Park Chung-Hee and Taiwan's Chiang Kai-Shek, pursued encompassed developmental policies precisely to contain potential domestic unrest (Doner, Ritchie, and Slater 2005). Likewise, there is no reason to believe political confidence is uniformly present in all democracies. The frequent government turnovers in some parliamentary systems such as Italy's suggest that regularized electoral competition for political office is not sufficient for government confidence. If there is variation in confidence, then there must also be variation in generalized trust. It therefore seems that under certain conditions, democracy can have no effect on social capital, as institutional confidence can develop regardless of the regime type.

Wealth

Wealth can also be relevant to social capital generation for two different reasons. First, wealth moderates conflict. Poverty exacerbates the gap between the haves and have-nots (see Lipset 1959: 83). In these situations, it is easy for the former to lord their economic assets over the latter. The rich develop norms that it is acceptable to treat the poor badly or unjustly. And for the poor, feelings of being subordinated inevitably develop. These behaviors and attitudes can impede the building of a larger community. In contrast, economic cleavages become less salient with the general diffusion of wealth. When the distinctions between the rich and the poor are muted (often by the emergence of a middle class), this allows for a sense of a collective community, and with this community, there is trust (Knack and Keefer 1997).

There is a second explanation linking wealth to social capital. There is evidence that social capital is influenced by the government's overall economic performance (Chanley, Rudolph, and Rahn 2000; Espinal, Hartlyn, and Kelly 2006; Hetherington 1998; Mishler and Rose 1997). When the population owns a sizable amount of capital, it provides the government with a substantial base from which to collect revenues. The government can then use these monies to provide basic public goods and to pursue other community-building policies. Given this discussion, it seems that whether by means of conflict moderation or public goods provision, diffused wealth has a positive effect on generalized trust. The next section empirically tests the leverage of these rival hypotheses against that of the language regime.

Language Regimes and Social Capital in Asia

To gauge the effects of language regime on social capital, I employ data from the Asian Barometer Survey. The Asian Barometer Survey is a survey that has been conducted in eighteen countries in 2003–2007. It has evolved from its original East Asian emphasis to become pan-Asia's "first systematic and more careful comparative survey of attitudes and orientations toward political regime, democracy, governance, and economic reform" (Asian Barometer, Program Overview). Approximately one thousand respondents are surveyed in each country in each year. The unit of analysis is the *respondent*.

Research Design

Generalized Trust: The dependent variable of interest is generalized trust. The Asian Barometer Survey asks the following question: "Generally, do you think people can be trusted or do you think that you can't be too careful dealing with people (that it pays to be wary of people)?" Respondents have the choice of "most people can be trusted," "can't be too careful in dealing with people," and "don't know." The answers have been recoded such that a value of 1 corresponds to the positive "people can be trusted" and a value of 0 for the negative "you can't be too careful." The "don't know" responses are treated as missing. In all, 30 percent of respondents answered "most people can be trusted." The most "trusting" country was South Korea (66.4 percent). The least trusting was Cambodia, where only 4.4 percent of respondents expressed interpersonal trust.

Altruism: While generalized trust is an important component of social capital, it is certainly not the only element in the concept. As an alternative, I use two other measures from the Asian Barometer Survey that involve altruism. The first focuses on the belief that people (in abstract) are altruistic: "Do you think that people generally try to be helpful or do you think that they mostly look out for themselves?" Again, answers to this yes or no question have been coded such that 1 corresponds to the positive "people generally try to be helpful." The second alternative measure focuses on the respondent's altruism and her own actual behavior: "If you saw somebody on the street looking lost, would you stop to help?" This question offers three responses, ranging from "I would always stop to help" (recoded and assigned a value of 1); "I would help if nobody else did" (0); and "It is highly likely that I wouldn't stop to help" (−1).

Language Regime: The key explanatory variable of interest is language regime. The coding for this variable remains unchanged. Specifically, the focus is on the medium of instruction at the public primary and secondary levels. There are two measures. One is the quadrachotomous measure: power-concentrating (i.e., exclusive recognition of the politically dominant language), power-sharing (i.e.,

recognition of multiple mother tongues), power-neutralizing (i.e., exclusive recognition of a lingua franca), and neutralized-sharing (i.e., recognition of mother
tongues and a lingua franca). Given its categorical nature, the variable has been
transformed into four dummy variables (*power-concentrating, power-sharing,
power-neutralizing,* and *neutralized-sharing*). With such models where the independent variable is a set of dichotomies that collectively constitute one singular
categorical variable, there needs to be a reference variable against which all the
other categorical variables are compared. In this model, the reference category is
power-concentrating. As an alternative, the other measure is continuous: the degree of linguistic neutralization in the education curriculum. As a reminder, this
variable is bounded from a minimum of 0 (no recognition of a lingua franca
whatsoever) to a maximum of 1 (complete recognition of a lingua franca).

Control Variables: To account for the effects of other variables on generalized
trust (see previous section), several control variables have been included. One
measure is politically relevant linguistic heterogeneity. The inclusion of this variable is critical for two reasons. First, the negative effects of heterogeneity on social capital levels are well established (Alesina et al. 2003; C. Anderson and
Paskeviciute 2006; Costa and Kahn 2003; Delhey and Newton 2005; Knack and
Keefer 1997; Putnam 2007; Rice and Steele 2001). Second, as shown in Chapter
4, politically relevant linguistic heterogeneity was the key independent variable
in explaining language regime choice. To assess how much of the effect of heterogeneity is mediated by language regimes, this necessitates the basic inclusion
of the antecedent explanatory variable.

Additionally, there are two other national level controls. One is regime type.
To measure democracy, I use the 21-point POLITY (Marshall and Jaggers 2008):
a minimum of −10 indicates complete authoritarianism and a maximum of 10 suggests complete democracy. The other national level control is wealth per capita, in
US$1000 units (GDP per capita). The data source for this variable is the IMF, as
reported in Kristian Gleditsch's (2002) Direction of Trade (DOT) Dataset.

There may be other factors accounting for generalized trust at the individual
level. There is evidence that partisanship and ideology matter the most for trust
(Stokes 1966). With the Asian Barometer Survey, however, questions that would
allow for some measure of these two concepts are absent. For instance, there is
no question that directly asks about the respondent's left-right position. There
are, however, questions that would allow for such inference indirectly. For instance, if a respondent indicated consistently "spend much more" on a number of
policy arenas (e.g., the environment, health, education, and pensions), this could

correspond to a leftist position. The problem with this approach is that this question was not asked—either in full or at all—in several of the countries (e.g., Brunei, China, Laos, Myanmar, and Vietnam). As an alternative, following Kelleher and Wolak (2007), I use demographics to tap into the mechanisms that would explain a respondent's level of trust. I focus on whether the respondent has at least a high school education, is a parent, is female, and is unemployed. All affirmative responses are assigned a value of 1. I also include a control for the respondent's income (measured on a four-point scale).

Empirical Evidence

To help structure the discussion, I have again relegated the technical discussions and statistical tables to the Appendix of this chapter. The first set of multilevel regressions includes four model specifications (Table 6.1). As a reminder, the theory posits a direct causal relationship between language regime and social capital levels. Specifically, there are a number of expectations: (1) the exclusive recognition of the politically dominant language has a negative effect; (2) the recognition of multiple mother tongues has a positive effect; (3) the recognition of a lingua franca, whether exclusively or not, has a positive effect; and (4) the effects of exclusive lingua franca recognition are more pronounced than recognition in conjunction with other mother tongues.

The first set of results indicate that language regime has no statistically significant effect whatsoever on generalized trust. There are several possible explanations. One is that, contrary to theoretical expectations, language regimes simply do not matter for social capital. Arguably, the only way to validate this explanation is the rejection of all others. It could also be the case that language regimes matter for social capital broadly but just not for generalized trust specifically. Since social capital is a broad encompassing concept, it is possible that the Asian Barometer Survey question is not tapping into the concept of interest. One way to assess this explanation is to use the altruism variables.

The use of alternative measures suggests language regimes do matter for social capital. Figure 6.1 shows the predicted effects of language regimes on perceived altruism of others. The baseline is that of a power-concentrating language regime: when linguistic power is concentrated in the politically dominant language, less than one-quarter of the respondents believe in the helpfulness of others. In contrast, holding all other factors equal, when a language regime is power-sharing, 41.2 percent of respondents believe in the affirmative. The shift to

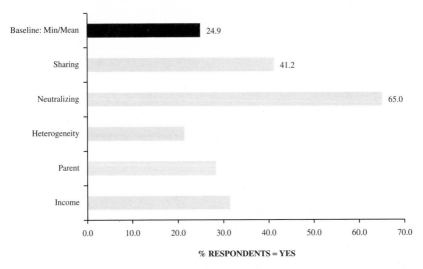

Figure 6.1. Expected values for altruism (one standard deviation shift).
Marginal effects reported only for significant coefficients in Table 6.1, Model 2.

power-neutralizing is even starker: 65 percent of the respondents believe people generally try to be helpful.

The above discussion is consistent with the hypotheses in Chapter 5. When a language regime is power-concentrating, this perpetuates inequality. From a practical standpoint, speakers of the one recognized language have an advantage when it comes to linguistic proficiency. This proficiency can translate into what is seen as an unfair advantage when it comes to job opportunities, university admissions, and other matters related to advancements in a community. Also from a psychological standpoint, when a person's language is not recognized, this suggests that her culture broadly and her identity specifically are both inferior. This asymmetry in respect can build resentment and hinder the integration of all into the imagined community.

In contrast, when there is linguistic concession, this can generate some semblance of equality, although the precise nature of this equality is different. Power-sharing language regimes, by affording multiple mother tongues legitimacy, evoke some sort of equality in *recognition*. In contrast, power-neutralizing language regimes, by employing a lingua franca, generate equality in *nonrecognition*. The results suggest these two language regimes do indeed cultivate a sense of equality— although note that the effects of power-neutralizing are larger than those of power-sharing.

Thus far, one language regime has escaped discussion: neutralized-sharing. Its absence in Figure 6.1 is because it is not statistically significant in any of the models. This is not consistent with theoretical priors. The expectation was that the effects would have been substantive, but less than those of power-neutralizing. But this does not seem to be the case. Instead, its effects on altruism are comparable to those of a power-concentrating language regime. One possible explanation for this unexpected finding is that while these regimes both share and neutralize power from a de jure standpoint, from a de facto perspective this is not the case. All languages are situated in some hierarchy (Safran and Liu 2012). Thus, this hybrid arrangement may be highlighting the differences between the haves and have-nots. It is possible that the asymmetrical use of mother tongues in conjunction with a lingua franca in the education system actually ghettoizes the different communities. Over time, this has negative implications for social capital.

Three of the control variables are statistically significant. First, at the national level, politically relevant linguistic heterogeneity levels matter. Consistent with the results of Habyarimana et al. (2009: 5–13) and with the broader political economy literature, social capital levels are higher in linguistically homogeneous countries. A shift of one standard deviation (0.26) from a mean of 0.44 can decrease the likelihood of respondents believing in the altruism of others from 24.9 to 21.4 percent.

The other two control variables of significance are at the individual level: parental status and income level. Respondents with children are more likely to believe in the altruism of others (28.3 percent), and those with more disposable income (31.4 percent) are as well. Note that these two variables are significant across all measures of social capital. With one exception (high school education), all other controls at the national and individual levels are significant as well but sensitive to model specification.

Additional Analyses: World Values Survey

The results for neutralized-sharing language regimes notwithstanding, Figure 6.1 illustrates the importance of language regimes. While other variables can affect altruism levels, none has the same impact. This highlights the initial findings suggesting that no link between language regimes and social capital may be a function of the measure—i.e., generalized trust—itself. There is also a third explanation for the nonfinding. It is possible that the results are due to some inherent feature of the Asian Barometer Survey, whether how the survey is conducted or with the respondent pool. To assess whether there is a survey effect, I employ an alternative survey.

The World Values Survey has grown from its European focus to include "97 societies containing almost 90 percent of the world's population" (World Values Survey Brochure 2008: 2). It has been administered over five waves (1981, 1990, 1995–1998, 1999–2000, 2005–2008). However, given the spatial (Asia) and temporal (1945–2005) parameters of this book, only the second, third, and fourth waves are included. The unit of analysis is the individual *respondent*. There are approximately 30,000 respondents.

The dependent variable of interest remains the same. The World Values Survey also asks a question about generalized trust: "Generally speaking would you say that most people can be trusted or that you need to be very careful in dealing with people?" The two possible responses are "you can't be too careful" and "most people can be trusted." Again, the responses have been recoded such that a value of 1 would suggest more trust (and 0 no trust). The "don't know" responses are treated as missing. Almost 30 percent of respondents answered "most people can be trusted."

The national level controls remain the same. The individual level controls, however, are different. The first control is the respondent's ideology: "In political matters, people talk of 'the left' and 'the right'. How would you place your views on this scale, generally speaking?" A higher value for this variable implies a more right-leaning respondent. To the extent that the right is more suspicious of governments (see Keele 2005), the expectation is that the coefficient for *ideology* is negative.

The other individual level control is the respondent's religiosity. There are several theoretical reasons why religion may matter. First, borrowing from Amaney Jamal and Irfan Nooruddin (2010), the logic is as follows. Since smaller groups are "better" at building cooperation and overcoming collective action problems (Olson 1965: 53–57), the expectation is that religiously observant individuals are more likely to display higher levels of social capital. Alternatively, the devout are also more likely to have faith in God. This faith, in turn, has externalities when it comes to trusting other people. Whatever happens is the result of God's will. To measure religiosity, I use a question about how often a respondent attends religious services. Higher values of the variable *religiosity* indicate more frequent attendance.

As a first glance, the results from the World Values Survey largely corroborate those from the Asian Barometer Survey: language regimes have no significant effect on generalized trust. However, the tests used thus far have made two implicit assumptions. The first is that the causal mechanism between language regimes and social capital is the same between members of the politically dominant group and those not. There is evidence, however, that this is not always the case (see Liu,

D. S. Brown, and Harrington 2014; Scherer and Curry 2010; Wong, Campbell, and Citrin 2006). In fact, there are good reasons to believe the effects are in opposite directions. Specifically, for those speaking a politically dominant language, the effects should be strong and positive when language regimes are power-concentrating and not so when otherwise. When language regimes do not concentrate power in one language, those in the politically dominant must share—if not forfeit— cultural egoism. In contrast, for those speaking a politically nondominant language, the effects are in the reverse direction: the link between language regimes and generalized trust is the strongest with power-sharing, followed by a regime that recognizes a lingua franca, and the weakest with power-concentrating.

The second assumption is that *all* politically nondominant groups respond in the same way to the recognition of *any* politically nondominant language. Again, there are theoretical reasons to believe a politically nondominant group may actually prefer no recognition of its language (power-concentrating) over another minority language having recognition (power-sharing). Stalin, for instance, believed the only way to solve the ethnic problems in the Caucasus was to assimilate the people into a "common stream of a higher culture" (quoted in Stern 1944: 231). This higher culture not only included that of Russia, but those of titular states such as Georgia. So although Georgian was a recognized minority language in the larger Soviet Union, Abkhazian, Ajarian and Ossetian (among many others) were not. This inequality among minorities generated resentment over the ensuing decades (Stern 1944) and culminated in open conflict in the early 1990s (Hewitt 1995; also see Suny 1994).

Here, the use of the World Values Survey allows for both assumptions to be relaxed. Unlike the Asian Barometer Survey, the World Values Survey asks: "What language do you normally speak at home?" The advantage of this question is twofold. First, it avoids assigning a respondent into a linguistic group based strictly on ancestry. Instead, it focuses on the actual language that this individual uses first and foremost—which can match the descriptive group classifications but not always.

The second advantage of the language-spoken-at-home question is that it also allows for the creation of three subsamples: politically dominant, largest nondominant, and other nondominant. If the respondent answers with a language that is spoken by the group with the highest level of political status—as identified in the ETH Ethnic Power Relations dataset (Cederman, Wimmer, and Min 2010)—she is placed into the "politically dominant sample." This would include the Japanese in Japan (1 = "monopoly"), the Javanese in Indonesia (2 = "dominant"), and the Hindis in India (3 = "senior partner").

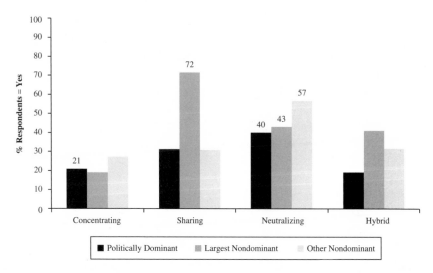

Figure 6.2. Majority versus minority trust (expected values). World Values Survey. Expected values based on Table 6.2, Models 5, 6, 8.

If a respondent is not classified into the "politically dominant" subsample, then she is considered to speak a politically nondominant language at home. Since there may be multiple such languages in a country, I identify a "largest nondominant" subsample. Those speaking the most populous politically nondominant language in each country are classified into this subsample. All others are considered in the "other nondominant" subsample. For example, in the aforementioned Indonesian example, the largest politically nondominant group would be the Sundanese speakers; and if a respondent in Indonesia were to have answered "Balinese" or "Madurese," she would have been assigned to the third subsample.

Figure 6.2 illustrates the effects of each language regime type on generalized trust based on the language spoken at home. Here, the importance of disaggregating the sample into politically dominant, largest politically nondominant, and other politically nondominant is evident. Among those whose mother tongue is a politically dominant language, trust levels are actually the highest when language regimes are power-neutralizing (40 percent). Surprisingly, trust levels are statistically comparable between power-concentrating, power-sharing, and neutralized-sharing language regimes. This is all contrary to Hypothesis 2.1(a) which argued power-concentrating would have the most substantive effects. It seems that for those who are already politically dominant, whether another language is recognized alongside theirs makes no difference. The recognition of the politically dominant language in any form, however, does reinforce group distinctions that a power-neutralizing language regime does not. When the bifurcation between "us" and "them" is less salient, it can help generate trust across a larger community.

The results for members of the largest politically nondominant group are consistent with theoretical priors. First and foremost, the link between language regimes and generalized trust is the weakest when linguistic power is concentrated in the hands of the politically dominant (19 percent). Power-concentrating language regimes cultivate narratives of one group's dominance; and with this inequality, respondents are less likely to trust another individual. The strength of this link increases once linguistic concessions—any concession—are made. However, not all concessions are equal. The impact from recognizing the group's mother tongue exclusively (72 percent) is much larger than that from employing a lingua franca in any capacity (exclusively: 43 percent; hybrid: 41 percent). In fact, additional tests reveal that while the recognition of a lingua franca is better than no recognition (i.e., power-concentrating) for trust, it is not the case that more recognition is always better than less. For the numerically present but politically nondominant group, what matters the most for trust is equality in recognition.

In contrast, for the other politically nondominant groups, what matters is equality in nonrecognition. The results highlight that members of this subset are the most likely to trust when language regimes are power-neutralizing (57 percent). The same cannot be said for the at-large recognition of other mother tongues: the effects for both power-sharing (31 percent) and a neutralized-sharing language regime (32 percent) are statistically no different from the effects of power-concentrating (27 percent). In fact, out of the three subsamples, those in this third subsample are the ones most likely to benefit from a power-neutralizing language regime, where there are perceptions of a collective community among speakers of the different languages. And it is precisely this sense of larger community that is necessary for generalized trust.

Language Regimes and Social Capital in Southeast Asia

The results from the statistical tests suggest there is a relationship between language regimes and social capital. In this section, I return to the controlled comparison of Malaysia and Singapore to demonstrate how the linguistic power distribution has affected community-building efforts, and how the particular type of community built (divided versus collective) has in turn affected social capital. Recall that the two cases were selected because they lend themselves very naturally to a most similar design (George and Bennett 2005: 153–60): the cases have a similar demographic composition; the continued dominance of a hegemonic party (the UMNO-led coalition in the former; the PAP in the latter); low levels of initial capital; and a history characterized by British colonialism. Moreover, the language regimes were comparable in the first periods after independence: neutralized-sharing with four languages (Chinese, English, Malay, and Tamil). All these similarities ensure that the alternative explanations discussed at length above—ethnic heterogeneity, regime type, and wealth—cannot account for the differences in observed social capital levels today. What can, however, is the subsequent language regime in each country.

As discussed in Chapter 4, the Malaysian language regime shifted in 1971. In 1969, when a series of ethnically charged protests turned deadly, the sultan declared a state of emergency, suspended Parliament, and ordered an immediate curfew. It was during this two-year period that Prime Minister Tunku was replaced by Razak. When Parliament reconvened in 1971, Razak and the UMNO-led National Front immediately adopted a new language regime where linguistic power was de jure power-sharing but de facto power-concentrating in the Malay language.

As in Malaysia, the language regime in Singapore also changed. Before 1965, Malay had been considered the lingua franca. It was seen as the language of inter-ethnic communication between the English faction of PAP led by Lee Kuan Yew and the Chinese faction controlled by Lim Chin Siong. But after Singapore separated from the Malaysian Federation, linguistic power was subsequently redistributed to power-neutralization. "Mother tongue" was redefined: it was no longer one's first-learned language but rather that of one's ancestry. This had the effect of combining the two former factions of PAP into one linguistic group. This reorganization also facilitated efforts to designate English as the new lingua franca. It was only a matter of time before English would become the exclusive medium of instruction.

Before turning to the specific details of each case, I first discuss the differences in social capital levels today. Specifically, generalized trust levels are much lower in Malaysia than in Singapore, even when controlling for an individual's mother tongue. I then process-trace through the two cases to demonstrate how language regimes have played a role in shaping social capital.

Social Capital Today

To measure social capital levels in Malaysia and Singapore, I begin with data from the Asian Barometer Survey. As discussed in the previous section, there are three

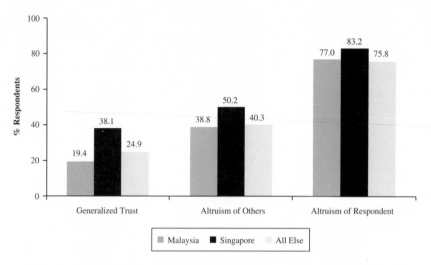

Figure 6.3. Social capital levels in Malaysia and Singapore. Asian Barometer Survey.

questions of interest. The first focuses on generalized trust ("Do you think most people can be trusted?"); the second, on the altruism of others ("Do you think that people generally try to be helpful?"); and the third, on the altruism of the respondent ("If you saw somebody on the street looking lost, would you stop to help?").

The survey results indicate social capital levels are high in Singapore but not in Malaysia. The specific percentages of respondents that answered "yes" to each question are illustrated in Figure 6.3. Each cluster of bars corresponds to one Asian Barometer Survey question. And within each cluster, there are three bars identified by different shades: dark gray (Malaysia), black (Singapore), and light gray (other surveyed countries).

It is evident from Figure 6.3 that across all three measures, there is a notable difference in social capital between Malaysia and Singapore. For instance, Malaysians are only half as likely to trust other people as their Singaporean counterparts (19.4 versus 38.1 percent). These numbers are striking. Not only is the relative difference between the two countries large, but from an absolute standpoint, Singaporeans simply trust at a higher frequency than the rest of Asia (38.1 versus 24.9 percent). Although the difference between Malaysia and Singapore is less extreme with the two altruism measures, the fact remains that Singaporeans display higher levels of social capital. Moreover, on two of the measures (generalized trust and altruism of others), social capital levels are actually lower in Malaysia than in the Asian sample.

As a preliminary observation, these patterns match two theoretical expectations. Consistent with Hypothesis 2.1, low levels of social capital in Malaysia

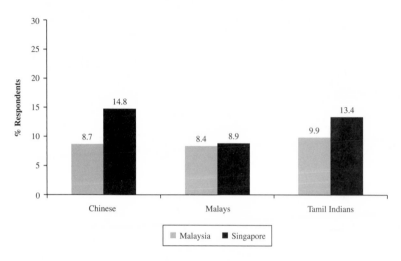

Figure 6.4. Generalized trust by linguistic groups in Malaysia and Singapore.
World Values Survey.

correspond to the de facto power-concentrating language regime since the 1970s.
Congruent with Hypothesis 2.3, high levels of trust and altruism in Singapore are
consistent with a power-neutralizing language regime.

The relationship between language regime and social capital still exists even
after changing surveys (World Values Survey) and disaggregating linguistic
groups. In the Malaysian and Singaporean cases, respondents are disaggregated
into three categories of interest: Chinese, Indians (Tamils), and Malays. The results are presented in Figure 6.4. Two observations merit discussion. The first is
about Malaysia. Consistent across all three linguistic groups, respondents in Malaysia are less likely to trust other people than their counterparts in Singapore.
For instance, in Malaysia, less than 9 percent of the Chinese-speaking respondents indicated they trusted other people. In contrast, almost 15 percent said
yes in Singapore. This gap is equally noticeable among the Tamil speakers (9.9
versus 13.4 percent).

The second observation is about the Malay speakers. Between the two countries, trust levels are comparable among the Malay speakers (8.4 versus 8.9 percent). This is quite surprising. Before the merger, Singapore aggressively pursued
pro-Malay policies including recognizing the language as the exclusive national
language and designating it as the lingua franca. But after the expulsion, the government enacted what were perceived as retractions and anti-Malay policies.
Given this flip-flop, it might be expected that Malays in Singapore would demon-

strate low trust levels. This, however, would not have been expected in Malaysia. In Malaysia, the Malays are the majority. Moreover, while the language regime is officially power-sharing, it is in reality power-concentrating. Malay not only dominates the education curriculum, but it is also recognized as the only official language of the state. Yet, these purported advantages have not translated into higher levels of trust.

If language regimes indeed do matter for social capital, then there should be what John Gerring (2007: 178–81) calls "pieces of evidence," that is, observable differences in how one linguistic group interacts with another as members of a larger community. To see whether this is so, I examine in detail the distribution of resources in the education sector between the politically dominant and the largest politically nondominant groups. The focus is on both the demands made by and the opportunities afforded to each group. Moreover, special attention is paid to the rhetoric of government officials. Specifically, do these statements suggest increasing harmony or fundamental distrust?

The two groups of interest here are the Chinese and the Malays. The Chinese-Malay relationship started at similar junctures for Malaysia and Singapore as both were British colonies. During colonial times, the Chinese were the commercial network. They were the middlemen between the British merchants and the Malay peasantry (Amrith 2011: 42–44). While the Chinese dominated the economic sector, the Malays were highly visible in the government administration. The British favored the Malays particularly in the uniformed security services (e.g., army, police, and firefighters) and in some related clerical, transport, and personal services (Li 1989: 108). The relationship between the Chinese and the Malays had always been tenuous at best. Even during the "honeymoon period immediately before and after [Malaysian] independence," the Malays saw relations in zero sum terms. There was a general fear that the Chinese would still come out as the winners (Bin Muhammad 1970: 10). These tensions would only continue to escalate during the two years when Singapore was a part of the Federation, prompting the Malaysian government to expel Singapore. Despite passionate pleas by PAP members, Tunku was "adamant that there was no other way, or in his other words, 'it will lead to bloodshed' " (K. C. Lee 1988: 80).

Malaysia

During his tenure, Tunku pursued as harmonious a language policy as possible. In 1966, the Central Committee passed a resolution denying recognition of

Chinese as an official language. This same resolution, however, did call for wider usage of the Chinese language in public domains. Moreover, in 1967, Parliament passed the National Language Act which designated Malay as the sole official language but provided for the continued use of Chinese and Tamil as mediums of public instruction at the primary level. This Act was described by MCA president Tan Siew Sin as a "compromise fair to all communities" (MCA 2010).[1]

After Tunku's removal in 1969, government rhetoric about a harmonious multicultural front where compromises were "fair" simply ceased. The Razak-led government pursued an "aggressive" policy whereby "significant resources and energy were devoted to the development" of a Malay curriculum (H. Lee 2007: 133–34). These expansions happened at all levels of education, including the establishment of a Malay-medium university. Questions regarding and public dissent over Malay as the main medium of instruction were banned with the passage of an amendment to the 1948 Sedition Act. This signaled very publicly "the finality of the National Language Policy" (Abdul Samad 1998: 86).

Despite a signal of finality, the conflict between the Malays and Chinese over education resources did not end. The fighting happened at all levels of schooling. At the primary level, the Chinese won in the sense that their language remained a medium of instruction. However, they also lost with the phasing out of the English schools. This was critical as these English schools, which had a large Chinese student body, were converted into Malay schools. As a result of these changes, the enrollment numbers in the Chinese primary schools increased. These rising enrollment demands (90 percent in the 1990s) were matched by severe limitations in the supply of schools. Overenrollment was a common problem in many urban areas. Yet, despite petitions by the Chinese community to build more Chinese schools, the UMNO-led government rejected these demands. Moreover, compared to the Malay schools, the Chinese schools received "far less funding" from the state and depended heavily on private donations (H. Lee 2007: 135).

The conflict was not always about money. In 1987–1988, a number of state education chiefs started posting non-Chinese teachers and staff to key positions in the Chinese primary schools. This move "caused concern amongst the Chinese community as they [sic] feared it would alter the characteristics of Chinese schools in [the] country" (MCA 2010). After failing to resolve the matter in the cabinet, Chinese community leaders organized a protest at a local temple. This protest incited strong reaction from the Malay community. The latter responded with another protest. The government was subsequently forced to invoke the Internal Security Act. After the situation stabilized, the MCA sought to resolve the issue again within the cabinet. They proposed that only those who knew the

Chinese language and had taught in Chinese schools could be eligible to hold key posts in the schools. The proposal was accepted with little publicity. In this situation, the MCA proved it still had the capacity to organize and be some sort of threat. As predicted in Chapter 3, governments make linguistic concessions when constrained by politically relevant minority groups.

The story plot is the same at the secondary level—but with a different ending. In 1975, the MCA submitted a Memorandum on Education to the UMNO-led government. In the memo, the MCA proposed extending Chinese as a medium of instruction to the secondary level as well. The argument was made on the grounds that it would provide students of various races a "better chance to improve and safeguard their mother tongue" (MCA 2010). The proposal fell on deaf ears. This is consistent with theoretical expectations. The MCA's political relevance was quite limited; much of it had been lost over the decades. The party was only able to extract some concessions at the primary level after a pair of protests that resulted in the invoking of the Internal Security Act.

At the tertiary level, the opportunities afforded to the Chinese community were "severely circumscribed" after 1971 (H. Lee 2007: 136). University admission had previously been based solely on merit. With that criterion, the Chinese accounted for almost 67 percent of the student body (Esman 1987: 403). The NEP, however, introduced a quota requiring that 75 percent of the enrollment be reserved for Malays. In 1978, the MCA president Datuk Lee San Choon raised the issue. He proposed an alternate ratio of 50 percent Malays to 50 percent non-Malays. One year later, after an UMNO-MCA meeting, the quota was changed to 55 percent Malays to 45 percent non-Malays (MCA 2010).

In response, a large number of Chinese high school graduates continued their tertiary education abroad. Singapore and Taiwan were common destinations[2] since universities in the two countries recognized Malaysian degrees. However, the UMNO-led government would refuse accreditation to these foreign universities. Given these developments, the Chinese community proposed the establishment of a privately funded Chinese-medium university (Merdeka University). Despite the overwhelming support from the Chinese community, both in finances and morale, these efforts also failed. The UMNO-led government had challenged the legality of the proposition in court—and won (H. Lee 2007: 136–37).

In the 1980s when large numbers of educated (and wealthy) Chinese started emigrating from Malaysia, someone expressed concerns to Prime Minister Mahathir about a possible brain drain (see Rahman Putra 1978: 215–19). The response from Mahathir reflected little love lost: "It's not a brain drain; it's a trouble drain. We are draining our country of our troubles" (K. Y. Lee 2000: 166). For

the Chinese, the biggest source of "malaise" has been the "general feeling of being used for political support by the government while being largely ignored in
policy matters deemed to be of vital interest to the non-Malay communities"
(Means 1991: 57). Despite harmonious efforts early on, the drama since then
in the education sector—where linguistic power is concentrated in the majority
language—is clear evidence that tensions of distrust, if not outright hostility, per-
sist. Many Chinese demands have gone unanswered. Opportunities have been
limited, and in some instances (e.g., tertiary) there have been clear contractions.
And with respect to government rhetoric, the emphasis has been on the Malays:
the amendment to the 1948 Sedition Act and the NEP are evidence of such. In
line with Hypothesis 2.1, these feelings of being used and largely ignored have
played a large role in stunting social capital levels in the country.

Singapore

The Chinese-Malay conflict is also present in the Singapore case. But unlike the
UMNO in Malaysia, the PAP has made efforts publicly to show equality in the
treatment of Chinese and Malays in their educational interests. Even before independence, some of the Chinese were disgruntled with what was perceived as interference in traditional education by the PAP-led government. As discussed in
Chapter 4, the PAP believed in the necessity of a nationalized primary and secondary education curriculum "united by a common language policy" (E. Tan 2007:
79). To achieve standardization, the PAP restructured the Chinese curriculums.

The treatment of the Chinese was similar at the tertiary level. Nanyang University, opened by the British governor in 1956, was a Chinese-medium university. Shortly after the separation of Singapore from Malaysia, there were concerns
regarding education quality at Nanyang. Compared to their counterparts at the
English-language University of Singapore, Nanyang graduates struggled to find
employment. As more ethnic Chinese students pursued higher education at the
University of Singapore, Nanyang responded by lowering admission requirements
and graduation standards. All this only further reduced the perceived quality of
Nanyang education. Initially, the PAP tried to convert Nanyang into an English-
language university. Yet despite a large faculty and staff educated abroad, most
could not make the transition to English and teach effectively. In response to this
structural problem, the PAP merged Nanyang with the University of Singapore,
thereby forcing the new, larger campus (National University of Singapore) to use
English. This policy clearly targeted the Chinese speakers directly. As one might

have expected, the Nanyang alumni challenged these changes (K. Y. Lee 2000: 174–79).

Another source of major opposition came from Malay community members who saw these changes as a signal of the PAP's indifference to the development of the Malay language (K. Y. Lee 2000: 174–77). The injustices perceived by the Chinese community were mirrored in the Malay community, who also felt that their traditional autonomy was now under threat. In the post-merger era, the PAP had reaffirmed the "special status" of the Malays as the indigenous people of Singapore (Li 1989: 111). This status afforded the Malay language continued recognition as Singapore's national language. Despite this distinction, the government has been largely neutral toward the Malays. Certainly, there have been proactive policies. These have included exemption of full school fees (111), expansion of Malay secondary education (Z. Ibrahim 1999: 117–18), and the establishment of a Mosque Building Fund (117–18). All in all, these policies were not unfavorable. However, the prevailing attitude among the Malays was that the special position granted by the constitution was merely symbolic (Kassim 1974: 73–75).

For the Malays, one particularly sensitive issue was the development of their language curriculum. Before independence, Malay was a medium only at the primary level. This changed with the establishment of the first Malay secondary school (San Nila Utama). This marked the first time in Singapore history that Malay was available in a curriculum from primary school to preuniversity level (Gopinathan 1974). Despite this success, it is important to recognize that the survival of the Malay curriculum depended heavily on Singapore government resources (as a point of contrast, the Chinese in Malaysia had independent financial resources). This effectively meant the Malays of Singapore were at the PAP's mercy. Thus, it is not a surprise that the Malays expressed grievances on a number of issues including facility shortages, insufficient higher level certificate courses, and the lack of support for the Malay Studies Department at Nanyang (Kassim 1974: 73).

Despite these issues, the PAP-led government in Singapore has also gone to great lengths to avoid playing favorites. As an Indian community leader summarized, "the government can always do more. But at least it's fair to everyone . . . . In Malaysia, the government doesn't even pretend." Since the separation, the PAP has increasingly emphasized English as the primary language of integration. This has allowed the Singapore state to be set "apart from the interests of all racial groups" (E. Tan 2007: 87). Opportunities (whether actual or perceived) in mother-tongue education have steadily decreased, but at the same time those available in English have increased at exponential rates. The PAP-led government rhetoric has matched its policies. English has become the first language of instruction; it is also now the only language of instruction at the tertiary level. The use of English has allowed the racially Chinese government to pursue public policies without appearing to kowtow to the Chinese majority and without being captured by the interests of that community. Additionally, the PAP-led government has been able to "make all these concessions to the Malay minority community mainly because the Chinese majority was an immigrant community in a predominantly Malay archipelago" (Kassim 1974: 79).

Discussion

In both the Malaysian and Singapore cases, language regimes have had pronounced social effects. Arguably, these effects have had greater impact than ethnic heterogeneity, regime type, wealth, and colonial legacy—three alternative explanations that have very similar values in the two countries. Language regimes can exacerbate or ameliorate the negative effects of linguistic heterogeneity. In Malaysia, although the language regime is de jure power-sharing, de facto it is power-concentrating. The fact that Malay dominates above all else generates a well-founded sense of inequality and perceptions of ethnic chauvinism. These feelings and beliefs, in turn, can retard social capital development. In contrast, when linguistic power is neutralized through a lingua franca—as in Singapore—people are more likely to feel that they belong to a larger collective community and to trust other people. We see evidence of these different social capital levels in the distribution of scarce education resources and in the government rhetoric.

Conclusion

Taken altogether, the evidence offers compelling support for the argument that language regimes matter for social capital levels. Of greatest interest here is the effect of a power-neutralizing language regime. Evidence suggests when a lingua franca is the only language recognized, this has a strong positive effect (1) on multiple dimensions of social capital including generalized trust, belief in the altruism of others, and expected altruism of respondent; and (2) across all groups regardless of the mother tongue spoken at home. The adoption of a lingua franca breeds equality. There is equality in terms of opportunity to use a language and in terms of proficiency. No one is more disadvantaged from learning a language than the next person. Everyone is afforded the same prospects for learning the lingua franca. Moreover, the neutralization of linguistic power removes views of ethnic chauvinism. There is no image of a state dominated and controlled by one singular group. Instead, in its place, there is the notion of a panethnic community, where the state is owned by all.

Interestingly, the effects of a neutralized-sharing language regime are less pronounced than expected. The results are robust across surveys and samples: with one exception (trust among the largest nondominant subsample), the effects are no different from those of power-concentrating. If the exclusive recognition of a politically dominant language can discourage trust and altruism, the results suggest that neutralized-sharing hybrids—David Laitin's 3 ± 1—can be just as guilty of perpetuating inequality.

"Social capital" has been attacked for being conceptually vague, thus making theoretical discussions and empirical tests difficult. Yet, it is hard to dismiss the importance of generalized trust, one specific and very important dimension of social capital, for economic growth. In fact, the absence of trust is arguably a sufficient condition for nongrowth (Knack and Keefer 1997; Ostrom 1990; Putnam 1993). Without trust, every commercial transaction incurs some cost, whether it is time spent contracting, enforcing, or punishing. These costs in aggregate can be quite taxing on any economy. If generalized trust is important for growth, and if the way linguistic power is distributed matters for generalized trust levels, then it would seem language regime type should also matter—albeit indirectly—for economic growth. The next chapter explores another mechanism linking language regime to economic growth: foreign capital.

Appendix

The first set of results uses the Asian Barometer Survey (see Table 6.1). To examine the effects of language regime on generalized trust, I first estimate a model with the three variables for language regime: *power-sharing*, *power-neutralizing*, and *neutralized-sharing*. Note that the reported coefficients are in reference to *power-concentrating*. The results in Model 1 suggest language regimes have no significant effect whatsoever on whether an individual is more likely to report generalized trust. Five control variables, however, are statistically significant. One is politically relevant heterogeneity levels. As expected, as linguistic diversity increases, the probability of a respondent expressing trust in other people decreases ($\beta = -2.30$; SE $= 1.03$). Interestingly, neither of the other two national level variables (democracy and wealth) has a significant effect. What seems to matter is at the individual level. Specifically, child-rearing, female, employed, or wealthy respondents are more likely to express trust toward other people than those without children, of the male gender, unemployed, or with less disposable income.

Model 2 replicates the first model but shifts the outcome of interest from generalized trust to the altruism of others. Here, the coefficients for language regimes are statistically significant. The results suggest respondents are more likely to believe in the altruism of others when the language is either power-sharing ($\beta = 0.56$; $SE = 0.34$) or power-neutralizing ($\beta = 1.55$; $SE = 0.29$) than when it is either power-concentrating or neutralized-sharing. Note that the non-significance of the hybrid coefficient ($\beta = 0.24$; $SE = 0.27$) renders the effects of the neutralized-sharing regime statistically no different from those of power-concentrating. Of the two altruism-generating language regimes, the magnitude of power-neutralizing is significantly larger than that of power-sharing. With one exception (neutralized-sharing), these results are consistent with the hypotheses. In Model 2, female and unemployed both lose significance.

Model 3 focuses not on the altruism of others but on that of the individual respondent. Here, only one language regime coefficient is statistically significant. Power-neutralizing language regimes can increase a respondent's willingness to help a stranger by 10 percent. The coefficient for neutralized-sharing language regime is still not significant, but interestingly it is in the positive direction. The same cannot be said for power-sharing. Not only is the coefficient negative, the lack of significance suggests language regimes that recognize multiple mother tongues are no better at generating actual altruism than those that recognize only the language of the politically dominant. In this model, heterogeneity is no longer statistically significant, but at the national level, regime type now is.

The results from Models 2 and 3 suggest that the nonsignificance of language regimes in Model 1 may be (partially) the result of "trust" not capturing the relevant dimensions of social capital, which can also include norms and networks (see Putnam 1993: 167). To assess whether the results are also being driven by the survey, I alternatively use data from the World Values Survey (which also has a question about generalized trust) and replicate Model 1. The results suggest that the nonsignificance of language regimes in the Asian Barometer Survey are not exclusive to that survey. When using the World Values Survey, none of the coefficients for the three language regimes are significant at the $p \leq 0.10$ level.

In all four models discussed thus far, the results ignore whether the respondents speak a politically dominant language or not. The nonfindings for generalized trust

Table 6.1: Language Regimes and Generalized Trust

	Model 1 Generalized trust (Asian Barometer)	Model 2 Altruism of others	Model 3 Altruism of respondent	Model 4 Generalized trust (world values)
National level factors				
Power-Sharing Language Regime	-0.29 (0.33)	0.56 (0.34)*	-0.21 (0.21)	0.29 (0.39)
Power-Neutralizing Language Regime	0.42 (0.41)	1.55 (0.29)‡	0.42 (0.18)†	0.86 (0.67)
Neutralized-Sharing Language Regime	0.43 (0.56)	0.24 (0.27)	0.44 (0.45)	-0.06 (0.74)
Politically relevant: Herfindahl index	-2.30 (1.03)†	-1.41 (0.57)†	-0.04 (0.28)	1.38 (1.12)
Democracy	0.01 (0.02)	0.02 (0.02)	-0.06 (0.02)‡	-0.03 (0.04)
GDP/capita (1000)	-0.004 (0.03)	-0.01 (0.02)	-0.01 (0.01)	0.08 (0.02)‡
Individual level Factors				
> High school education	-0.03 (0.24)	-0.11 (0.19)	0.14 (0.13)	
Parent	0.07 (0.04)*	0.17 (0.05)‡	0.21 (0.06)‡	
Female	-0.20 (0.08)†	0.05 (0.04)	-0.12 (0.06)†	
Unemployed	-0.18 (0.10)*	-0.11 (0.13)	0.06 (0.09)	
Income	0.20 (0.06)‡	0.15 (0.06)†	0.09 (0.04)†	
Ideology				-0.02 (0.01)†
Religiosity				0.03 (0.02)
Number of observations (countries)	14987 (14)	15014 (14)	15071 (14)	29900 (15)
Pseudo R^2	0.0645	0.0414	0.0277	0.0410

Standard errors are reported in parentheses. $*p \leq 0.100$; $†p \leq 0.050$; $‡p \leq 0.010$.

could be the result of this aggregation. Unlike the Asian Barometer Survey, the World Values Survey has a question allowing for the classification of respondents into three categories: politically dominant, largest nondominant, and other nondominant.

Model 6 (see Table 6.2) focuses only on the respondents who identify as speaking the politically dominant language at home. Two results warrant discussion. First, neither power-sharing nor neutralized-sharing is statistically significant. This suggests that so long as the mother tongue is recognized, whether in isolation or with another language, the distribution of linguistic power has no effect on trust levels for the politically dominant. It seems that for the politically dominant, the negative effects of sharing recognition (i.e., the relative costs to cultural egoism) are not as important so long as they are politically advantaged. Second, the coefficient for power-neutralizing is not only positive but it is also significant ($\beta = 0.93$; SE $= 0.53$). Individuals are almost twice as likely to trust others when a lingua franca is recognized (40 versus 21 percent for power-concentrating).

The results, not surprisingly, change once the sample shifts to the largest politically nondominant group (Model 6). As theoretically expected, trust levels are significantly higher so long as the language regime is not power-concentrating. If there is a linguistic concession, whether it is to the group's mother tongue ($\beta = 2.52$; SE $= 0.65$), a lingua franca ($\beta = 1.18$; SE $= 0.60$), or both ($\beta = 1.27$; SE $= 0.71$), trust levels are more than double of those in a power-concentrating language regime (19 percent). In fact, as would be expected, trust levels increase more than threefold with power-sharing (72 percent). Trust levels are statistically the same between the two regimes that use a lingua franca.

These results would suggest that for members of the largest politically nondominant group, while the recognition of a lingua franca is better than no recognition, more is neither better nor worse than less. Model 7 examines this corollary using the continuous measure of linguistic neutralization. The model also includes a control for power-sharing because not all regimes that do not recognize a lingua franca are the same. It is important to account for those that do not employ a lingua franca because they have not made any concessions, and those that opted for other mother tongues. The results confirm that the degree of linguistic neutralization has no bearing on trust levels, but the recognition of mother tongues does.

Finally, Model 8 takes into consideration all the other politically nondominant groups. The results show that for those without the political advantage or the numerical presence, the only language regime that benefits trust is one that

Table 6.2: Majority Versus Minority Trust

	Model 5 Politically dominant	Model 6 Largest minority only	Model 7 Largest minority only	Model 8 Other minorities
National level factors				
Power-Sharing Language Regime	0.53 (0.56)	2.52 (0.65)‡	1.45 (0.18)‡	0.16 (0.24)
Power-Neutralizing Language Regime	0.93 (0.53)*	1.18 (0.60)†		1.24 (0.57)†
Neutralized-Sharing Language Regime	−0.11 (0.63)	1.27 (0.71)*		0.20 (0.73)
Degree of Linguistic Neutralization			−0.07 (0.15)	
Politically Relevant Linguistic Heterogeneity	1.68 (1.18)	3.19 (0.67)‡	3.65 (0.58)‡	0.23 (0.74)
Democracy	−0.02 (0.04)	0.08 (0.01)‡	0.08 (0.01)‡	−0.06 (0.03)*
GDP/capita (1000)	0.08 (0.02)‡	0.11 (0.04)‡	0.04 (0.01)‡	0.07 (0.01)‡
Individual level factors				
Ideology	−0.02 (0.01)	−0.09 (0.01)‡	−0.09 (0.01)‡	−0.02 (0.01)
Religiosity	0.04 (0.02)†	0.02 (0.03)	0.02 (0.03)	−0.01 (0.03)
Number of observations (countries)	12700 (14)	1344 (8)	1344 (8)	16685 (14)
Pseudo R^2	0.0510	0.0636	0.0628	0.0335

Note: Standard errors are reported in parentheses. $*p \leq 0.100$; $†p \leq 0.050$; $‡p \leq 0.010$.

recognizes a lingua franca exclusively. While the likelihood of trust is the lowest when only the politically dominant language is recognized (27 percent), this number is statistically comparable to those of power-sharing (31 percent) and neutralized-sharing language regimes (32 percent). In contrast, when the language regime is power-neutralizing, trust levels can more than double to 57 percent—incidentally a magnitude larger than that for the politically dominant (40 percent) or the largest politically nondominant (43 percent).

The results in Table 6.2 indicate that the initial nonfindings for language regimes on generalized trust in Table 6.1 are also driven by the aggregation of different groups into one larger sample. Taking both tables into consideration corroborates the overall claim of this chapter: language regimes—in how they distribute linguistic power—matter for social capital.

CHAPTER 7

Mechanism 2: Foreign Capital

The previous chapter demonstrated a link between language regimes and social capital. Specifically, power-neutralizing language regimes have a positive effect on generalized trust, belief in the altruism of others, and expected altruism of survey respondents. Moreover, the effects from recognizing a lingua franca exclusively are consistent across all ethnolinguistic groups regardless whether their mother tongue is the language of the politically dominant, largest politically non-dominant, or others. This chapter continues in the same vein but shifts the focus to a different capital type. The argument is that language regimes can affect economic performance by attracting foreign direct investment (FDI). In addition to an influx of money and employment opportunities, FDI also promotes technology transfers and knowledge spillovers (Borensztein, De Gregorio, and Lee 1998; De Mello 1999).

It is because of these purported advantages that governments adopt various strategies to attract foreign investors. One strategy is the reduction of transaction costs. Another strategy is an emphasis on the workforce quality (Globerman and Shapiro 2002; Mody and Srinivasan 1998). Quality can be measured by a number of indicators including educational attainment or linguistic skills. A workforce proficient in a lingua franca can make the country more attractive to foreign investors, especially those that speak the lingua franca. Translation costs are minimal when the lingua franca of the receiving state is also the language of the politically dominant group in the sending state.

This chapter begins with a literature review, focusing on several alternative explanations for why some countries are better than others at attracting FDI. It then presents the argument, followed by the empirical tests. In the same structure as the previous chapter, the first test is the large N statistical analysis, the second the comparative process-tracings of Malaysia and Singapore. The concluding sections discuss the indirect effects of language regimes on economic growth.

Language Regimes and FDI

What explains variance in FDI levels? Why do some countries attract more than others? Broadly speaking, there are two sets of explanations. One set (monadic) focuses on the characteristics of the country, such as regime type, market size, and colonial legacy. The other set (dyadic), drawing on the trade flow literature, examines the relationship between the sending and receiving states (Bénassy-Quéré, Coupet, and Mayer 2007). Typically, the principal factors have included the market size of the two states and the geographical distance between them (see J. Anderson and Van Wincoop 2003). The logic is that larger economies are more likely to send and receive investments. However, large distances between the two states can deter economic exchanges. Other variables that also capture potentially important bilateral relationships include cultural affinity (Guiso, Sapienza, and Zingales 2005; Habib and Zurawicki 2002; Kogut and Singh 1988; R. White and Tadesse 2008), bilateral investment treaties (Elkins, Guzman, and Simmons 2006), common exchange rate pegs (Froot and Stein 1991), dual tax treaties (De Mooij and Ederveen 2001), preferential trade agreements (Büthe and Milner 2008; Makki and Somwaru 2004; Tomz, Goldstein, and Rivers 2007), and common international organization memberships (Blomstrom and Kokko 2003). Given the monadic nature of the statistical dataset used throughout this book (the unit of analysis is *country-year*, not *country-country-year*), in the remainder of this section, I discuss the three competing hypotheses that focus on the characteristics of the country and consider each in turn.

Regime Type

Nathan Jensen (2008) identifies a number of mechanisms linking democracy to FDI levels. For instance, one mechanism has to do with policy stability. By construction, democracies are embedded with multiple veto players (Cox and McCubbins 2001; Tsebelis 1995, 2002). This is not to say that veto players are absent in authoritarian regimes. Instead, compared to their democratic counterparts, the actors constraining governments from predatory behavior are fewer. When there are more veto players, the government's ability to change policies at will becomes less likely. Collective approval is necessary. Such consensual requirements ensure policy stability. When investors can be guaranteed that policies will not change arbitrarily on entering a market and investing, it makes the country more attractive.

A second possible mechanism has to do with transparency. Since democracies have larger winning coalitions, they are also more transparent than nondemocracies (Bueno de Mesquita et al. 2003). Larger firms have the opportunity to observe legislative processes and have the necessary information when policy changes are expected. This provision of information is important because it allows firms to influence policy making or to respond effectively when the outcome is considered not favorable.

The third mechanism is related to the previous two. Democracies provide channels for the public to influence policy making and outcomes. Fundamentally, with democracies, the costs of participation and mobilization are lower than in dictatorships (Baum and Lake 2003). Although foreign investors may not have direct access to affect policy making, they do, however, have legal and formal channels to influence politicians.

Finally, democracies force leaders to build their country's reputation as a destination for secure investments. Since entry and exit barriers for political office are low (Baum and Lake 2003), democratic leaders are constrained from expropriating assets (North and Weingast 1989). When governments do expropriate, they incur a negative reputation cost with the foreign investors. Under such conditions, foreign firms have little incentive to reinvest or invest in the first place. Democracy—and its bundles of political institutions, including the rule of law— can protect investors against random government confiscation. Governments are electorally constrained. It is this tenure threat that separates democracies from their authoritarian counterparts. In the latter, legislatures can pass laws and the courts can uphold these laws, but the government can never credibly commit to protect property rights. There are most certainly signals the government can send to increase its credibility (e.g., allowing parties to contest legislative elections and joining international organizations), but the credibility will never be equal to that of a functioning democracy.

While there are compelling reasons to believe democracy has a positive effect on foreign capital, there are also reasons to believe democracy can hinder FDI levels (N. Jensen 2008). First and foremost, democracy cannot insulate leaders from either popular demands or particularistic pressures. Because democratic leaders are "single-minded seekers of reelection" (Mayhew 1974: 17), this makes governments much more responsive to popular preferences. When the demand is to confiscate property or to nationalize unpopular foreign firms, the outcome may be a democratic government reneging on its commitments. Democracies have institutionalized channels to allow for such violations: legislative majorities and executive discretion. If an electoral majority supports the expropriation of some foreign asset, the government—"of the people, by the people, for the people"—may be incentivized to break its commitments to investors.

Second, democratic governments are more likely than their authoritarian counterparts to be captured by competing interest groups. The influence of interest groups can be magnified by electoral rules. Because proportional rules create a multiparty system, well-organized groups can ensure their interests remain protected through logrolls and regulations (Rosenbluth and Schaap 2002). In contrast, when bureaucracies can implement policies freely though still tied to the state and society—embedded autonomy (Evans 1995: 10–18)—governments have institutionalized channels for pursuing investment-friendly policies. This discussion highlights the simple fact that regime type matters. But how they matter is subject to debate (see Boix and Stokes 2003; Przeworski and Limongi 1997).

Market Size

Market size is also important for investment levels. There are several different reasons (Asiedu and Lien 2011). First, from a demand standpoint, a larger market suggests more people who will want the goods and services provided by the firm. Second, from a supply standpoint, firms prefer larger markets when investing abroad. There are costs to any investment, and these costs are both necessary and substantive. Firms naturally prefer larger yields for each unit of cost, and increasing returns to scale. Bigger markets are also more likely to have common market regulation that will minimize the costs accrued from tweaking products, services, or methods, or those associated with diversifying beyond the initial investments. This discussion suggests that all else being equal, market size has a positive effect on investment levels. This comes, however, with a caveat: there is a threshold effect. When GDP levels are too low, there is simply no foreign investment (Asiedu and Lien 2003).

Colonial Legacy

Colonial origins may also shape FDI levels. The historical origins of a country's legal system—often the product of colonial legacy—has implications for government quality today. Specifically, British colonies or those employing the common law interfere less with the private sector (e.g., better property rights protection and business regulations), are more efficient (e.g., less corruption and bureaucratic delays), and have better public good outputs (e.g., lower infant mortality and illiteracy rates), among other indicators of predictable and law-bound governments (La Porta et al. 1999). Since foreign investors care about the receiver state's quality of government, this would suggest an indirect importance of colonial legacies.

The colonial past also matters because it affects economic cooperation between a former colonizing state and its former colonies. The colonial legacy includes a set of institutions such as the aforementioned legal system and a population proficient in (or at least familiar with) the colonizer's language. These factors can increase familiarity with a country's investment opportunities, regulations and procedures, and culture and customs. This familiarity, in turn, can reduce transaction costs, thereby increasing FDI levels (see Lane and Milesi-Ferretti 2004).

Aside from British investments, British colonies have another inherent advantage over other colonies. The presence of an English-speaking workforce can make a receiver state more attractive than its French- or Portuguese-speaking competitor to American investors (who account for the largest share of total global FDI). The English language is without a doubt *the* global lingua franca (Ostler 2010: xvi). It is the language with the greatest utility on the international scale. It cuts across more territorial borders than any other language. This discussion suggests that all else being equal, investment levels will be higher in British colonies. The next two sections assess these different claims, first quantitatively and then qualitatively.

Language Regimes and Foreign Capital in Asia

The first test looks at the effects of a country's language regime on foreign capital. The sample is all Asian countries theoretically 1945–2005. In reality, however, because of data limitations on FDI, the sample is thirty-seven countries 1980–2005. International organizations such as the UN and the World Bank only began collecting FDI numbers globally in the 1970s and in the region in the 1980s. The absence of FDI numbers in historical sources such as the *International Historical Statistics* volume (Mitchell 2008) confirms this general trend. There are some exceptions, but many of these countries (e.g., the United States) are not in Asia. The unit of analysis is *country-year*.[1] In this section, I begin with a description of the data followed by the empirical results.

Research Design

FDI: To operationalize foreign capital, I look at FDI levels. Specifically, following convention in the political economy literature (see N. Jensen 2008; Kim et al. 2015; Leblang 2010), the focus is on the reporting economy's inflow levels. To ensure comparability of each unit invested across countries and over time, all numbers have been standardized to constant USD. Data came from the World Bank, which compiled numbers from various sources including the IMF and the International Financial Statistics and Balance of Payments database.

The average FDI level across the entire sample is US$5,537.916 million, which is significantly higher than the median FDI level: $577.387 million. This suggests that in some *country-year* observations, the FDI level is substantially larger than the rest of the sample. A look at the FDI numbers confirms this is the case. China's lowest FDI-attracting years (early 1980s) is roughly the entire sample's median. This discussion highlights the very large numbers and very skewed (nonnormal) distribution of FDI in this sample. To account for the large numbers, I rescale FDI levels to the million USD unit. And to adjust for the nonnormal distribution, I transform all numbers to their logarithmic equivalent.[2] The advantage of using a logarithm here is that such math operators attenuate the effects of the extreme outliers, such as China.

Language Regime: Language regime is the primary independent variable in this analysis here. Language regime is operationalized using the same coding schemes discussed extensively in Chapter 2. The first scheme is the quadrachotomous categorical measure which is subsequently transformed into four dummy variables: *power-concentrating, power-sharing, power-neutralizing,* and *neutralized-sharing language regime*. To maintain consistency with previous chapters, *power-concentrating* is again the reference category. The second coding scheme is the continuous measure, where a larger value (maximum of 1) indicates more neutralization, and a smaller value indicates less neutralization (minimum of 0). Since a language regime that has no linguistic neutralization whatsoever can be either power-concentrating or power-sharing, I also include a control for whether the language regime is power-sharing to differentiate between the two possibilities.

Control Variables: To account for other confounding factors, I include additional variables in the regression analyses based on prior theoretical expectations. First, since FDI levels are highly contingent on levels from the previous year(s), I include a lagged dependent variable to control for temporal autocorrelation. The second control is politically relevant linguistic heterogeneity (Cederman, Wimmer, and Min 2010). Recall that this variable measures the likelihood of randomly coming across two people who speak two different languages. Lower values (minimum of 0) suggest greater levels of homogeneity, and vice versa (maximum of 1). The inclusion of this variable is important. If politically relevant linguistic heterogeneity matters for language regime choice, and if language regime is to matter for foreign capital levels, then it is critical to assess whether—and if so, to what extent—heterogeneity matters directly for FDI.

Another variable of theoretical interest is regime type. On the one hand, as discussed above, there are reasons to believe democracies have a positive effect: policy stability, channels for policy influence, transparency of politics, and reputation costs (N. Jensen 2008). But on the other hand, democracies can also have a negative effect: centripetal policies (resulting from electoral politics) and competing interest groups can both undermine investment levels (N. Jensen 2008). To measure regime type, I again use the 21-point POLITY index (Marshall and Jaggers 2008).

Market size is also important (Asiedu and Lien 2011). When investing abroad, firms prefer markets where their goods and services will be in demand. Demand levels should be higher in receiving states with bigger economies and larger populations. The data source for both variables is the IMF, as reported in Kristian Gleditsch's (2002) Direction of Trade (DOT) Dataset. Given the magnitude of both variables, GDP has been rescaled to the billion USD unit and population to the 100,000 unit.

Colonial legacy matters as well, specifically one that is British. In their colonies, the British and the continental Europeans adopted different policies. These policies had long-term implications when the colonial authorities departed: the British were more likely to leave institutions that were conducive to market economies (La Porta et al. 1999). The British colonies were (not surprisingly) also more likely to have incorporated English into their education curricula. If colonial legacy matters for institutional quality and transaction cost reduction, then it should also matter for investment levels.

Empirical Evidence

As with previous chapters, the technical discussion and statistical tables can be found in the appendices to this chapter. The results suggest that language regime type affects investment levels. The effects, however, are not always in line with theoretical expectations. First, the range of investment levels that power-concentrating language regimes can attract, while positive, is substantially no larger than those of power-sharing. In fact, this range overlaps heavily with another range: neutralized-sharing. This is contrary to the claim that when language regimes recognize only one language, they reduce transaction costs and consequently attract foreign capital. And conversely, when language regimes afford multiple languages recognition, this increases translation volumes, thereby deterring foreign investors.

Consistent with prior expectations, however, is the effect of recognizing a lingua franca, specifically when exclusively. The range of possible investments attracted by a power-neutralizing language regime ($651.56 million to $1,290.27 million) is not only substantive but also much greater than any of the other three regimes. This highlights that it is not the mere recognition of a lingua franca that matters, but that more recognition is definitely important. The bottom graph in Figure 7.1 plots this supposition: as the language regime becomes increasingly characterized by lingua franca usage, FDI levels increase. This suggests that efficiency and transaction cost reduction are important considerations to foreign investors.

Of course, one alternative explanation is that countries that were bound to have high investment levels were also inherently bound to recognize a lingua franca. And as we know from Chapters 3 and 4, language regimes are in and of themselves anything but exogenous. They are institutional choices constrained by cultural egoism, communicative efficiency, and collective equality. The results from a number of alternative model specifications suggest there is neither a selection effect nor an omitted variable bias. For instance, across all models, politically relevant linguistic heterogeneity has no significant effect on investment levels. This suggests that foreign investors, when choosing where to invest, make decisions based on a country's linguistic repertoire and not on its demographic landscape. From a normative standpoint, this is welcome news: the supposed effects of ethnolinguistic diversity—if they exist—can be mitigated through language regimes.

Of course, other factors in addition to language regimes matter for FDI. Although sensitive to model specifications, results show that democracies attract more investments than their authoritarian counterparts. This suggests that foreign

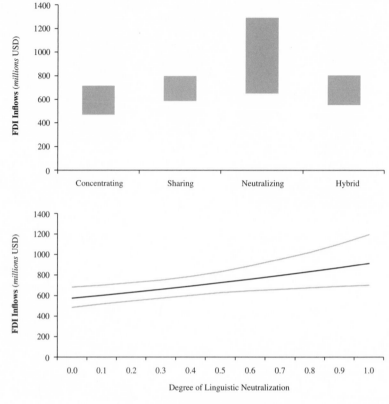

Figure 7.1. Expected values of FDI.

investors, when choosing where to put their money, do consider the reputation of
the government (e.g., whether the government has expropriated unlawfully in the
past) and the policy-making process: how transparent the process for making policy is, how much influence the firm can have in the actual policy making (even if
the channels are informal), and how stable the policies are once implemented.
Also important for FDI is market size: bigger markets attract more investments.
When countries have large economies or large populations, or both, this can signal to foreign investors not just a stock of potential consumers but also an abundance in resources and workforce.

A country's colonial legacy, specifically, one that is British, has no impact on
FDI levels. There is a theoretical and empirical explanation for this nonfinding.
Theoretically, it is possible that while the British left their colonies with institu-
tions better equipped to handle a market economy, the fact that English is such an

important language nowadays has meant non-British colonies are also learning it. As a result, whatever linguistic comparative advantage the British colonies had upon independence has since then dissipated. And empirically, since the World Bank did not begin collecting FDI numbers in Asia until the 1980s (and even then it was only a sample of the countries), it is possible that a period in which the linguistic comparative advantage did exist is not being captured.

Language Regimes and Foreign Capital in Southeast Asia

We now explore the relationship between language regimes and FDI levels specifically in the context of Malaysia's National Front Era and Singapore's Post-Merger Era. These two cases allow for substantial analytical leverage. At the start of their respective second periods, both countries were characterized by a hegemonic party increasing the centralization of power (the UMNO-led coalition in the former; the PAP in the latter); a struggling economy with small markets, low wages, and high unemployment; and a colonial history shaped very much by the British. These similarities ensure that none of these alternative country-level (*monadic*) explanations are the reasons for the divergent investment levels observed today.

Additionally, some explanations for FDI flows focus on the *dyadic* nature. With the way language regime was operationalized and coded in Chapter 2, the statistical test above could not assess the impact of dyadic variables. But in this section, with these two countries, we can consider the relationship of the FDI-sending state with Malaysia and with Singapore and the effects of this relationship. Here, we see that the two countries are again very similar on a number of alternative explanations. First and foremost, as the two countries are contiguous, geographically, the distance between any sending state and either Malaysia or Singapore is substantively comparable. If large distance between countries is a deterrent for FDI, then the same logic should apply to both countries. Second, as both periods of interest began during the height of the Cold War, both governments committed to noncommunist ideologies and allied with the United States. The convergent foreign policy choices meant the two countries were largely comparable regarding the extent and nature of their global integration: both were signatories of the General Agreement on Tariffs and Trade;[3] both lacked preferential trade agreements;[4] and their currencies were initially pegged to the British pound and then later to the U.S. dollar.[5] Taken together, the similarities across a number of dimensions allow us to discount many of these monadic and dyadic explanations. One factor that remains unaccounted for is the language regime.

Below I highlight the general patterns of FDI levels, first at the monadic level. Then I show that while the two countries started at similar points, investment levels in Singapore have dwarfed Malaysia's. I then examine the link between language regimes and FDI dyadically in each case. Specifically, I demonstrate how the distribution of linguistic power attracted foreign investors toward Singapore but not toward Malaysia.

Foreign Capital Today

Compared to the postwar world at large, Malaysia's and Singapore's economic development have been very impressive if not outright "miraculous." An important element of this growth was driven by foreign capital. Figure 7.2 compares foreign investment levels across Malaysia, Singapore, Southeast Asia (averaged), and global Asia (averaged) between 1980 and 2005. Investment levels in Malaysia (black solid line) and Singapore (gray solid line) have always been high, especially when compared to the other two samples. In 2000, investment level in Malaysia ($9,653.271 million) was twice that of global Asia's average ($4,741.309 million) and ten times that of Southeast Asia's ($974 million). Singapore's numbers are even more extreme. This pattern is consistent with theoretical priors: countries that recognize one language are attractive destinations for investment because of lower transaction costs. Additionally, consistent with a corollary (and

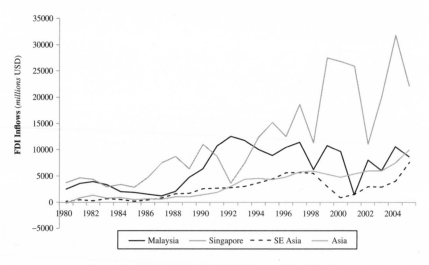

Figure 7.2. FDI in Malaysia and Singapore. World Bank.

with the empirical results from the statistical tests), language regime effects are most pronounced when a lingua franca is recognized.

In both countries investment levels have increased over time. The pace of these increases, however, has been different. While investment shares in Malaysia have almost doubled, this trajectory has been subjected to several fluctuations. After a weak showing in the late 1980s and early 1990s, investment levels tripled in the mid-1990s. In the wake of the 1997–1998 East Asian Financial Crisis, we see a drop. However, since the early years of this century's first decade, the numbers have steadily increased. In contrast, Singapore's numbers, which initially dropped in the early 1980s, have steadily if not exponentially increased. In 2005, Singapore attracted three times as much investment as Malaysia.

What explains this divergence? One answer, I suggest, is language regime. Although the language regimes in both countries are, in principle, efficient, there is one substantive difference. The power-neutralizing language regime in Singapore was inherently more efficient with the recognition of English. The use of the global lingua franca, however, was not the only reason for investment differences. If language regimes attract (or deter) foreign capital, then there should be evidence of linguistically motivated economic activities. To probe this question, I focus on whether changes in the education curriculum have had an effect on workforce proficiency, and whether this proficiency matched the interests of the investment-sending states, especially the English-speaking states. Additionally, I examine government rhetoric. Specifically, do these statements suggest any sort of ethnic preference?

Malaysia

In 1971, Parliament reconvened in Kuala Lumpur with the newly formed UMNO-led National Front in government. The distribution of linguistic power correspondingly changed. The government adopted an aggressive de facto shift towards Malay. English, a lingua franca, was abandoned. Similarly, although the status of Chinese and Tamil remained technically unchanged, in reality, as demonstrated in the previous chapter, recognition contracted. The government viewed these languages, especially English, with "considerable consternation" (Nunan 2003: 602). There was an intense fear that the English language could prove detrimental to the Malay-dominant Malaysian state.

To solidify the position of the Malay language, the government charged the Institute of Language and Literature (Dewan Bahasa dan Pustaka) to develop the national language. The task included cultivating literary growth and publishing books in Malay (Hassan 1988). To this end, a team of language planners from the Institute met with their Bruneian and Indonesian counterparts multiple times over the course of two decades to standardize new vocabulary (Kaplan and Baldauf 2003: 105–6, 120). The success of this endeavor is reflected in the introduction of half a million new words (Hassan 1988).

The Malay emphasis was evident in the economic sphere. In 1971, the government introduced the New Economic Plan (NEP). The NEP was a comprehensive strategy for eradicating poverty. At the start, 37 percent of the population (World Bank 1993: 4) and 50 percent of all households in Peninsular Malaysia (Means 1991: 46) lived below the poverty line. Whatever capital existed was controlled mostly by the foreigners or the local Chinese. The NEP also aimed to restructure society so that social classes were less congruent with ethnic lines. At the time, the Chinese were on average much wealthier than their Malay counterparts. This was due in large part to colonial policies. The Chinese resided in urban areas where commercial activities prevailed. The Chinese controlled 68 percent of the commercial and industrial workforce. In contrast, Malays were predominantly confined to the agrarian sector. Among employed Malays, only 7 percent were engaged in either commerce or industry. A shocking 73 percent earned their living from peasant agriculture (Abdul Samad 1998: 62–65). Despite this inequality, Tunku had avoided addressing this matter because of a "politics for the Malays, economics for the Chinese" arrangement struck between the UMNO and the MCA as a part of the Merdeka Agreement.

Under the NEP, the government did not expropriate Chinese assets. However, the government would afford Malays and their language special privileges, especially in the public sector. Although the NEP rhetoric was not overtly anti-Chinese, the set of policies was fundamentally an ethnic redistribution program (Shoup 2011: 790–91). Judged in aggregate, the NEP appeared a great success: the incidence of poverty fell to below 5 percent of the population in 2005. It was also instrumental in restructuring the economy: Malay (Bumiputera) ownership stakes in the private sector have increased to 20 percent, the number of Malays employed in the industrial sector has increased exponentially, and a Malay middle class has emerged.

From another perspective, however, the Malay language emphasis specifically and the NEP generally have incurred some economic costs as well. The downgrading of English has led to a decreased proficiency in the language, especially among the Malays (K. Y. Lee 2013: 162–63) and those in the rural areas (Kaplan and Baldauf 2003: 115). The implication was most notable in the 1990s when Malaysia found itself struggling "to stay relevant and competitive in the increasing globalized knowledge economy" (H. Lee 2007: 139). This struggle manifested in two ways (Gill 2005): (1) in the endeavor to ensure there was a workforce with the necessary linguistic skills for a knowledge-oriented economy (in which English is the language of science and technology); and (2) in keeping up with the required translations. The explosion of the English language in global industries has meant intense demands for translations between Malay and English. While Malay is historically indigenous to the area, recall that the language did not modernize and develop until the NEP era.

The effects of emphasizing Malay over English are evident when the focus is shifted from monadic to dyadic investment levels. The top plot in Figure 7.3 shows investment levels from the United Kingdom in the two countries during the same period. Recall that Malaysia and Singapore were both British colonies. The numbers show that a British colonial legacy in and of itself cannot account for varying levels of investment. Today, British investment levels in Malaysia are barely a quarter of those in Singapore ($40.68 million versus $144.20 million).

The deemphasis of English had implications beyond just the United Kingdom. Theoretically, we should see similar investment patterns from other English-speaking countries, for example, Australia and New Zealand (geographical proximity), the United States (the largest market in size), and Canada (another English-speaking OECD country). The bottom plot shows that investment levels from these four countries have mirrored those of the United Kingdom: some investments in Malaysia but substantial investments in Singapore. From Figure 7.3, it is evident that even when focusing only on the influential English-speaking sending states, Malaysia has attracted far less English investment than Singapore.

Singapore

The story was completely different in Singapore. After being expelled from the Malaysian Federation, the PAP-led government initially maintained its bilingual curriculum with mother tongue first and English second. When Britain announced it would withdraw its military by the early 1970s, the government was faced with an inevitable crisis. As noted previously in Chapter 4, the British military was more than just a defense presence. It provided economic support as well. Defense spending accounted for almost 20 percent of Singapore's GDP, and the military base, which occupied 11 percent of the island's total area, provided over 30,000

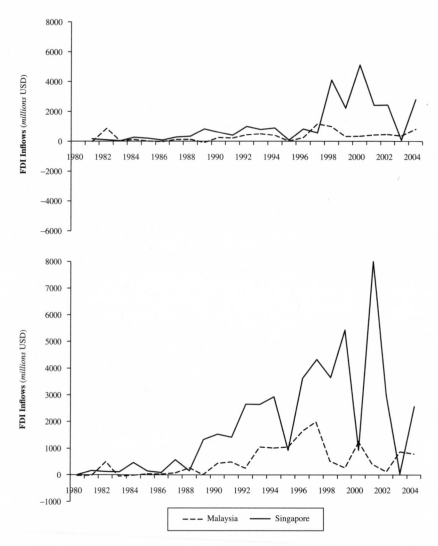

Figure 7.3. English FDI in Malaysia and Singapore. Top: investments from UK.
Bottom: investments from Australia, Canada, New Zealand, United States.
OECD Direct International Investment (Leblang 2010).

jobs in direct employment and just under 40,000 in support services (K. Y. Lee
2000: 69–73).

Given this systemic vulnerability (Doner, Ritchie, and Slater 2005), the PAP
chose to elevate the standing of English vis-à-vis the mother tongue, much to the

chagrin of the Chinese parents (Gopinathan 1998; Kaplan and Baldauf 2003). Singapore's policy makers hoped that with an English-first, mother-tongue-second linguistic arrangement in the classrooms, the students would be exposed to English earlier and hence develop better proficiency. Lee Kuan Yew argued, "If a student is unable to understand a language, then he is unable to receive information or knowledge in that language. It is therefore crucial that a breakthrough must be made in the English language as early in life as possible" (*Strait Times*, May 29, 1982).

With the country in desperate need of foreign capital, top PAP officials traveled to the likes of London and New York City to lobby English-speaking foreign investors. Along with access to a strategic port, a workforce proficient in English— thanks to the government's commitment to its use in the classrooms and in technical training—provided a powerful component of their sales pitch. These efforts paid off with the arrival of the first set of entrepreneurs from then English-speaking Hong Kong. The firms helped build up a successful textile and garment industry (K. Y. Lee 2000: 135–44).

The emphasis on English would continue to grow. In 1979, the Goh Report criticized the extant bilingual curriculum for failing to teach either English or the mother tongue adequately. For Education Minister Goh, his biggest concern was the continued weak proficiency in English. As he recalled, many of the "teachers [simply] did not know what they were teaching" (Nair 2008: 13). In response, the government restructured the education curriculum so that English would serve as the sole medium of instruction. Mother tongue languages would still be available as subjects (Gopinathan 1998: 35–37). This shift in linguistic emphasis would prove essential in the 1990s as Singapore moved towards a banking and service-based economy (K. Y. Lee 2000). It is important to also note that in addition to investment, the PAP also worked to attract skilled foreign labor. Embassy personnel in Australia, Britain, Canada, New Zealand, the United Kingdom, and the United States frequently met with promising Asian (not just Singaporean) students at the university level to recruit them for Singaporean jobs. Without these foreigners, Singapore "would not have done as well" (K. Y. Lee 2000: 168).

Compared to Malaysia, Singapore has been able to attract far more investments from English-speaking countries. As illustrated in Figure 7.3, this has not always been the case. In the 1980s, the two countries started out on similar trajectories. But ever since the late 1980s—exactly one decade after the Goh Report— English-language investment levels in Singapore have significantly outpaced those of Malaysia.

Undoubtedly, in the Singapore story, the choice to neutralize linguistic power has had substantial, positive effects in attracting FDI. The efficiency that comes with recognizing English has attracted foreign capital not only from English-speaking countries. For instance, a representative from a Japanese company was once quoted as saying, "We have high standards. You must be able to communicate . . . . You must know English. . . . That's why we are here [in Singapore]."

Discussion

As illustrated in Figure 7.2, compared to the averages of Southeast Asia and global Asia, FDI levels in both Malaysia and Singapore have been high. This pattern is consistent with theoretical priors that language regimes that are able to reduce transaction costs and promote greater efficiency are better advantaged. One European firm, for example, was attracted to Malaysia because it was "easy." However, also consistent with the statistical tests is the recognition that the efficiency effects are not uniform. Countries that neutralize linguistic power by using a lingua franca attract more investments. FDI levels in Malaysia, although positive, have suffered in comparison to Singapore's. This difference was in part due to the UMNO-led government's nationalizing pursuit of a Malay-dominant Malaysian state, which has included the de facto concentration of linguistic power. In contrast, investment levels in Singapore exploded in part because of the PAP's choice to neutralize linguistic power by prioritizing English.

Language Regimes and Economic Growth

Language regimes matter for foreign capital. When a language regime recognizes one language across an entire population, it reduces the translation volume necessary for communication. When transacting barriers are low, a country can be attractive to foreign investors. In addition to foreign capital, language regimes also matter for social capital. As discussed at length in the previous chapters, when a language regime neutralizes linguistic power, it can break down group boundaries. It can aid speakers of politically nondominant languages in the development of their own culture and identity. These opportunities consequently have a positive effect for community-building. In the presence of a collective community, people are more likely to trust each other and help others in need. If power-neutralizing language regimes can generate social capital and attract FDI, and if both social and foreign capital are important for economic growth, then the logical extension is that language regimes matter indirectly for economic growth. These arguments are tested below.

Research Design

<u>Economic Growth</u>: The dependent variable is economic growth, measured as the annual percentage growth rate of GDP. To make GDP figures comparable across countries and over time, all numbers have been standardized to market prices based on constant prices in the country's local currency. The data source is the World Bank. In the sample, the lowest growth rate by *country-year* observation is Georgia-1992 (-44.9 percent). This sizable contraction was influenced largely by the collapse of the Soviet Union and the subsequent civil conflicts in Abkhazia and South Ossetia. In contrast, the highest was Oman-1968 (81.89 percent). This expansion was due to oil discovery. Oil extraction began in 1967. The Georgia-1992s and Oman-1968s notwithstanding, 90 percent of the observations fall in the range from −7.1 to 13.82 percent. Note that the World Bank only began collecting these data in 1961.

Although GDP increases can be indicators of a growing economy, it does not necessarily imply increasing equality or quality of living standards. A country like Oman in 1968 can experience surges in its economy, but because it is driven primarily by oil, this does not mean everyone benefits equally from the cash influx. Even if many were to benefit, this can still be the result of a rentier effect where governments spend much but tax little. Over time, while GDP expansions continue and social services such as education continue to be funded heavily, actual human development remains stunted (see Doner, Ritchie, and Slater 2005; Ross 2001).

<u>Language Regime</u>: As with previous tests, language regime is again measured with both the quadrachotomous-turned-into-four-dummies and continuous coding schemes. In the former, power-concentrating language regimes are the reference category (i.e., interpretation of the effects of the other language regimes is in relation to that of power-concentrating).

<u>Generalized Trust</u>: Consistent with the previous chapter, social capital is again operationalized as generalized trust. One caveat bears mention. In Chapter 6, the empirical tests focused on the individual respondent. Specifically, how does language regime affect an individual's propensity to trust? But now, the unit of

analysis has shifted to the country level. Presumably, if language regimes affect trust at the individual level, this should also be reflected at the national level. For example, assume that one country has a power-concentrating language regime and another has power-neutralizing. Based on the previous results, we would expect people to be less trusting in the former than in the latter: The first country would have citizens who are on average less trusting than those in the second country. In this section, I use the World Values Survey and take the average scores for the question about generalized trust.

FDI: This variable also remains unchanged. As with the previous models, foreign capital is measured by taking the log transformation of the net inflow of FDI (reported in the million USD unit) plus one.

Empirical Evidence

The results of the estimated models can be found in Table 7.3 in Appendix 2. Consistent across all four models are three important findings. First, language regimes—regardless of measurement—have no direct effect on economic growth. This nonfinding is robust across a number of model specifications. Second, instead, what matters are trust and FDI levels. Countries with a more trusting population have higher levels of economic growth. Similarly, countries that are able to attract more FDI net inflows experience larger expansions in their economies over time. When considering these two findings together, the story about the link between language regimes and economic growth becomes clear: the effects of the former are mediated through social or foreign capital. But Figures 6.1 and 7.1 established that the positive effects of language regimes on both generalized trust and FDI are most pronounced when a lingua franca is recognized—exclusively. This lends support to Hypotheses 4.1 and 4.2 that power-neutralizing language regimes can have positive, albeit indirect, implications for a country's economic performance.

The third finding pertains to the effects of politically relevant linguistic heterogeneity. The negative economic effects of ethnic diversity have been well documented (see Habyarimana et al. 2009: 5–13). Yet consistent across all models, the coefficient is never statistically significant. Moreover, the direction of the coefficient flips from positive in some models to negative in others. These results cast some doubt on the claim that ethnolinguistic heterogeneity is a cause for a country's "growth tragedy" (Easterly and Levine 1997: 1203). This is not to say

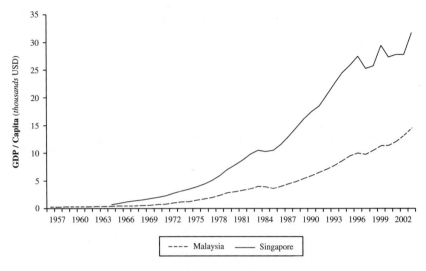

Figure 7.4. GDP/capita in Malaysia and Singapore. World Bank.

heterogeneity in and of itself does not matter. On the contrary, if ethnolinguistic differences do impede economic performance, then the effects are indirect—first through language regime and then through social capital and foreign capital. However, given the number of other variables mediating this effect, there is welcome news: countries endowed with high levels of heterogeneity are not trapped and have institutional tools to spur economic growth.

These effects are clearly illustrated when comparing Malaysia and Singapore. As shown in Figure 7.4, when compared to the world at large, Malaysia's and Singapore's economic growth trajectories have been impressive. However, as illustrated in Figures 6.3 and 7.2, their trust and FDI levels diverge substantially. This difference is hard to miss. Singapore's journey from the third to the first world (not coincidentally the title of one of Lee Kuan Yew's memoirs) was partly the result of a strategic language regime choice: increasing linguistic neutralization. In contrast, Malaysia's growth was handicapped by the shift away from neutralization toward Malay concentration.

Conclusion

The empirical tests in the previous chapter and this one demonstrate that language regimes matter for economic performance, albeit indirectly. The effects can manifest through different channels. One mechanism is social capital. When language regimes perpetuate equality, this can aid in the development of a collective community. When such communities exist, we are more likely to find trust and willingness of individuals to help others in need. And with social capital, countries are more likely to experience growth. The results suggest that the link between language regimes and social capital is the strongest when language regimes are power-neutralizing.

Another mechanism is foreign capital. Some language regimes necessitate translations across multiple languages, thereby increasing transaction costs. These costs can come in the form of money or time. Regardless of the source of the costs, in aggregate, they render the language regime inefficient. This inefficiency in turn can make a country unattractive to potential foreign investors. Although foreign capital is not absolutely necessary for growth, its absence (or low levels of it) can impede growth. The results in this chapter suggest that the effects of efficiency are most pronounced with a lingua franca, especially when it is recognized exclusively.

The implications of the empirical tests are twofold. First, lingua franca recognition matters for trust and for FDI levels. But it is not the case that *any* lingua franca recognition is better than *none*. Instead, what is of great importance is that *more* recognition is better than *less*, specifically, that the recognition is exclusive. This suggests that adopting a power-neutralizing language regime can play an important role in cultivating economic growth. Second, if the effects of language regimes on economic growth are mediated through two different channels, then the supposed negative effects of ethnolinguistic heterogeneity can also be mitigated with the proper choice of rules delineating which languages can be used when and where. To condemn a country with high levels of diversity ignores the institutional options available to the government to respond appropriately. One such institution is language regime. In fact, it is under conditions of extreme heterogeneity that linguistic power is neutralized. If linguistic neutralization is normatively desired because of its equality and efficiency properties, this would suggest the effects of heterogeneity are not necessarily those commonly argued in the literature.

Appendix 1: Foreign Capital

The first set of results is presented in Table 7.1. Model 1 is the baseline model. Language regime is measured using the quadrachotomous measure. Recall, *power-concentrating* is the reference category. The results suggest that of the

Table 7.1: Language Regimes and FDI

	Model 1 Quadrachotomous language regime	Model 2 Continuous neutralization
Power-Sharing Language Regime	**0.17 (0.14)**	0.16 (0.11)
Power-Neutralizing Language Regime	**0.47 (0.18)**[†]	
Neutralized-Sharing Language Regime	**0.14 (0.15)**	
Degree of Power-Neutralization		**0.46 (0.18)**[‡]
Politically Relevant Linguistic Heterogeneity	−0.23 (0.36)	−0.23 (0.30)
Democracy	0.01 (0.01)	0.01 (0.01)
GDP (billions)	0.05 (0.06)	0.05 (0.06)
Population (100,000)	0.04 (0.02)*	0.05 (0.02)[†]
Colonialism: British	−0.13 (0.09)	−0.11 (0.09)
FDI (t–1)	0.85 (0.03)[‡]	0.85 (0.03)[‡]
Constant	1.02 (0.16)[‡]	1.02 (0.15)[‡]
Number of observations (clusters)	642 (38)	642 (38)
F Statistic / Wald χ^2	3959.04[‡]	4157.15[‡]
R^2	0.8397	0.8399

Note: Standard errors clustered by country. *$p \le 0.100$; [†]$p \le 0.050$, [‡]$p \le 0.010$.

four language regimes, those that neutralize linguistic power have a significant and positive effect ($\beta = 0.47$; SE $= 0.18$). When language regimes are power-neutralizing, the expected FDI inflow is US$927.72 million. This is significantly larger than those with power-concentrating ($580 million), power-sharing ($684.94 million), and neutralized-sharing ($670.41 million).

Model 2 replicates the baseline model with one difference: language regime is operationalized using the continuous measure of linguistic neutralization. The coefficient is again positive and significant ($\beta = 0.46$; SE $= 0.18$). A shift from where a lingua franca is half the education curriculum (0.50) to one where the lingua franca is the exclusive language can increase FDI inflow levels by more than 25 percent, from $725.21 million to $914.073 million. Interestingly, the coefficient for whether a language regime is power-sharing (to account for differences in language regimes when there is no linguistic neutralization) is not statistically significant. The results for language regimes from these two models suggest that language regimes have a positive effect on FDI inflow levels, but only when they are power-neutralizing.

Among the controls, population is statistically significant. As expected, countries that are more populated attract more investment. Additionally, the lagged dependent variable is highly significant. This is consistent with theoretical priors: FDI levels are heavily influenced by those in the previous year. Interestingly, politically relevant linguistic heterogeneity, while significant for language regime choice, is not significant for FDI levels.

FDI by nature is very dynamic. The models in Table 7.1 take this into consideration with the use of a lagged dependent variable. However, it is also possible the lagged dependent variable is driving the findings. To ensure this is not the case, I run several additional tests (see Table 7.2). The first (Model 3) is a difference-in-difference model: it accounts for changes from one year to the next. Specifically, it looks at the effects of a changing value in each of the independent variables on the changing FDI levels. Since FDI levels do not change drastically (i.e., in the magnitude of the billions), I do not log the dependent variable. Consequently, the coefficients are quite large. The results suggest that when a language regime shifts from a neutralized-sharing where a lingua franca is half the curriculum (0.5) to one that is power-neutralizing, FDI inflows can increase by US$1.679 million.

Alternatively, in Model 4, I rerun Model 2 (with the continuous measure of linguistic neutralization) without the lagged dependent variable. Although the magnitude of the coefficients does change, most notably for power-neutralization (0.46 versus 1.67), the substantive results remain largely consistent. As linguistic neutralization increases, FDI inflow levels also increase.

It is also possible that there is some nonrandomness in which countries attract more investment. To account for this possibility, I employ a Heckman selection model. The first model (Model 5.1) explains the level of linguistic neutralization. This model should largely mirror that from Chapter 4. The second model (5.2) then estimates a model for FDI levels.

In the first (selection) model, politically relevant linguistic heterogeneity has a statistically significant effect on the degree of linguistic neutralization ($\beta = 2.47$; $SE = 1.45$). As theoretically argued, countries endowed with higher heterogeneity levels are more compelled to recognize a lingua franca, whether exclusively or in conjunction with other mother tongues. We also see that in this model, other variables are also significant. Democracies, post-Soviet republics, and federations are all less likely to neutralize exclusively. Note that this does not necessarily mean that lingua franca recognition is unequivocally absent; instead, it may suggest tendencies toward the recognition of a neutralized-sharing language regime.

Moving on to the second (outcome) model, the coefficient for power-neutralization is still positive and significant ($\beta = 1.41$; $SE = 0.85$). This is impor-

Table 7.2: Sensitivity Tests

	Model 3 Change	Model 4 No Lagged DV	Model 5.1 Neutralization	Model 5.2 FDI
Degree of Power-Neutralization	1679.07 (579.08)‡	1.67 (0.51)‡		1.41 (0.85)*
Power-Sharing	−601.92 (427.53)	0.77 (0.52)		−0.48 (3.01)
Politically Relevant Linguistic Heterogeneity	−655.81 (905.53)	−1.13 (1.85)	2.47 (1.45)*	0.05 (0.13)
Democracy	2.81 (25.25)	0.14 (0.03)‡	−0.06 (0.03)*	0.96 (0.40)†
GDP (billions)	14333.13 (2010.62)‡	0.81 (0.20)‡		−0.10 (0.10)
Population (100,000)	838.631 (6281.62)	0.50 (0.10)‡		
GDP/capita (1000)			−0.001 (0.04)	
Colonialism: British		0.40 (0.71)	0.94 (0.74)	−0.10 (0.44)
Colonialism: Russia			2.04 (1.01)†	
Federal			−1.22 (0.71)*	
FDI (t−1)	22.14 (54.39)			0.72 (0.08)‡
Number of observations (clusters)	642 (38)	713 (39)	582 (32)	
F Statistic / Wald χ^2	132.58‡	153.88‡		
R^2	0.0467	0.2528		
Log Pseudo-likelihood			−294.0861	
ρ			−0.76 (0.63)	

Note: Standard errors clustered by country. *$p \leq 0.100$; †$p \leq 0.050$; ‡$p \leq 0.010$. Constants not reported.

tant. Taking into consideration the nonrandom fact that heterogeneous countries are more likely to recognize a lingua franca, it seems lingua franca recognition—and more of it—does attract more investments. Two other results merit attention. First, the effects of heterogeneity are not significant in the latter model ($\beta = -0.48$; $SE = 3.01$). This suggests the effects are indirect and mediated through language regimes. Second, the rho value for the Heckman model is not statistically significant. The 95 percent confidence band ranges from -0.9993 to 0.96. This clearly confirms the absence of a selection effect between the model for explaining language regimes and the one for accounting FDI levels.

Appendix 2: Economic Growth

Four models are used to test the link between language regimes and economic growth (see Table 7.3). The first two test the effect of social capital on economic growth while controlling for language regime. Model 6 uses the quadrachotomous measure. If the effects of language regimes are indirect, none of the coefficients of interest should be statistically significant. The results indicate this is the case. All three coefficients, while negative, are statistically no different from the effects of power-concentrating. In addition to these results, generalized trust has a significant and positive effect on economic growth ($\beta = 7.07$; $SE = 4.06$).

This finding is robust in Model 7. Again, language regime has no significant effect on economic growth. The coefficient for the degree of linguistic neutralization is not statistically significant; additionally, the control for whether a language regime is power-sharing is also not significant. But the effect of generalized trust is still significant and the magnitude of this effect is largely comparable to that in Model 6 ($\beta = 7.75$; $SE = 3.92$).

The last two columns examine the independent effects of language regime and FDI on economic growth. Consistent with the previous models, one uses the quadrachotomous measure; the other, the continuous measure. Across both Models 8 and 9, the coefficients for language regime are not statistically significant. This corroborates the larger claim that the effects of language regime, when they matter, manifest indirectly through other channels. Specifically, when people feel they are part of a larger collective community, this sense of trust can promote growth. Alternatively, language regimes can also promote growth by attracting foreign capital. FDI effects are highly robust: in both models, the coefficient is positive and significant. As expected, when countries are able to attract investments from abroad, this makes high growth much more likely.

Table 7.3: Language Regimes and Economic Growth

	Model 6 Quadrachotomous language regime	Model 7 Continuous neutralization	Model 8 Quadrachotomous language regime	Model 9 Continuous neutralization
Power-Sharing Language Regime	**-7.34 (5.10)**	-4.33 (3.81)	**-0.18 (3.07)**	0.53 (2.72)
Power-Neutralizing Language Regime	**-9.51 (8.18)**		**-1.30 (3.19)**	
Neutralized-Sharing Language Regime	**-8.10 (6.30)**		**-2.23 (3.77)**	
Degree of Power-Neutralization		**-3.36 (5.83)**		**-1.76 (2.68)**
Generalized Trust	**7.07 (4.06)***	**7.75 (3.92)**[†]		
FDI			**0.84 (0.35)**[†]	**0.84 (0.35)**[†]
Politically Relevant Linguistic Heterogeneity	13.38 (9.13)	4.87 (5.05)	-6.19 (10.76)	-7.15 (9.65)
Democracy	-0.40 (0.16)[†]	-0.39 (0.16)[†]	-0.09 (0.12)	-0.09 (0.12)
GDP/capita (1000)	-0.05 (0.15)	-0.11 (0.16)	-0.22 (0.10)[†]	-0.20 (0.10)[†]
Colonialism: British	3.89 (3.76)	0.77 (2.46)	2.39 (1.86)	2.03 (1.52)
Colonialism: continental	6.80 (6.62)	2.11 (5.23)	-3.38 (5.20)	-3.25 (5.33)
Colonialism: Russian	7.28 (4.78)	4.18 (3.33)	-2.42 (2.50)	-3.12 (1.79)*
Number of observations (clusters)	35 (19)	35 (19)	711 (39)	711 (39)
F Statistic	41.66[‡]	21.54[‡]	16.54*	19.33[†]
R^2	0.5174	0.4587	0.0513	0.0480

Note: Standard errors clustered by country. *$p \le 0.100$; [†]$p \le 0.050$; [‡]$p \le 0.010$. Constants not reported.

A disclaimer warrants mention. Since the argument is that the effects of language regimes manifest through two different channels, from a research design perspective, the models should include both generalized trust and FDI in the same regression. However, surveys are administered neither widely in a number of countries (in this case 19 compared to 39 countries reported FDI levels) nor across multiple time periods (the average is less than two years per surveyed country). As a result, the total number of observations at the country level is quite small ($N = 35$). The fact that there is any significance to Models 6 and 7 is no small feat. To run a full model that includes both generalized trust and FDI renders statistical inferences limited.

CHAPTER 8

Conclusion: Standardizing Diversity

People of Seattle! Listen to me! We are not barbarians!
We are not Neanderthals and we are NOT FRENCH!
—Frasier Crane in *Frasier*, Season 3, Episode 17
("High Crane Drifter")

Language is a vehicle of communication, but it is also a potential tool for demarcating group boundaries. It may distinguish members of the in-group (e.g., French-speakers) from those in the out-group (e.g., non-French-speakers). This possibility is what makes language regimes inherently political. Language regimes can be classified into four types. The first type recognizes one mother tongue, that of the politically dominant. Moreover, with a few exceptions, the language of the politically dominant is also the language of the largest ethnolinguistic group. The exclusive promotion of standard Thai throughout Thailand is an example of a power-concentrating language regime. The second type distributes linguistic power across multiple mother tongues. At least one of these languages must, by definition, be that of a politically nondominant group. The use of Malay, Chinese, and Tamil in Malaysian classrooms today is an example of a de jure power-sharing language regime. The third type employs a lingua franca exclusively. The linguistic arrangement in Indonesia with Indonesian monopolizing the education curriculum is an illustration of linguistic neutralization. And finally, the fourth language regime is a hybrid of power-sharing and power-neutralizing: a lingua franca is recognized in conjunction with at least one other mother tongue. An example of this neutralized-sharing type is pre-merger Singapore with its recognition of English alongside Chinese, Malay, and Tamil. With this typology, this book asked two related questions: what explains language regime choice, and what are the economic implications of this choice? The answers to both questions suggest much larger implications beyond just language regimes.

Power-Neutralizing Institutions

Language regimes are institutional choices made by governments in response to politically relevant linguistic heterogeneity levels. When choosing language regimes, governments must find the optimal balance between the three Es: cultural egoism, communicative efficiency, and collective equality. If politically relevant linguistic heterogeneity levels are low, the government has an incentive to concentrate linguistic power exclusively in the politically dominant language. Doing so ensures there are egoism and efficiency benefits for a minimal equality cost.

This calculation, however, changes once politically relevant linguistic heterogeneity levels increase. When constrained by multiple linguistic minority groups, the government must make concessions. One form of concession is to recognize other mother tongues. The advantage of sharing linguistic power is that it yields a greater sense of collective equality, but there are severe costs regarding communicative efficiency. These costs accrue exponentially with the addition of each minority linguistic group. Moreover, the cultural egoism benefits start to diminish drastically. Under such conditions, another form of linguistic concession may be preferable: the recognition of a lingua franca. When a lingua franca is recognized, whether exclusively or in conjunction with other mother tongues, such arrangements require all linguistic groups to forfeit some—if not all—claims to their mother tongue.

By focusing on how the balance of power among linguistic groups shapes institutional designs, this book shifts the attention away from the efficiency-enhancing properties of institutions (North 1990) to their distributional consequences (Knight 1992; Moe 2005). In doing so, I identify an institutional alternative that has been theoretically overlooked and empirically ignored. The literature, especially with respect to ethnic conflict resolution, has been long dominated by two types of designs (Reynolds 2002). The first type emphasizes moderation through power-concentration (Horowitz 1985). The logic is that when institutions concentrate power in the hands of a few actors, it encourages convergence toward a median voter. For example, in theory winner-takes-all electoral rules reward parties that speak to the median voter and punish those advocating extremist positions. The second type focuses on power-sharing (Lijphart 1968; Norris 2008).

When institutions distribute power across multiple actors, this mitigates tensions and creates the incentives for consensus-building. Returning to the example of electoral rules, proportional representation generates multiple parties. Since no party is likely to be sufficiently large to govern singularly, each party must reach out to other parties and make compromises if it hopes to be in any governing coalition.

The argument here is that in addition to the aforementioned concentration and sharing, power can also be neutralized. With power-neutralization, power is forfeited by the bargaining actors—who may have opposing preferences—and figuratively placed in the hands of a neutral third party. This alternative institutional design happens frequently. While the focus in this book has been on language regimes, power-neutralization can be found across a large spectrum of institutions. Here, I discuss four such institutions.

Secularism: Neutralization of Religious Power

Religion regimes are the rules that delineate which religions can be practiced when and where. Like their linguistic counterparts, religion regimes can be classified into three pure types. The first type is power-concentration. In Cambodia, for example, while Khmer citizens have the constitutional right to "enjoy the freedom of belief," "Buddhism is the state religion" (1993 Constitution, Article 43). Similarly, in Thailand, despite de jure secularism, religious power has been de facto concentrated in Buddhism. Much of the legitimacy of the Thai state rests on the convergence of political and spiritual powers (Ricks 2008). For instance, the Chakri king is constitutionally required to be a Buddhist (2007 Constitution, Chapter 2).

The second type is power-sharing where multiple religions are recognized. Indonesia's religious-management regime is one example. Despite having the largest Muslim population in the world, Indonesia's 1945 Constitution calls for the "belief in the one and only God" (Indonesian Constitution, Preamble). This "one God" has been officially recognized in the form of five different religions: Buddhism, Catholicism, Hinduism, Islam, and Protestantism (Drake 1989: 66–71). The Philippines is another example. There, religious power is shared between the majority Catholics (85 percent) and the minority Muslims (Von der Mehden 1963).

Finally, the third type is power-neutralization where religious power is removed from the hands of political actors. In this case, power-neutralization is secularism, where there is "religious freedom and . . . [the] separation of religion and state" (Fox and Flores 2009: 1499). It is about the right to practice one's religion, however minor, free of state-authorized majority persecution. By the twenty-first century, almost 70 percent of the countries, including the United States, have at one point or another chosen no state religion (Barro and McCleary 2005). In effect, secularism is more than just abstention. The lack of institutionalization of a state religion is by no means synonymous with a lack of religiosity. Instead, it is the neutralization of religious power.[1]

Creation of Capitals: Neutralization of Geographical Power

Like language and religion regimes, the debate on where to place the capital can be resolved through concentration, sharing, or neutralization. Some capitals are intentionally chosen for power-concentrating purposes. Madrid, for example, was "deliberately selected by the centralizing government anxious to 'subordinate the parts'" (Spate 1942: 624). Similarly, the Chinese Nationalist Party (Kuomintang) in 1911 chose Nanjing so as to "restore [it] to the supreme position it had occupied in the fourteenth century" (Chang 1965: 313).

Other capitals are chosen so that there is some sense of power-sharing. There are several different ways to achieve this. One way is to divide the political functions of the government across multiple cities. The choice of three capitals in South Africa is a good example. Bloemfontein is home to the judiciary; Cape Town, the legislature; and Pretoria, the executive. Another way is to designate one city as the political center but to grant a rival city nonpolitical power. In Switzerland, for example, power is shared between Bern politically and Zurich economically. And in Turkey, Ankara has maintained its status as the political capital. But in exchange, both Istanbul and Izmir have been able to claim their rights as cultural, economic, and historic centers. There is still a third means of power-sharing although its use today is less common: rotation. During the American Revolution, Connecticut and Rhode Island both opted for rotating capitals so that it would "equalize representation" (Zagarri 1988: 1240).[2]

Finally, capitals can also be artificially "created" (Lavedan 1936: 9) to neutralize "the vested sectional interests that might attach to a city whose historic traditions or economic ties were with one of the components rather than with the country as a whole" (Spate 1942: 623). It is not a coincidence that Washington, D.C., sits between the industrial North and the agrarian South. Similarly, Ottawa is on the border between the English and French territories. Canberra was also chosen because it was "outside a radius of 100 miles from Sydney" (H. King 1954: 102). There were even discussions in Nigeria to relocate the capital to a new, separate site so that "absolute neutrality [could] be assured" (Moore 1984: 169). In this scenario, to create a capital is to neutralize geographical power.

Judicial Review: Neutralization of Law-Making Power

If power-neutralization happens when all relevant bargaining actors forfeit power and place it in the hands of a third party, the creation of an independent judiciary is another such example. There are two (not mutually exclusive) ways to conceptualize this power-neutralization. The first is when the judiciary exists to be the "judgment" between the legislature and executive (Hamilton, *Federalist* 78). When the judiciary has the power to exercise judicial review, it can by definition "set aside ordinary legislative or administrative acts if judges conclude they conflict with the constitution" (Vanberg 2005: 1). In the American context, for example, the Supreme Court has played an important role mediating between Congress and the president.

Power-neutralization can also happen when an independent judiciary exists as a form of insurance. This is especially prominent in newly democratizing countries. As countries transition and undergo constitutional bargaining, if political interests are diffused across multiple parties, the choice of an independent judiciary becomes attractive to those who may fear electoral losses. In South Korea, for instance, the strength of the Constitutional Court today has its roots in the bargaining process over the 1987 Constitution. Then, each of the three major parties, all roughly of equal political strength, was uncertain of its electoral prospects. Given this uncertainty, there was a collective incentive to create a strong judiciary (Ginsburg 2003: chap. 7).

Today, an independent judiciary is a hallmark of democracy (Helmke 2002, 2005: 1–7; Hirschl 2000, 2004). Seventy-two of the third-wave democracies—including nearly every post-Soviet state—legally recognize constitutional review (Ginsburg 2003: 3–11). By granting the branch that has neither the sword nor the purse that authority, the constitution effectively neutralizes bargaining power between the legislative and executive branches.

Independent Central Banks: Neutralization of Monetary Power

While independent central banks can constrain a government's ability to manipulate monetary policies (and therefore be conceptualized as a rival bargaining actor to the government), a central bank's sheer existence is an example of a power-neutralizing institution. The logic is that government ministries, backbench legislators, and coalition partners (in multiparty governments) can have conflicting preferences over monetary policies. These conflicts can be adjudicated by removing all monetary power from those actors and placing it in the hands of a third party. In this case, the third party is a central bank (Bernhard 1998, 2002).

Consider the U.S. Federal Reserve as an example. Before the Federal Reserve, there had been no institution to oversee the nation's credit or to handle the country's money. Instead, there had been a collection of state-chartered banks that generally behaved with little fiscal restraint. Despite several efforts to create a National Banking Act, it was not until a 1907 financial crisis that the desperate need for reform was highlighted. Yet disagreements between the radical agrarians (mostly in the southern and western states) and the private bankers (mostly in the eastern states) ensued. It was in 1913, when President Woodrow Wilson signed the Federal Reserve Act, that monetary power was effectively neutralized. Neither the agrarians nor the bankers could influence monetary policy at will. In addition to creating a centralized national bank, the control of the Board of the Directors would be in the hands of the government (Johnson 2010). In short, the presence of an independent central bank is the neutralization of monetary power.

Because third party options are by definition alternatives that involve none of the relevant bargaining actors, they are easy to theoretically overlook when modeling bargaining dynamics. They are also easy to empirically miscode into some residual category if not the error term. But as argued in this book, without taking into consideration this distinct, frequently employed alternative, scholars risk drawing incorrect inferences.

Standardizing Diversity

If language regimes institutionalize the distribution of linguistic power, then they matter for economic growth. They matter for two different mechanisms. The first has to do with social capital. When language regimes generate equality, this can create a collective community much larger than those dictated by linguistic group boundaries. And when there is such a community, people are more likely to trust, more likely to believe in the helpfulness of others, and more likely to actually help others. It is precisely this mechanism—social capital—that facilitates economic growth. While the concept of "social capital" has been criticized for being too fuzzy (see Woolcock 2010: 482), the effects of a power-neutralizing language regime are robust (1) on multiple dimensions of social capital and (2) across all groups regardless of the mother tongue at home. The second mechanism has to do with foreign capital. Some linguistic arrangements are inherently more efficient than others. When only one language is necessary to conduct business transactions, this can drastically reduce translation volumes. All else being equal, foreign firms prefer to invest in a country where costs are minimal. These costs can include paying taxes, hiring lawyers, and translating all relevant documents. Some of these costs are inevitable, but the last one—linguistic—can be minimized if not completely avoided. So when there is efficiency, countries are better able to attract FDI. Of the four language regimes, exclusive recognition of a lingua franca has the most pronounced effect on FDI.

Taken altogether, the results suggest that it is not that *any* lingua franca recognition is better than *no* recognition for trust and investment levels. Instead, it is that *more* recognition is better than *less*, especially when the lingua franca recognition is exclusive. If social capital and foreign capital are both conducive to economic growth, this discussion would suggest that power-neutralizing language regimes can be as well. If economic growth is to be desired, then the implication is that lingua franca recognition can be normatively good.

Language regimes, however, are not exogenous. Recall that they are endogenous institutions. They are choices made in response to politically relevant linguistic heterogeneity levels. Specifically, language regimes that recognize a lingua franca—whether exclusively or in conjunction with other mother tongues—are ideal when governments are constrained by high levels of heterogeneity. As illustrated in Figure 8.1, it seems that extreme diversity can actually facilitate normatively desired outcomes such as economic growth. This finding is encouraging. Despite the oft-argued claim that diversity is a cause for some sort of "growth tragedy" (Easterly and Levine 1997: 1203), the evidence in this book suggests otherwise. This is welcome news: the purported negative effects of diversity can be mitigated—if not flipped—with certain language regime choices.

The implications are much larger than just economic growth. Returning to the Indonesian example, it is hard not to be impressed with the successful state-building story. Despite the extreme poverty, a conflict-ridden legacy, and high levels of ethnic diversity in 1949, today Indonesia is the world's third largest democracy, after India and the United States. This is not to say its development has been a fairy tale. Its history does include the Chinese massacres of 1965. It also includes several civil conflicts in the peripheral regions (e.g., Aceh, Papua, and Timor-Leste). These atrocities notwithstanding, the Indonesian story deserves praise—especially when considering there have been at least two other challenges.

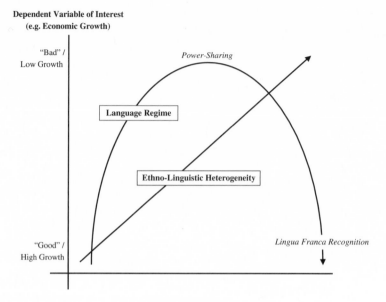

Figure 8.1. Standardizing diversity.

First, the country is predominantly Muslim (almost 90 percent). For Samuel Huntington (1996), the prevalence of Islam makes Indonesia especially vulnerable to the "free-elections trap," whereby democracy brings to power a nondemocratic government (see Stepan 2000: 47–52). The second challenge is the thirty-two-year legacy of military dictatorship. That, coupled with the choice of presidentialism following the 1998 transition, makes democracy highly unstable (Cheibub 2007: 3–15). But despite pockets of Islamic fundamentalism (Chalk 2001) and party cartels (Slater 2004), Indonesia remains, according to Pepinsky, Liddle, and Mujani (2010), the only consolidated Muslim democracy.

This finding highlights how governments, such as Indonesia's, can take a bad hand and play it to their advantage. This book thus contributes to the line of thought that identity, whether it is ethnicity, language, or religion, is very much structured by institutions (see Birnir 2007; Chandra 2004; Posner 2004). All in all, the take-home message from this book should be welcome news for policy makers. This argument is less fatalistic than those found in the likes of Alesina et al. (2003). Countries endowed with high levels of ethnolinguistic heterogeneity are not trapped. Ethnolinguistic identity is, without a doubt, important. It affects preferences; it identifies a larger network; and it affects how coethnics interact with each other (Habyarimana et al. 2009: 5–13). But all these purported mechanisms are reasons why heterogeneity is normatively good: it facilitates the recognition of a lingua franca. In some ways, this discussion is in stark contrast to the rhetoric emanating from the EU, the UN, and parts of the U.S. government. There is the normative argument in these bodies that minority language recognition constitutes some form of human right, and therefore, minorities should be able to use their own mother tongues. Even if language recognition were a right, this book cautions against the blanket praise of minority languages and power-sharing—and even against a neutralized-sharing hybrid (Laitin's 3 ± 1). Instead, it calls attention to the merits of a neutralizing lingua franca.

NOTES

Chapter 1. Introduction

1. The Javanese are roughly half the population. Estimates range from 41 to 53 percent. There are two possible explanations for this range. One is that upon independence, there was dispute over what constituted "Indonesia." This would have altered the estimated size of the larger Indonesian population (and subsequently the denominator) when trying to calculate the proportion of the Javanese. Another explanation is that the Dutch did not maintain books for a centralized "Indonesia." Instead, the census was conducted across each individual island and so while the numbers for Java are largely reliable, the same cannot be said for the whole archipelago.

2. In the Norwegian language, there are two "dialects." One has its roots in Old Norwegian (Nynorsk) and the other is Modern Norwegian (Bokmal). Incidentally, the latter shares more similarity with Danish than with its namesake (Leclerc 2010).

3. Unless otherwise noted, I list all countries, groups, and languages in the English alphabetical order so that their placement in my prose has no hierarchical suggestion.

4. The four official languages of Singapore are Chinese, English, Malay, and Tamil.

5. Dialects are, however, commonly used during election campaigns when candidates (from both the government party and the opposition) go door-to-door to reach out to older Chinese Singaporeans (E. Tan 2007: 91).

6. While the common language was technically a number of dialects, the mutual intelligibility of all was sufficient to establish their speakers as one ethnic group.

7. The Hungarian-Romanian tension was certainly not one-sided. When Transylvania was still under Hungarian control (dating as far back as 1003 CE), the treatment of ethnic Romanians by the Hungarians was largely similar (Sugar 1990: 122–24).

8. The Kurdistan region of Iraq now has Kurdish as its official language. Moreover, Kurdish is one of the two official languages of Iraq (McGarry and O'Leary 2007).

9. In the literature, heterogeneity is commonly operationalized as either the weighted number of ethnic groups (fractionalization) or the intensity and division between the larger groups (polarization).

10. Conflict regulation recognizes that many differences will require constant management (see McGarry, O'Leary, and Simeon 2008).

11. This, of course, assumes the "majority" is moderate.

12. In a paper discussing alternatives to consensual power-sharing in Northern Ireland, Brendan O'Leary identifies another institutional arrangement: arbitration. Arbitration is

characterized by the presence of a "supposedly neutral authority above the rival subcultures" (O'Leary 1989: 568). O'Leary notes that the British relied on arbitration as a solution to the Northern Ireland conflict. By creating an office of the Secretary of State for Northern Ireland that was independent of local authorities and their interests, the government was able to create an image of a neutral arbiter. This categorization of power-arbitration conceptually parallels power-neutralization.

13. Not all lingua francas connote the same sense of neutrality. Lingua francas that are the result of colonialism (e.g., English in South and Southeast Asia, French in West Africa, and Russian in Central Asia and Eastern Europe) are inherently less neutral than the likes of Malay in Indonesia or Swahili in Tanzania. Colonial lingua francas can potentially benefit certain segments of the population—regardless of this group's own mother tongue—that had been advantaged during colonial times. But what is of importance here is not the comparison between Malay in Indonesia and English in Singapore but between English (lingua franca), Chinese (politically dominant), and Malay (politically nondominant), and so forth, in Singapore. This distinction will be discussed in greater detail in Chapter 2.

14. Despite U.S. president William McKinley's efforts to promote the use of Philippine languages, English was considered the proper vehicle for the "inculcation of 'progressive' ideas about business and civil government" (Hau and Tinio 2003: 340). Incidentally, even after the United States granted the Philippines independence, the dominance of Tagalog over other Philippine languages was due to a U.S. legacy of promoting it (Gonzalez 1999; Kaplan and Baldauf 2003: 67–69).

15. According to the Graded International Disruption Scale (Fishman 1991), there are eight different stages of endangerment. At one end (stage 1), a language is used widely in government services, higher education, and mass media. A stage 1 language is at the lowest risk of extinction. At the other end (stage 8), a language is mostly spoken by socially isolated elders. Such languages are considered vestigial and are at the highest risk of extinction.

16. Here, it is necessary to clarify that what is important is *whether* one mother tongue is legally recognized and not *how* this mother tongue is recognized. In other words, a "power-concentrating" language regime can be found in a country where the majority is 99.9 percent, a country that has adopted coercive assimilation (the intentional killing of a minority group language), and a country that has allowed for integration (a dominant language is publicly recognized but minority language rights in the private sphere are protected). Although the de facto status of minority languages differs quite substantively in these three scenarios, de jure the status is the same: exclusive public recognition of one language.

17. The recognition of multiple minority languages can also include consociation (i.e., minority languages are recognized collectively as equal) and partition (i.e., each linguistic group has the right to its own language and each group attends to matters that exclusively affect the community). Although consociation and partition are very different

strategies for resolving conflicts, again, the focus is *not* on how the multiple languages are recognized but whether they are de jure recognized.

Chapter 2. Typology of Language Regimes

1. Note that the Framework Convention for the Protection of National Minorities (1998) has not been ratified by France. Additionally, the European Convention on Human Rights embeds no clear language rights (see McCrudden and O'Leary 2013).

2. Note that the 1977 Charter of the French Language recognizes French as the singular official language of Quebec. With the Charter, French is the exclusive language of the legislature, judiciary, public administration, education, labor, trade, etc. However, since 1984 when the Superior Court of Quebec invalidated sections of the Charter (later upheld in 1988 by the Supreme Court of Canada), the Quebecois government has walked the fine line between having the right to impose the use of French and prohibiting English (see 1998 Act 178, 1993 Act 76, 1997 Act 40, 2000 Act 171, 2002 Act 104, 2010 Act 103, 2010 Act 115, and 2012 Act 14).

3. See O'Leary (2010) for a review and critique of the variations of federalism.

4. At the state (*pradesh*) level, there are even more official languages.

5. Although Cyprus is in the EU and is culturally European, geographically it is sometimes considered part of the Middle East and other times part of Asia. The removal of Cyprus from any of the statistical analyses does not substantively change the results.

6. For other comparative works focusing on ethnicity and language broadly in Asia, see Bertrand and Laliberté (2010), M. Brown and Š. Ganguly (2003), and Kaplan and Baldauf (2003).

7. Initially, there was a fourth group: Europeans. They have since been removed from the census.

8. As early as 1786, the British established three types of colonies in British Malaya: Strait Settlements, Federated Malay States, and Unfederated Malay States. Singapore was a Strait Settlement (others included Dinding, Malacca, and Penang—all in present-day Malaysia).

9. There are a few exceptions. For example, as noted previously, in Cambodia under Khmer Rouge, there was no education system whatsoever.

10. See Appendix to this chapter on the differences in places and periods covered between these data sources.

Chapter 3. Language Regime Choice: Theory

1. Even the privately run "wild schools" established by the indigenous populations operated in the Dutch language (Groeneboer 1998: 233).

2. While the focus of this book is on language regimes, the conditions under which governments will prefer state instability can be inferred in the Appendix to this chapter.

3. It is possible that a minority linguistic group may have little interest in having its maternal language recognized. There is some evidence of this lack of interest in Cameroon (Albaugh 2007) and Ghana (Laitin 1994). In these accounts, the choice was between the indigenous language and that of the colonial authorities. Given the economic benefits associated with the latter, minorities often expressed little preference for the former. This is a rational ordering of preferences (recognition of lingua franca > recognition of mother tongue). However, if the menu of options included being schooled in the mother tongue or the language of another indigenous group, the ordering would most likely change (recognition of mother tongue > recognition of another indigenous language). This point touches on the relativity of cultural egoism.

4. This is also true regardless whether the one recognized language was forcibly imposed upon the population or is the result of some organic development where everyone coincidentally coordinated on the same lingua franca. While there are some coercion costs in the former, what matters is that the population at large can speak the same language.

5. How a country's heterogeneity is operationalized and subsequently coded will be discussed at length in Chapter 4.

6. Note that because the choice variable is discrete (i.e., how many languages to recognize), we cannot solve for D's utility by simply taking the derivative and finding the maximum. Instead, we have to solve with induction. The logic behind proof by induction is as follows. To test whether a pattern holds true for all whole numbers, we first assume the pattern holds for some value q. Given this assumption, if we can then prove the pattern holds as well for some generic value plus one ($q + 1$), we will have effectively proved that the pattern holds at all values.

Chapter 4. Language Regime Choice: Evidence

1. This dataset relies on the expertise of country specialists.

2. Recall that these figures measure the number of *politically relevant* linguistic groups, not the simple *demographic number* of groups.

3. Recall that while colonialism is the most common source for a lingua franca, it is not the only one. Other sources include religion and commerce.

4. One change was made to the existing coding. Hadenius and Teorell (2005) code all the former Soviet states as having never been colonized by a "western" power. Yet there are reasons to consider the post-Soviet states as having been colonized. First, while Russian colonialism is in some ways different from its British or Spanish counterparts, the fact is that the effects today in Uzbekistan are in many ways similar to those in Uganda and Uruguay. Russian is spoken in Tashkent much like English in Kampala and Spanish in Montevideo. Second, while Russia may not be part of Western Europe, it has at some point been considered a "western" power. In some circles, the Russo-Japanese War (1904–1905) is considered the first instance of an Asian country having defeated a western power (Osborne 1997; SarDesai 2010).

5. Countries coded as never having been colonized by a western power include Afghanistan, China, Israel, Iran, Mongolia, North Korea, Saudi Arabia, South Korea, Russia, Taiwan, Thailand, and Turkey.

6. "Bumiputera" is derived from the Sanskrit "Bhumiputra."

7. Eurasians are descendants of Europeans who intermarried with the locals (e.g., Chinese, Indians, and Malays). At the time of independence, the Eurasian community was by far the smallest.

8. The country Malaya did not assume the name "Malaysia" until 1963.

9. The Emergency would end in 1960 with the defeat of the MCP. MCP leader Chin Peng tried renewing the insurgency in 1967 but with little success.

10. Gerakan, People's Progressive Party (both from Peninsular Malaysia), Sabah Chinese Association, Sarawak Chinese Association, and Sarawak United People's Party.

11. Officially, the NEP ended in 1990 and was followed by the National Development Policy. Whether the NEP was successful is subject to debate. On the one hand, the NEP did promote economic growth and reduce the socioeconomic disparity between the Chinese and Malays (Jomo 2004; World Bank 1993). On the other hand, the NEP and its aggressive pro-Malay position has damaged national (i.e., interethnic) unity (Jomo 2004) and encouraged a mass migration of ethnic Chinese out of the country (K. Y. Lee 2000: 166; H. Lee 2007: 140–41).

12. In his memoirs, Lee Kuan Yew recalls feelings of alienation while studying at Cambridge. He was aware that he did not share the same sentiments as the other Chinese students. It did not help that his proficiency in the Chinese language was lacking. This made him an easy target for being branded as non-Chinese. This issue was quickly resolved once the campaigns started (K. Y. Lee 1998).

13. The Chinese in aggregate—communists and noncommunists combined—accounted for 70–80 percent of the island's population.

14. Four years of primary, two years of senior primary, three years of junior middle, and three years of senior middle.

15. As a part of a gentlemen's agreement the Alliance Party reciprocated and promised to not field candidates in Singapore's elections.

16. The ban on Malay conscription was eventually lifted in 1973, but even then the extent of recruitment was limited. Full conscription did not happen until the 1980s.

17. There are exceptions. Schools under the Special Assistance Plan have curricula that allow for more extensive use of a mother tongue. While theoretically "mother tongue" can mean any of the other three official languages, empirically it has meant only Chinese (Gopinathan 1998: 30–31).

Chapter 5. Economic Effects of Language Regimes: Theory

1. Transaction costs can include time, money, and other resources. While theoretically important, transaction costs are difficult to measure because of possible conceptual

heterogeneity in the component terms and empirical challenges to gauging the counterfactual what-if costs.

2. The name "Indonesian" first gained prominence at the 1928 Youth Congress but did not get formally acknowledged until Indonesia declared independence in 1945.

3. Figures based on 2011. Ranking excludes the EU. Its combined economy of $15.39 trillion would make it the largest in the world (United States: $15.04 trillion).

4. Other countries that achieved both feats included the other High-Performing Asian Economies (HPAEs): Hong Kong, Korea, Malaysia, Singapore, Taiwan, and Thailand.

5. Brazil, China, Egypt, India, **Indonesia,** Mexico, Russia, South Korea, Taiwan, and Turkey.

6. Bangladesh, China, Egypt, India, **Indonesia,** Iraq, Mongolia, Nigeria, the Philippines, Sri Lanka, and Vietnam.

7. Colombia, **Indonesia,** Vietnam, Egypt, Turkey, and South Africa.

8. Argentina, Brazil, Chile, China, Colombia, India, **Indonesia,** Mexico, Russia, and Turkey.

9. Mexico, **Indonesia,** South Korea, and Turkey.

10. Bangladesh, Egypt, **Indonesia,** Iran, Mexico, Nigeria, Pakistan, the Philippines, Turkey, South Korea, and Vietnam.

11. Brazil, Russia, India, China, **Indonesia,** and South Korea.

12. Admittedly, this argument ignores the heterogeneity across British colonies. Additionally, it is possible that the British selected colonies that would have performed economically well regardless of the colonial authority (A. Lee and Schultz 2012). But even if we take into consideration these points, the fact that Indonesia was Dutch colonized but still experienced "British-colony-like" growth renders this colonial explanation dubious.

13. With Bali and Maluku as two of the more notable exceptions, the dominance of Islam across the archipelago offers another (possibly more convenient) ethnic marker for nation-building. However, the fact that the Indonesian founding fathers never recognized Islam as the official religion of the country (e.g., the Preamble and Chapter 11 of the constitution call for the belief in the abstract "One God") but recognized Indonesian as the official language (Chapter 15) suggests there was a calculated strategy to use language as the tool to bring "unity in diversity."

14. See Note About Interviews, page vii.

15. Until recently, the concept of a larger Indonesian state was still a contested matter, most notably in three regions: Aceh, Papua, and Timor-Leste. All three regions were home to separatist movements during the New Order. Efforts at accommodating these separatist demands included a 2001 Special Autonomy Law that afforded Aceh and Papua both rights over various matters. In 2002, Timor-Leste became independent following a 1999 referendum; in 2005, Aceh was given special autonomy and national troops were withdrawn.

16. Note that these questions are commonly asked in other regional barometers.

17. Admittedly, this manufacturing was at times perceived as coercive. This was especially true for the Chinese, who saw severe restrictions on the use of their language:

Chinese schools were banned, public displays of Chinese prohibited, Chinese New Year banned, and as mentioned earlier, all Chinese surnames replaced (Bertrand 2003: 278–81).

18. As another example, outside Asia, in Northeast Brazil, industrial managers and business elites provide subsidized workforce training as an alternative to quality basic education to keep wages low. Low wages make the region more attractive than the South (Tendler 2002).

Chapter 6. Mechanism 1: Social Capital

1. These fair arrangements were not seen as "fair" by all. First, Tunku and some UMNO members were attacked by the Malay community for perpetuating Chinese chauvinism. There was a common belief that it was a "necessity to limit display of Chinese and Indian supremacy" (Abdul Samad 1998: 94). Second, Tunku and MCA members were criticized by the Chinese for having been too soft. Many felt MCA did not do enough to demand the official recognition of their language (MCA 2010).

2. Australia and the United Kingdom were also popular destinations for wealthy parents.

Chapter 7. Mechanism 2: Foreign Capital

1. While the unit of analysis is monadic here, I do consider dyadic interactions in the two case studies.

2. Since the logarithmic transformation of 0 does not exist (and the log of 1 is 0), I add a value of 1 to all FDI levels before taking the log.

3. Although Singapore did not sign until 1973—much later than Malaysia (1957)—this is not an empirical concern. In fact, the lag should bias *against* Singapore. Specifically, in the period between 1957 and 1973, Malaysian FDI should be higher. Yet this is not the case.

4. Both countries did not sign their first preferential trade agreement until 1988 (Global System of Trade Preferences)—many years after the two periods began.

5. Between 1967 and 1973, the Malaysian ringgit and the Singapore dollar were exchangeable at par (Monetary Authority of Singapore 2013). After 1973 and until 1985, the Singapore dollar was pegged to a fixed basket of currencies.

Chapter 8. Conclusion: Standardizing Diversity

1. While a state may be hard pressed to be absolutely equidistant from all religions, from a relative standpoint, by adopting secularism the government is signaling noninterference in all religions.

2. Nine other states (Delaware, Georgia, New Hampshire, New Jersey, New York, North Carolina, Pennsylvania, South Carolina, and Virginia) moved their capital from the coast to a more centralized inland city so that the government would be equally accessible, from a geographic standpoint, to all (Zagarri 1988).

REFERENCES

Abdelal, Rawi, Yoshiko M. Herrera, Alastair Iain Johnston, and Rose McDermott. 2009. *Measuring Identity: A Guide for Social Scientists.* New York: Cambridge University Press.

Abdul Samad, Paridah. 1998. *Tun Abdul Razak: A Phenomenon in Malaysian Politics.* Kuala Lumpur: Affluent Master Sdn. Bhd.

Acemoglu, Daron, Simon Johnson, and James Robinson. 2000. "The Colonial Origins of Comparative Development: An Empirical Investigation." National Bureau of Economic Research Working Paper 7771.

Achen, Christopher H. 2000. "Why Lagged Dependent Variables Can Suppress the Explanatory Power of Other Independent Variables." Paper presented at Annual Meeting of the Political Methodology Section of the American Political Science Association, Los Angeles.

Adams, Cindy. 1966. *Sukarno: An Autobiography as Told to Cindy Adams.* Hong Kong: Gunung Agung.

Aitken, Brian J., and Ann E. Harrison. 1999. "Do Domestic Firms Benefit from Direct Foreign Investment? Evidence from Venezuela." *American Economic Review* 89: 605–18.

Alba, Richard, John Logan, Amy Lutz, and Brian Stults. 2002. "Only English by the Third Generation? Loss and Preservation of the Mother Tongue Among the Grandchildren of Contemporary Immigrants." *Demography* 39, 3: 467–84.

Albaugh, Ericka A. 2007. "Language Choice in Education: A Politics of Persuasion." *Journal of Modern African Studies* 45: 1–32.

———. 2009. "The Colonial Image Reversed: Language Preferences and Policy Outcomes in African Education." *International Studies Quarterly* 53: 389–420.

———. 2014. *State-Building and Multilingual Education in Africa.* New York: Cambridge University Press.

Alesina, Alberto, and Robert J. Barro. 2001. "Dollarization." *American Economic Review* 91: 381–85.

Alesina, Alberto, Arnaud Devleeschauwer, William Easterly, Sergio Kurlat, and Romain Wacziarg. 2003. "Fractionalization." *Journal of Economic Growth* 8: 155–94.

Alesina, Alberto, and Eliana La Ferrara. 2002. "Who Trusts Others?" *Journal of Public Economics* 85: 207–34.

Alesina, Alberto, and Eliana La Ferrara. 2005. "Ethnic Diversity and Economic Performance." *Journal of Economic Literature* 43: 762–800.

Althusser, Louis. 1971. "Ideology and Ideological State Apparatuses." In *Lenin and Philosophy and Other Essays*, ed. Louis Althusser. New York: Monthly Review Press.

Amrith, Sunil S. 2011. *Migration and Diaspora in Modern Asia*. New York: Cambridge University Press.

Anderson, Benedict. 1983. *Imagined Communities: Reflections on the Origin and Spread of Nationalism*. London: Verso.

———. 2006. *Language and Power: Exploring Political Cultures in Indonesia*. Singapore: Equinox Publishing (Asia).

Anderson, Christopher, and Aida Paskeviciute. 2006. "How Ethnic and Linguistic Heterogeneity Influence the Prospects for Civil Society: A Comparative Study of Citizenship Behavior." *Journal of Politics* 68: 783–802.

Anderson, James E., and Eric van Wincoop. 2003. "Gravity with Gravitas: A Solution to the Border Puzzle." *American Economic Review* 93: 170–92.

Anderson, Leslie E. 2010. *Social Capital in Developing Democracies: Nicaragua and Argentina Compared*. New York: Cambridge University Press.

Annett, Anthony. 2001. "Social Fractionalization, Political Instability, and the Size of Government." *IMF Staff Papers* 48: 561–92.

Arellano, Manuel, and Olympia Bover. 1995. "Another Look at the Instrumental Variable Estimation of Error-Components Models." *Journal of Econometrics* 68: 29–51.

Arrow, Kenneth J. 1972."Gifts and Exchanges." *Philosophy and Public Affairs* 1: 343–362.

Asian Barometer Survey. 2011. http://www.asianbarometer.org/newenglish/surveys/

Asiedu, Elizabeth, and Donald Lien. 2003. "Capital Controls and Foreign Direct Investment." *World Development* 32: 479–90.

———. 2011. "Democracy, Foreign Direct Investment and Natural Resources." *Journal of International Economics* 84: 99–111.

Aslan, Senem. 2007. " 'Citizen, Speak Turkish!': A Nation in the Making." *Nationalism and Ethnic Politics* 13: 245–72.

Baker, Andy, James R. Scarritt, and Shaheen Mozaffar. 2014. "Ethnopolitical Demograpjhy and Democracy in Sub-Saharan Africa." Typescript. University of Colorado and Bridgewater State University.

Bandelj, Nina. 2002. "Embedded Economies." *Social Forces* 81, 2: 411–44.

Banerjee, Abhijit, Lakshmi Iyer, and Rohini Somanathan. 2005. "History, Social Divisions, and Public Goods in Rural India." *Journal of the European Economic Association* 3: 639–47.

Barro, Robert J. 1991. "Economic Growth in a Cross Section of Countries." *Quarterly Journal of Economics* 106: 407–443.

Barro, Robert J., and Rachel M. McCleary. 2005. "Which Countries Have State Religions?" *Quarterly Journal of Economics* 120: 1331–70.

Baum, Matthew, and David A. Lake. 2003. "The Political Economy of Growth: Democracy and Human Capital." *American Journal of Political Science* 47: 333–47.

Beck, Thorsten, George Clarke, Alberto Groff, Philip Keefer, and Patrick Walsh. 2001. "New Tools in Comparative Political Economy: The Database of Political Institutions." *World Bank Economic Review* 15: 165–176.

Bénassy-Quéré, A., M. Coupet, and T. Mayer. 2007. "Institutional Determinants of Foreign Direct Investment." *World Economy* 30: 764–82.

Bennett, Andrew. 2008. "Process Tracing: A Bayesian Approach." In *Oxford Handook of Political Methodology*, ed. J. M. Box-Steffensmeier, Henry Brady, and David Collier. New York: Oxford University Press. 702–21.

Bernhard, William. 1998. "A Political Explanation of Variations in Central Bank Independence." *American Political Science Review* 92: 311–27.

———. 2002. *Banking on Reform: Political Parties and Central Bank Independence in the Industrial Democracies*. Ann Arbor: University of Michigan Press.

Bertrand, Jacques. 2003. "Language Policy and the Promotion of National Identity in Indonesia." In *Fighting Words: Language Policy and Ethnic Relations in Asia*, ed. Michael E. Brown and Šumit Ganguly. Cambridge, Mass.: MIT Press. 263–90.

Bertrand, Jacques, and André Laliberté. 2010. *Multination States in Asia: Accommodation or Resistance*. New York: Cambridge University Press.

Bin Muhammad, Mahathir. 1970. *The Malay Dilemma*. Singapore: Asia Pacific Press.

Birdsall, Nancy, David Ross, and Richard Sabot Sabot. 1997. "Education, Growth, and Inequality." In *Pathways to Growth: Comparing East Asia and Latin America*, ed. Nancy Birdsall and F. Jaspersen. Baltimore: Johns Hopkins University Press.

Birnir, Jóhanna Kristín. 2007. *Ethnicity and Electoral Politics*. New York: Cambridge University Press.

Bjork, Christopher. 2003. "Local Responses to Decentralization Policy in Indonesia." *Comparative Education Review* 47: 184–216.

Blomstrom, Magnus, and Ari Kokko. 2003. "The Economics of Foreign Direct Investment Incentives." National Bureau of Economic Research Working Paper 9489.

Bobo, Lawrence. 1988. "Group Conflict, Prejudice, and the Paradox of Contemporary Racial Attitudes." In *Eliminating Racism: Profiles in Controversy*, ed. Phyllis A. Katz and Dalmas A. Taylor. New York: Plenum.

Boix, Carles. 2003. *Democracy and Redistribution*. New York: Cambridge University Press.

Boix, Carles, and Susan Stokes. 2003. "Endogenous Democratization." *World Politics* 55: 517–49.

The Book of Mormon: Another Testament of Jesus Christ. 1981. Salt Lake City, Utah: Church of Jesus Christ of Latter-Day Saints.

Borensztein, Eduardo, Jose De Gregorio, and Jong-Wha Lee. 1998. "How Does Foreign Direct Investment Affect Economic Growth?" *Journal of International Economics* 45: 115–35.

Bourdieu, Pierre. 1991. *Language and Symbolic Power*. Trans. Gino Raymond and Matthew Adamson. Malden, Mass.: Polity Press.

Bovingdon, Gardner. 2001. "The History of the History of Xinjiang." *Twentieth-Century China* 26: 95–139.

Brambor, Thomas, William Roberts Clark, and Matt Golder. 2006. "Understanding Interaction Models: Improving Empirical Analyses." *Political Analysis* 14: 63–82.

Brehm, John, and Wendy M. Rahn. 1997. "Individual Level Evidence for the Causes and Consequences of Social Capital." *American Journal of Political Science* 41: 999–1023.

Brimble, Peter, and Richard F. Doner. 2007. "University-Industry Linkages and Economic Development: The Case of Thailand." *World Development* 35, 6: 1021–36.

Brock, William, and Steven Durlauf. 2001. "What Have We Learned from a Decade of Empirical Research on Growth? Growth Empirics and Reality." *World Bank Economic Review* 15: 229–72.

Brown, David. 2009. "Ethnic and Nationalist Politics in Southeast Asia." In *Contemporary Southeast Asia*, ed. Mark Beeson. Hampshire: Palgrave Macmillan.

Brown, David S., and Wendy Hunter. 1999. "Democracy and Social Spending in Latin America, 1980–92." *American Political Science Review* 93: 779–90.

———. 2004. "Democracy and Human Capital Formation: Education Spending in Latin America 1980 to 1997." *Comparative Political Studies* 37: 842–64.

Brown, Michael E. 1993. "Causes and Implications of Ethnic Conflict." In *Ethnic Conflict and International Security*, ed. Michael E. Brown. Princeton, N.J.: Princeton University Press.

Brown, Michael E., and Šumit Ganguly. 2003. "Introduction." In *Fighting Words: Language Policy and Ethnic Relations in Asia*, ed. Michael E. Brown and Šumit Ganguly. Cambridge, Mass.: MIT Press. 1–18.

Bueno de Mesquita, Bruce, James D. Morrow, Randolph M. Siverson, and Alastair Smith. 2003. *The Logic of Political Survival*. Cambridge, Mass.: MIT Press.

Burhanudeen, Hafriza. 2006. "Language and Social Behavior: Voices from the Malay World." Ph.D. Dissertation, Political Science, Universiti Kebangsaan Malaysia, Bangi.

Bussman, Hadumod. 1996. *Routledge Dictionary of Language and Linguistics*. Trans. G. P. Trauth and K. Kazaazi. London: Routledge.

Büthe, Tim, and Helen V. Milner. 2008. "The Politics of Foreign Direct Investment into Developing Countries: Increasing FDI Through International Trade Agreements?" *American Journal of Political Science* 52: 741–62.

Caddick, Brian. 2010. "Perceived Illegitimacy and Intergroup Relations." In *Social Identity and Intergroup Relations*, ed. Henri Tajfel. New York: Cambridge University Press. 137–54.

Callahan, Mary P. 2003. "Language Policy in Modern Burma." In *Fighting Words: Language Policy and Ethnic Relations in Asia*, ed. Michael E. Brown and Šumit Ganguly. Cambridge, Mass.: MIT Press.

Campbell, John L., and John A. Hall. 2010. "Defending the Gellnerian Premise: Denmark in Historical and Comparative Context." *Nations and Nationalism* 16, 1: 89–107.

Cardinal, Linda, and Anne-Andrée Denault. 2007. "Empowering Linguistic Minorities: Neo-Liberal Governance and Language Policies in Canada and Wales." *Regional and Federal Studies* 17: 437–56.

Casper, Jonathan D., Tom Tyler, and Bonnie Fisher. 1988. "Procedural Justice in Felony Cases." *Law and Society Review* 22: 483–507.

Cederman, Lars-Erik, Andreas Wimmer, and Brian Min. 2010. "Why Do Ethnic Groups Rebel? New Data and Analysis." *World Politics* 62: 87–119.

Central Intelligence Agency (CIA). 2008. "The World Factbook." https://www.cia.gov /cia/publications/factbook/ index.html.

Chalk, Peter. 2001. "Separatism and Southeast Asia: The Islamic Factor in Southern Thailand, Mindanao, and Aceh." *Studies in Conflict and Terrorism* 24: 241–69.

Chambers, J .K., and Peter Trudgill. 1998. *Dialectology.* New York: Cambridge University Press.

Chan, Heng Chee, and Obaid ul Haq. 1987. *The Prophetic and the Political: Selected Speeches and Writings of S. Rajaratnam.* Singapore: Graham Brash.

Chandra, Kanchan. 2004. *Why Ethnic Parties Succeed: Patronage and Ethnic Head Counts in India.* New York: Cambridge University Press.

———. 2005. "Ethnic Parties and Democratic Stability." *Perspectives on Politics* 3: 235–52.

———. 2006. "What Is Ethnic Identity and Does It Matter?" *Annual Review of Political Science* 9: 397–424.

Chandra, Kanchan, and Steven Wilkinson. 2008. "Measuring the Effect of 'Ethnicity'." *Comparative Political Studies* 41, 4–5: 515–63.

Chang, Sen-Dou. 1965. "Peking: The Growing Metropolis of Communist China." *Geographical Review* 55: 313–27.

Chanley, Virginia A., Thomas J. Rudolph, and Wendy M. Rahn. 2000. "The Origins and Consequences of Public Trust in Government." *Public Opinion Quarterly* 64: 239–56.

Cheibub, Jose Antonio. 2007. *Presidentialism, Parliamentarism, and Democracy.* New York: Cambridge University Press.

Cheibub, Jose A., Jennifer Gandhi, and James R. Vreeland. 2009. "Democracy and Dictatorship Revisited." *Public Choice* 143: 67–101.

Chua, Beng Huat. 2005. "Taking Group Rights Seriously: Multiracialism in Singapore." Asia Research Centre Working Paper 124.

Cleary, Matthew, and Susan Stokes. 2006. *Democracy and the Culture of Skepticism: Political Trust in Argentina and Mexico.* New York: Russell Sage.

Coleman, James S. 1990. *Foundations of Social Theory.* Cambridge, Mass.: Harvard University Press.

Collier, David, Henry Brady, and Jason Seawright. 2004. "Sources of Leverage in Causal Inference: Toward an Alternative View of Methodology." In *Rethinking Social Inquiry,* ed. Henry Brady and David Collier. Lanham, Md.: Rowman and Littlefield.

Collier, David, Jody LaPorte, and Jason Seawright. 2012. "Putting Typologies to Work: Concept-Formation, Measurement, and Analytic Rigor." *Political Research Quarterly* 65: 217–32.

Collier, David, and Steve Levitsky. 1997. "Democracy with Adjectives: Conceptual In-
    novation in Comparative Research." *World Politics* 49: 430–51.
Collier, David, Jason Seawright, and Gerardo Munck. 2004. "The Quest for Standards:
    King, Keohane, and Verba's *Designing Social Inquiry.*" In *Rethinking Social Inquiry*,
    ed. Henry Brady and David Collier. Lanham, Md.: Rowman and Littlefield.
Collier, Paul, and Jan Willem Gunning. 1999. "Why Has Africa Grown Slowly?" *Journal
    of Economic Perspectives* 13: 3–22.
Collier, Ruth, and David Collier. 1991. *Shaping the Political Arena: Critical Junctures,
    the Labor Movement and Regime Dynamics in Latin America.* Princeton, N.J.: Prince-
    ton University Press.
Connor, Walker. 1973. "The Politics of Ethnonationalism." *Journal of International Affairs*
    27, 1: 1–21.
Costa, Dora L., and Matthew E. Kahn. 2003. "Civic Engagement in Heterogeneous Com-
    munities." *Perspectives on Politics* 1: 103–12.
Cowen, Robert, and Martin McLean. 1983. *International Handbook of Education Systems:
    Asia, Australasia, and Latin America.* Chichester: Wiley.
Cox, Gary W. 1997. *Making Votes Count: Strategic Coordination in the World's Electoral
    Systems.* New York: Cambridge University Press.
Cox, Gary W., and Matthew McCubbins. 2001. "The Institutional Determinants of Eco-
    nomic Policy." In *Presidents, Parliaments, and Policy*, ed. Stephan Haggard and
    Matthew McCubbins. New York: Cambridge University Press. 21–63.
Cribbs, Robert. 2008. "The Indonesian Massacres." In *Century of Genocide: Critical Es-
    says and Eyewitness Accounts*, ed. Samuel Totten and William S. Parsons. New York:
    Garland.
Crosby, Faye. 1976. "A Model of Egoistic Relative Deprivation." *Psychological Review*
    83: 85–113.
Crowley, Tony. 2005. "Whose Language Is It Anyway? The Irish and the English Language."
    In *The Contest of Language*, ed. W. Martin Bloomer. Notre Dame, Ind.: Notre Dame
    University Press. 165–84.
Crystal, David. 2003. *A Dictionary of Linguistics and Phonetics.* Malden, Mass.: Blackwell.
Darwin, John. 2008. *After Tamerlane: The Global History of Empire since 1405.* New
    York: Bloomsbury Press.
Das Gupta, Jyotirindra. 1970. *Language Conflict and National Development: Group Poli-
    tics and National Language Policy in India.* Berkeley: University of California Press.
Day, Peter. 2011. "Can Indonesia Join the BRIC Countries?" *BBC News*, February 17. Jakarta.
De Cremer, David, Daan van Knippenberg, Marius van Dijke, and Arjan E. R. Bos. 2004.
    "How Self-Relevant Is Fair Treatment?" *Social Justice Research* 17: 407–19.
De Mello, Luiz R., Jr. 1999. "Foreign Direct Investment-Led Growth: Evidence from
    Time Series and Panel Data." *Oxford Economic Papers* 51: 133–51.
De Mooij, Ruud A., and Sjef Ederveen. 2001. "Taxation and Foreign Direct Investment: A
    Synthesis of Empirical Research." CESifo Group Munich.

Deighton, Lee C. 1971. *The Encyclopedia of Education*. New York: Macmillan Free Press.

Delhey, Jan, and Kenneth Newton. 2005. "Predicting Cross-National Levels of Social Trust: Global Pattern or Nordic Exceptionalism?" *European Sociological Review* 21: 311–27.

Deschamps, Jean-Claude. 2010. "Social Identity and Relations of Power Between Groups." In *Social Identity and Intergroup Relations*, ed. Henri Tajfel. New York: Cambridge University Press. 85–98.

Deutsch, Karl W. 1953. *Nationalism and Social Communication: An Inquiry into the Foundations of Nationality*. Cambridge, Mass.: MIT Press.

DeVotta, Neil. 2003. "Nationalism and Ethnic Conflict in Sri Lanka." In *Fighting Words: Language Policy and Ethnic Relations in Asia*, ed. Michael E. Brown and Šumit Ganguly. Cambridge, Mass.: MIT Press.

Dick, William G. 1974. "Authoritarian Versus Nonauthoritarian Approaches to Economic Development." *Journal of Political Economy* 82: 817–27.

Dixon, L. Quentin. 2005. "Bilingual Education Policy in Singapore: An Analysis of Its Sociohistorical Roots and Current Academic Outcomes." *International Journal of Bilingual Education and Bilingualism* 8, 1: 25–47.

Doner, Richard F., Bryan K. Ritchie, and Dan Slater. 2005. "Systemic Vulnerability and the Origins of Developmental States." *International Organization* 59: 327–61.

Doshi, Tilak, and Peter Coclanis. 1999. "The Economic Architect: Goh Keng Swee." In *Lee's Lieutenants: Singapore's Old Guard*, ed. Penger Lam and K. Y. L. Tan. St. Leonards, N.S.W.: Allen and Unwin.

Drake, Christine. 1989. *National Integration in Indonesia*. Honolulu: University of Hawaii Press.

Dreyer, June Teufel. 2003. "The Evolution of Language Policies in China." In *Fighting Words: Language Policy and Ethnic Relations in Asia*, ed. Michael E. Brown and Šumit Ganguly. Cambridge, Mass.: MIT Press.

Duverger, Maurice. 1963. *Political Parties: Their Organization and Activity in the Modern State*. New York: Wiley.

Dworkin, Ronald. 2006. *Is Democracy Possible Here?* Princeton, N.J.: Princeton University Press.

Dwyer, Arienne M. 2005. *The Xinjiang Conflict: Uyghur Identity, Language Policy, and Political Discourse*. Washington, D.C.: East-West Center.

Eagle, Sonia. 2000. "The Language Situation in Nepal." In *Language Planning in Nepal, Taiwan and Sweden*, ed. Richard B. Baldauf, Jr., and Robert B. Kaplan. Clevedon: Multilingual Matters.

Easterly, William. 2001. *The Elusive Quest for Growth*. Cambridge, Mass.: MIT Press.

Easterly, William, and Ross Levine. 1997. "Africa's Growth Tragedy: Policies and Ethnic Divisions." *Quarterly Journal of Economics* 112: 1203–50.

Easton, David. 1953. *The Political System: An Inquiry into the State of Political Science*. New York: Knopf.

Elbadawi, Ibrahim, and Nicholas Sambanis. 2002. "How Much War Will We See? Estimating the Incidence of Civil War in 161 Countries, 1960–1999." *Journal of Conflict Resolution* 46: 307–34.

Elkins, Zachary, Andrew T. Guzman, and Beth A. Simmons. 2006. "Competing for Capital: The Diffusion of Bilateral Investment Treaties 1960–2000." *International Organization* 60: 811–46.

Engerman, Stanley L., and Kenneth L. Sokoloff. 1994. "Factor Endowments: Institutions and Differential Paths of Growth Among the New World Economies." National Bureau of Economic Research Historical Working Paper 66.

Englebert, Pierre. 2000. *State Legitimacy and Development in Africa*. Boulder, Colo.: Lynne Rienner.

EPP Group in the European Parliament. 2009. "New Slovak Language Law Does Not Comply with European Standards. " Press release, July 9.

Ericksen, Thomas Hylland. 1993. *Ethnicity and Nationalism: Anthropological Perspectives*. London: Pluto Press.

Esman, Milton J. 1987. "Ethnic Politics and Economic Power." *Comparative Politics* 19: 395–418.

Espinal, Rosario, Jonathan Hartlyn, and Jana Morgan Kelly. 2006. "Performance Still Matters." *Comparative Political Studies* 39: 200–223.

European Radio Network. 2009. "Hungary Attacks Slovak Language Law." August 4.

Evans, Peter. 1989. "Predatory, Developmental, and Other Apparatuses: A Comparative Political Economy Perspective on the Third World State." *Sociological Forum* 4: 561–587.

———. 1995. *Embedded Autonomy: States and Industrial Transformation*. Princeton, N.J.: Princeton University Press.

Farzad, Roben. 2010. "The BRIC Debate: Drop Russia, Add Indonesia?" *Bloomberg Businessweek*, November 10.

Fearon, James D. 2004. "Why Do Some Civil Wars Last So Much Longer Than Others?" *Journal of Peace Research* 41: 275–301.

Fearon, James D., Kimuli Kasara, and David D. Laitin. 2007. "Ethnic Minority Rule and Civil War Onset." *American Political Science Review* 101: 187–93.

Fearon, James D., and David D. Laitin. 1996. "Explaining Interethnic Cooperation." *American Political Science Review* 90: 715–35.

Feldstein, Martin. 2000. "Aspects of Global Economic Integration: Outlook for the Future." National Bureau of Economic Research Working Paper 7899.

Ferguson, Charles A. 1959. "Diglossia." *Word* 15: 325–40.

Fidrmuc, Jan, Victor Ginsburgh, and Shlomo Weber. 2007. "Ever Closer Union or Babylonian Discord? The Official-Language Problem in the European Union." CEPR Discussion Paper 6367.

Fierman, William. 2006. "Language and Education in Post-Soviet Kazakhstan: Kazakh-Medium Instruction in Urban Schools." *Russian Review* 65: 98–116.

Findlay, Ronald. 1990. "The New Political Economy: Its Explanatory Power for the LDCs." *Economics and Politics* 2: 193–221.

Fishman, Joshua A. 1989. *Language and Ethnicity in Minority Sociolinguistic Perspective*. Clevedon: Multilingual Matters.

———. 1991. *Reversing Language Shift: Theoretical and Empirical Foundations of Assistance to Threatened Languages*. Clevedon: Multilingual Matters.

Folger, Robert. 1984. "Perceived Injustice, Referent Cognitions, and the Concept of Comparison Level." *Representative Research in Social Psychology* 14: 88–108.

Fong, Sip Chee. 1979. *The PAP Story: The Pioneering Years*. Singapore: Times Periodicals.

Fox, Jonathan, and Deboray Flores. 2009. "Religions, Constitutions, and the State: A Cross-National Study." *Journal of Politics* 71: 1499–1513.

Frazer, James George. 1918. *Folk-Lore in the Old Testament*. London: Macmillan.

Froot, Kenneth A., and Jeremy C. Stein. 1991. "Exchange Rates and Foreign Direct Investment: An Imperfect Capital Markets Approach." *Quarterly Journal of Economics* 106, 4: 1191–1217.

Gambetta, Diego, and Heather Hamill. 2005. *Streetwise: How Taxi Drivers Establish Their Customers' Trustworthiness*. New York: Russell Sage.

Gandhi, Jennifer. 2008. *Political Institutions Under Dictatorship*. New York: Cambridge University Press.

Ganguly, Rajat. 2003. "Introduction." In *Ethnic Conflict and Secessionism in South and Southeast Asia*, ed. Rajat Ganguly and Ian Macduff. New Delhi: Sage.

Ganguly, Šumit. 2003. "The Politics of Language Policies in Malaysia and Singapore." In *Fighting Words: Language Policy and Ethnic Relations in Asia*, ed. Michael E. Brown and Šumit Ganguly. Cambridge, Mass.: MIT Press.

Geddes, Barbara. 1999. "What Do We Know About Democratization After Twenty Years?" *Annual Review of Political Science* 2: 115–44.

Geertz, Clifford. 1994. "Primordial and Civic Ties." In *Nationalism*, ed. John Hutchinson and Anthony D. Smith. New York: Oxford University Press.

Gellner, Ernest. 1983. *Nations and Nationalism*. Ithaca, N.Y.: Cornell University Press.

George, Alexander L., and Andrew Bennett. 2005. *Case Studies and Theory Development in the Social Sciences*. Cambridge, Mass.: Belfer Center for Science for International Affairs, Harvard University.

Gerring, John. 2007. *Case Study Research: Principles and Practices*. New York: Cambridge University Press.

Gilberg, Trond. 1992. "The Multiple Legacies of History: Romania in the Year 1990." In *The Columbia History of Eastern Europe in the Twentieth Century*, ed. Joseph Held. New York: Columbia University Press. 277–305.

Gill, SaranKaur. 2005. "Language Policy in Malaysia: Reversing Direction." *Language Policy* 4, 3: 241–60.

Ginsburg, Tom. 2003. *Judicial Review in New Democracies: Constitutional Courts in Asian Cases*. New York: Cambridge University Press.

Ginsburgh, Victor, and Shlomo Weber. 2011. *How Many Languages Do We Need?* Princeton, N.J.: Princeton University Press.

Gleditsch, Kristian S. 2002. "Expanded Trade and GDP Data." *Journal of Conflict Resolution* 46: 712–24.

Globerman, Steven, and Daniel Shapiro. 2002. "Global Foreign Direct Investment Flows: The Role of Governance Infrastructure." *World Development* 30: 1899–1919.

Gonzalez, Andrew. 1999. "The Language Planning Situation in the Philippines." In *Language Planning in Malawi, Mozambique, and the Philippines*, ed. Robert B. Kaplan and Richard B. Baldauf, Jr. Clevedon: Multilingual Matters.

Gopinathan, S. 1974. *Towards a National System of Education in Singapore 1945–1973*. Singapore: Oxford University Press.

———. 1998. "Language Policy Changes 1979–1997: Politics and Pedagogy." In *Language, Society and Education in Singapore: Issues and Trends*, ed. S. Gopinathan, A. Pakir, W. K. Ho, and V. Saravanan. Singapore: Times Academic Press.

Gradstein, Mark, Moshe Justman, and Volker Meier. 2005. *The Political Economy of Education: Implications for Growth and Inequality*. Cambridge, Mass.: MIT Press.

Grenoble, Lenore A. 2003. *Language Policy in the Soviet Union*. Dordrecht: Kluwer Academic.

Grier, Kevin B., and Gordon Tullock. 1989. "An Empirical Analysis of Cross-National Economic Growth." *Journal of Monetary Economics* 24: 259–76.

Grin, François. 2003. *Language Policy Evaluation and the European Charter for Regional or Minority Languages*. Basingstoke: Palgrave Macmillan.

Groeneboer, Kees. 1998. *Gateway to the West: The Dutch Language in Colonial Indonesia 1600–1950*. Trans. Myra Scholz. Amsterdam: University of Amsterdam.

Grossman, Gene M., and Elhanan Helpman. 1994. "Technology and Trade." National Bureau of Economic Research Working Paper 49264926.

Guiso, Luigi, Paola Sapienza, and Luigi Zingales. 2005. "Cultural Biases in Economic Exchange." National Bureau of Economic Research Working Paper 11005.

Gurr, Ted Robert. 1970. *Why Men Rebel*. Princeton, N.J.: Princeton Univesity Press.

Habib, Mohsin, and Leon Zurawicki. 2002. "Corruption and Foreign Direct Investment." *Journal of International Business Studies* 33: 291–307.

Habyarimana, James, Macartan Humphreys, Daniel N. Posner, and Jeremy Weinstein. 2007. "Why Does Ethnic Diversity Undermine Public Goods Provision?" *American Political Science Review* 101: 709–25.

———. 2009. *Coethnicity: Diversity and the Dilemmas of Collective Action*. New York: Russell Sage.

Hadenius, Axel, and Jan Teorell. 2005. "Cultural and Economic Prerequisites of Democracy: Reassessing Recent Evidence." *Studies in Comparative International Development* 39: 87–106.

Haji Omar, Asmah. 1979. *Language Planning for Unity and Efficiency: A Study of the Language Status and Corpus Planning of Malaysia*. Kuala Lumpur: University of Malaya Press.

Hakimzadeh, Shirin, and D'Vera Cohn. 2007. *English Usage Among Hispanics in the United States*. Washington, D.C.: Pew Hispanic Center.

Hall, Robert E., and Charles I. Jones. 1999. "Why Do Some Countries Produce So Much More Output per Worker Than Others?" *Quarterly Journal of Economics* 114: 83–116.

Hamilton, Alexander, James Madison, and John Jay. 1788/1961. *Federalist Papers*, ed. Clinton Rossiter. New York: Mentor Book. Cited in text by author and number.

Handoko, Francisca. 2008. "Mandarin the Educational Systems in the Indonesian Archipelago: Past, Present and Future." Paper presented at the International Workshop Language Change in Post New Order Indonesia. Depok, Indonesia.

Hardin, Russell. 2002. *Trust and Trustworthiness*. New York: Russell Sage.

Hashim, Azirah. 2003. "Language Policies and Language Education Issues in Malaysia." In *Babel or Behemoth: Language Trends in Asia*, ed. Jennifer Lindsay and Ying Ying Tan. Singapore: Asia Research Institute, National University of Singapore.

Hassan, Ahmad. 1988. *Bahasa Sastera Buku Cetusan Fikiran*. Kuala Lumpur: Dewan Bahasa dan Pustaka.

Hau, Caroline S., and Victoria L. Tinio. 2003. "Language Policy and Ethnic Relations in the Philippines." In *Fighting Words: Language Policy and Ethnic Relations in Asia*, ed. Michael E. Brown and Šumit Ganguly. Cambridge, Mass: MIT Press.

Helmke, Gretchen. 2002. "The Logic of Strategic Defection: Court-Executive Relations in Argentina Under Dictatorship and Democracy." *American Political Science Review* 96: 291–303.

———. 2005. *Courts Under Constraints: Judges, Generals, and Presidents in Argentina*. New York: Cambridge University Press.

Henisz, Witold J. 2000. "The Institutional Environment for Economic Growth." *Economics and Politics* 12: 1–31.

Hetherington, Marc J. 1998. "The Political Relevance of Political Trust." *American Political Science Review* 92: 781–808.

Hewitt, B. George. 1995. "Demographic Manipulation in the Caucasus (with Special Reference to Georgia)." *Journal of Refugee Studies* 8: 48–74.

Hirschl, Ran. 2000. "The Political Origins of Judicial Empowerment Through Constitutionalization: Lessons from Four Constitutional Revolutions." *Law and Social Inquiry* 25: 91–149.

———. 2004. "The Political Origins of the New Constitutionalism." *Indiana Journal of Global Legal Studies* 11: 71–108.

Hirschman, Charles. 1987. "The Meaning and Measurement of Ethnicity in Malaysia." *Journal of Asian Studies* 46: 555–82.

Hobsbawm, Eric. 1990. *Nations and Nationalism Since 1780*. New York: Cambridge University Press.

Hogan-Brun, Gabrielle, and Stefan Wolff. 2003. *Minority Languages in Europe: Frameworks, Status, and Prospects*. New York: Palgrave Macmillan.

Horowitz, Donald L. 1985. *Ethnic Groups in Conflict*. Berkeley: University of California Press.

———. 1991. *A Democratic South Africa? Constitutional Engineering in a Divided Society*. Berkeley: University of California Press.

Hull, Geoffrey. 2000. "Current Language Issues in East Timor." Public lecture, University of Adelaide, Adelaide, Australia, March 29.

Huntington, Samuel P. 1996. *The Clash of Civilizations and the Remaking of World Order.* New York: Simon and Schuster.

Huo, Y. Juen, Heather J. Smith, Tom R. Tyler, and E. Allan Lind. 1996. "Superordinate Identification, Subgroup Identification and Justice Concerns." *Psychological Science* 7: 40–45.

Ibrahim, Muhammad H. 1985. "Communicating in Arabic: Problems and Prospects." Paper at Conference on Vernacular Languages for Modern Societies, Bad Homburg, West Germany, June 11–15.

Ibrahim, Zuraidah. 1999. "The Malay Mobilisers: Ahmad Ibrahim, Othman Wok, Yaacob Mohamed, and Rahim Ishak." In *Lee's Lieutenants: Singapore's Old Guard,* ed. Peng Er Lam and Kevin Y. L. Tan. St. Leonards, N.S.W.: Allen and Unwin.

Ignatius, Adi. 2000. "Asia Buzz: Korean Kut-Up." *Time,* March 27.

Inglehart, Ronald. 1990. *Culture Shift in Advanced Industrial Society.* Princeton, N.J.: Princeton University Press.

International Monetary Fund (IMF). 2013. "Direction of Trade Statistics." https://www .imf.org/external/pubs/cat/longres.cfm?sk=19305.0.

Iwasaki, John. 2002. "Bilingual Ballots Draw Protests." *Seattle Post-Intelligencer,* October 17.

Jamal, Amaney, and Irfan Nooruddin. 2010. "The Democratic Utility of Trust: A Cross-National Analysis." *Journal of Politics* 72: 45–59.

Jensen, John B. 1989. "On the Mutual Intelligibility of Spanish and Portuguese." *Hispania* 72: 848–52.

Jensen, Nathan. 2008. "Political Risk, Democratic Institutions, and Foreign Direct Investment." *Journal of Politics* 70: 1040–52.

Johnson, Roger T. 2010. *Historical Beginnings . . . The Federal Reserve.* Boston: Federal Reserve Bank of Boston.

Jomo, K. S. 2004. "The New Economic Policy and Interethnic Relations in Malaysia." Identities, Conflict and Cohesion, Program Paper 7. Geneva: UN Research Institute for Social Development.

Kaplan, Robert B., and Richard B. Baldauf, Jr. 1997. *Language Planning.* Clevedon: Multilingual Matters.

———. 2003. *Language and Language-in-Education Planning in the Pacific Basin.* Dordrecht: Kluwer Academic.

Kaske, Elisabeth. 2008. *The Politics of Language in Chinese Education 1895–1919.* Boston: Brill.

Kassim, Ismail. 1974. *Problems of Elite Cohesion: A Perspective from a Minority Community.* Singapore: Singapore University Press.

Kawachi, Ichiro, S.V. Subramanian, and Daniel Kim. 2010. *Social Capital and Health.* New York: Springer.

Keefer, Philip. 2012. "Database of Political Institutions." http://econ.worldbank.org/WB SITE/EXTERNAL/EXTDEC/EXTRESEARCH/0,,contentMDK:20649465 ~pagePK:64214825~piPK:64214943~theSitePK:469382,00.html

Keele, Luke. 2005. "The Authorities Really Do Matter: Party Control and Trust in Government." *Journal of Politics* 67: 873–86.

Keeler, Ward. 1984. *Javanese: A Cultural Approach.* Athens: Ohio University Press.

Kelleher, Christine, and Jennifer Wolak. 2007. "Explaining Public Confidence in the Branches of State Government." *Political Research Quarterly* 60: 707–21.

Keyes, Charles F. 1997. "Cultural Diversity and National Identity in Thailand." In *Government Policies and Ethnic Relations in Asia and the Pacific*, ed. Michael E. Brown and Šumit Ganguly. Cambridge, Mass.: MIT Press.

———. 2003. "The Politics of Language in Thailand and Laos." In *Fighting Words: Language Policy and Ethnic Relations in Asia*, ed. Michael E. Brown and Šumit Ganguly. Cambridge, Mass.: MIT Press.

Kim, Moonhawk, Amy H. Liu, Kim-Lee Tuxhorn, David S. Brown, and David Leblang. 2015. "Lingua Mercatoria: Language and Foreign Direct Investments." *International Studies Quarterly* (Forthcoming).

King, Charles. 2000. *The Moldovans.* Stanford, Calif.: Stanford University Press.

King, Herbert W. H. 1954. "The Canberra-Queanbeyan Symbiosis: A Study of Urban Mutualism." *Geographical Review* 44: 101–18.

Kirton, John. 1999. "The G7 and China in the Management of the International Financial System." Paper for forum China in the 21st Century and the World, sponsored by China Development Institute, China International Center for Economic and Technical Exchange, and the National Institute for Research Advancement, Japan, at Shenzen, China, November 11–12.

Knack, Stephen, and Philip Keefer. 1997. "Does Social Capital Have an Economic Payoff? A Cross-Country Investigation." *Quarterly Journal of Economics* 112: 1251–88.

Knight, Jack. 1992. *Institutions and Social Conflict.* New York: Cambridge University Press.

Kogut, Bruce, and Harbir Singh. 1988. "The Effect of National Culture on the Choice of Entry Mode." *Journal of International Business Studies* 19: 411–32.

Koper, Gerda, Daan Van Knippenberg, Francien Bouhuijs, Riel Vermunt, and Henk Wilke. 1993. "Procedural Fairness and Self-Esteem." *European Journal of Social Psychology* 23: 313–25.

Kukathas, Chandran. 2003. *The Liberal Archipelago: A Theory of Diversity and Freedom.* Oxford: Oxford University Press.

Kwok, Kian-Woon. 1999. "The Social Architect: Goh Keng Swee." In *Lee's Lieutenants: Singapore's Old Guard*, ed. Peng Er Lam and Kevin Y. L. Tan. St. Leonards, N.S.W.: Allen and Unwin.

Kymlicka, Will. 1995. *Multicultural Citizenship: A Liberal Theory of Minority Rights.* Oxford: Clarendon.

La Porta, Rafael, Florencio Lopez-de-Silanes, Andrei Shleifer, and Robert W. Vishny. 1999. "The Quality of Government." *Journal of Law, Economics, and Organization* 15: 222–79.

Laitin, David D. 1977. *Politics, Language, and Thought.* Chicago: University of Chicago Press.

———. 1988. "Language Games." *Comparative Politics* 20: 289–302.

———. 1992. *Language Repertoires and State Construction in Africa.* New York: Cambridge University Press.

———. 1994. "The Tower of Babel as a Coordination Game: Political Linguistics in Ghana." *American Political Science Review* 88: 622–34.

———. 1998. *Identity in Formation.* Ithaca, N.Y.: Cornell University Press.

———. 2000. "What Is a Language Community?" *American Journal of Political Science* 44: 142–55.

Laitin, David D., and Rob Reich. 2003. "A Liberal Democratic Approach to Language Justice." In *Language Rights and Political Theory*, ed. Will Kymlicka and Allan Patten. Oxford: Oxford University Press.

Lake, David A., and Matthew Baum. 2001. "The Invisible Hand of Democracy: Political Control and the Provision of Public Services." *Comparative Political Studies* 34: 587–621.

Landau, Jacob M., and Barbara Kellner-Heinkele. 2001. *Politics of Language in the Ex-Soviet Muslim States.* Ann Arbor: University of Michigan Press.

Lane, Philip R., and Gian Milesi-Ferretti. 2004. *International Investment Patterns.* IMF Working Paper 04 (134).

Laponce, Jean A. 2006. *Loi de Babel et autres régularités des rapports entre langue et politique.* Lévis, Québec: Presses de l'Université Laval.

Lasswell, Harold D. 1936. *Politics: Who Gets What, When, How.* New York: McGraw-Hill.

Lavedan, Pierre. 1936. *Géographie des villes.* Paris: Gallimard.

Leblang, David. 2010. "Familiarity Breeds Investment: Diaspora Networks and International Investment." *American Political Science Review* 104: 584–600.

Leclerc, Jacques 2010. "L'aménagement linguistique dans le monde." http://www.tlfq.ula val.ca/axl/.

Lee, Alexander, and Kenneth A. Schultz. 2012. "Comparing British and French Colonial Legacies: A Discontinuity Analysis of Cameroon." *Quarterly Journal of Political Science* 7, 4: 365–410.

Lee, Hock Guan. 2007. "Ethnic Politics, National Development and Language Policy in Malaysia." In *Language, Nation and Development in Southeast Asia*, ed. H. G. Lee and L. Suryadinata. Singapore: Institute of Southeast Asian Studies.

Lee, Hock Guan, and Leo Suryadinata, eds. 2007. *Language, Nation and Development in Southeast Asia.* Singapore: Institute of Southeast Asian Studies.

Lee, Khoon Choy. 1988. *On the Beat to the Hustings.* Singapore: Times Centre.

Lee, Kuan Yew. 1998. *The Singapore Story: Memoirs of Lee Kuan Yew.* Singapore: Prentice Hall.

———. 2000. *From Third World to First: The Singapore Story*. Singapore: Times Media.

———. 2013. *One Man's View of the World*. Singapore: Strait Times.

Lenin, Vladimir I. 1905. "От Народничества К Марксизму" [From Populism to Marxism]. *Вперед* 24: 190–97.

Levi, Margaret. 1996. "Making Democracy Work: Review." *Politics and Society* 24: 45–55.

Lewis, Paul M. 2009. *Ethnologue: Languages of the World*. Dallas: SIL International.

Li, Tania. 1989. *Malays in Singapore: Culture, Economy, and Ideology*. Singapore: Oxford University Press.

Lieberman, Evan S. 2005. "Nested Analysis as a Mixed-Method Strategy for Comparative Research." *American Political Science Review* 99: 435–52.

Lien, Donald, Hoon Oh Chang, and W. Travis Selmier. 2011. "Confucius Institute Effects on China's Trade and FDI: Isn't It Delightful When Folks Afar Study Hanyu?" *International Review of Economics and Finance* 21: 147–55.

Lieven, Dominic, and John McGarry. 1993. "Ethnic Conflict in the Soviet Union and Its Successor States." In *The Politics of Ethnic Conflict Regulation: Case Studies of Protracted Ethnic Conflicts*, ed. John McGarry and Brendan O'Leary. London: Routledge.

Lijphart, Arend. 1968. *The Politics of Accommodation: Pluralism and Democracy in the Netherlands*. Berkeley: University of California Press.

Lijphart, Arend. 1977. *Democracy in Plural Societies: A Comparative Exploration*. New Haven: Yale University Press.

———. 1999. *Patterns of Democracy*. New Haven, Conn.: Yale University Press.

———. 2002. "The Wave of Power-Sharing Democracy." In *The Architecture of Democracy*, ed. Andrew Reynolds. New York: Oxford University Press. 37–54.

Lind, E. Allan, Ruth Kanfer, and P. Christopher Early. 1990. "Voice, Control, and Procedural Justice." *Journal of Personality and Social Psychology* 59: 971–80.

Linz, Juan. 1994. "Presidential or Parliamentary Democracy: Does It Make a Difference?" In *The Failure of Presidential Democracy: Comparative Perspectives*, ed. Juan Linz and Arturo Valenzuela. Baltimore: Johns Hopkins University Press.

Lipset, Seymour Martin. 1959. "Some Social Requisites of Democracy: Economic Development and Political Legitimacy." *American Political Science Review* 53: 69–105.

Liu, Amy H. 2011. "The Linguistic Effects of Political Institutions." *Journal of Politics* 73: 125–39.

Liu, Amy H., and Vanessa Baird. 2012. "Linguistic Recognition as a Source of Confidence in the Justice System." *Comparative Political Studies* 45: 1203–1229.

Liu, Amy H., David S. Brown, and Meghan Harrington. 2014 "Minority Language Recognition and Trust in Democracies." Typescript. University of Texas, University of Colorado, and University of California Berkeley.

Liu, Amy H., and Jacob I. Ricks. 2012. "Coalitions and Language Politics: Policy Shifts in Southeast Asia." *World Politics* 64: 476–506.

Lynch, Colum. 2010. "How a Translation Error Led to an International Incident." *Foreign Policy,* February 2.

Lopes, Armando Jorge. 1999. "The Language Situation in Mozambique." In *Language Planning in Malawi, Mozambique, and the Philippines*, ed. Robert B. Kaplan and Richard B. Baldauf, Jr. Clevedon: Multilingual Matters. 85–133.

Machiavelli, Niccolo. 1532/1997. *The Prince*. Trans. A. M. Codevilla. New Haven, Conn.: Yale University Press.

MacIntyre, Andrew. 2001. "Institutions and Investors: The Politics of the Economic Crisis in Southeast Asia." *International Organization* 55: 81–122.

Mahoney, James. 2000. "Path Dependence in Historical Sociology." *Theory and Society* 29: 507–48.

———. 2010. "After KKV: The New Methodology of Qualitative Research." *World Politics* 62: 120–47.

Mahoney, James, and Gary Goertz. 2004. "The Possibility Principle: Choosing Negative Cases in Comparative Research." *American Political Science Review* 98: 653–69.

Makki, Shiva S., and Agapi Somwaru. 2004. "Impact of Foreign Direct Investment and Trade on Economic Growth: Evidence from Developing Countries." *American Journal of Agricultural Economics* 86: 795–801.

Malik, Adam. 1980. *In the Service of the Republic*. Singapore: Gunung Agung.

Marschall, Melissa J., and Dietlind Stolle. 2004. "Race and the City: Neighborhood Context and the Development of Generalized Trust." *Political Behavior* 26: 125–53.

Marshall, Monty G., and Keith Jaggers. 2008. *Polity IV Project*. http://www.systemic peace.org/polity/polity4.htm.

Matthews, Roderic D. 2007. *Education in Arab Countries of the Near East*. Cookhill: Read Books.

May, R. J. 2003. "Harmonizing Linguistic Diversity in Papua New Guinea." In *Fighting Words: Language Policy and Ethnic Relations in Asia*, ed. Michael E. Brown and Šumit Ganguly. Cambridge, Mass.: MIT Press.

Mayhew, David. 1974. *Congress: The Electoral Connection*. New Haven, Conn.: Yale University Press.

MCA. 2010. "Party History." http://www.mca.org.my/en/about-us/about-mca/history-zone /party-history/.

McColm, R. Bruce. 1990. *Freedom in the World: Political Rights and Civil Liberties*. New York: Freedom House.

McCrudden, Christopher, and Brendan O'Leary. 2013. *Courts and Consociations: Human Rights Versus Power-Sharing*. Oxford: Oxford University Press.

McEvoy, Joanne, and Brendan O'Leary, eds. 2013. *Power-Sharing in Deeply Divided Places*. Philadelphia: University of Pennsylvania Press.

McGarry, John, and Brendan O'Leary. 2004. *The Northern Ireland Conflict: Consociational Engagements*. Oxford: Oxford University Press.

———. 2007. "Iraq's Constitution of 2005: Liberal Consociation as Political Prescription." *International Journal of Constitutional Law* 5: 670–98.

McGarry, John, Brendan O'Leary, and Richard Simeon. 2008. "Integration or Accommodation? The Enduring Debate in Conflict Regulation." In *Constitutional Design for Divided Societies: Integration or Accommodation?*, ed. Sujit Choudhry. Oxford: Oxford University Press. 41–88.

Means, Gordon P. 1991. *Malaysian Politics: The Second Generation*. Singapore: Oxford University Press.

Mill, John Stuart. 1859/1989. *On Liberty*. Ed. Stefan Collini. Cambridge: Cambridge University Press.

Mishler, William, and Richard Rose. 1997. "Trust, Distrust, and Skepticism: Popular Evaluations of Civil and Political Institutions in Post-Communist Societies." *Journal of Politics* 59: 418–51.

Mitchell, Brian R. 2008. *International Historical Statistics: Africa, Asia and Oceania, 1750–2005*. New York: Palgrave Macmillan.

Mody, Ashoka, and Krishna Srinivasan. 1998. "Japanese and US Firms as Foreign Investors: Do They March to the Same Tune?" *Canadian Journal of Economics* 31: 778–99.

Moe, Terry M. 2005. "Power and Political Institutions." *Perspectives on Politics* 3: 215–33.

Mohr, Marie V. 1984. *The Call of the Hibiscus*. Singapore: Gunung Agung.

Mohsin, Amena. 2003. "Language, Identity, and the State in Bangladesh." In *Fighting Words: Language Policy and Ethnic Relations in Asia*, ed. Michael E. Brown and Šumit Ganguly. Cambridge, Mass.: MIT Press.

"Monetary Authority of Singapore." 2013. http: //www.mas.gov.sg.

Montolalu, Lucy R., and Leo Suryadinata. 2007. "National Language and Nation-Building: The Case of Bahasa Indonesia." In *Language, Nation and Development in Southeast Asia*, ed. H. G. Lee and L. Suryadinata. Singapore: Institute of Southeast Asian Studies.

Moore, Elaine. 2012. "Civets, Brics and the Next 11." *Financial Times*, June 8.

Moore, Jonathan. 1984. "The Political History of Nigeria's New Capital." *Journal of Modern African Studies* 22: 167–75.

Mowbray, Jacqueline. 2012. *Linguistic Justice: International Law and Language Policy*. Oxford: Oxford University Press.

Muller, Edward N., and Mitchell Seligson. 1994. "Civic Culture and Democracy: The Question of Causal Relationships." *American Political Science Review* 88: 635–52.

Mydans, Seth. 2007. "A New Country's Tough Non-Elective: Portuguese 101." *New York Times*, July 31.

Nair, E. Shailaja. 2008. *The Master Sculptor: Goh Keng Swee*. Singapore: SNP Editions.

Newton, Kenneth. 1999. "Social Capital and Democracy in Modern Europe." In *Social Capital and European Democracy*, ed. Jan W. van Deth, Marco Maraffi, Kenneth Newton, and Paul F. Whiteley. New York: Routledge.

Norris, Pippa. 2008. *Driving Democracy: Do Power-Sharing Institutions Work?* New York: Cambridge University Press.

North, Douglass C. 1990. *Institutions, Institutional Change, and Economic Performance*. New York: Cambridge University Press.

North, Douglass C., and Barry R. Weingast. 1989. "Constitutions and Commitment: The Evolution of Institutions Governing Public Choice in Seventeenth-Century England." *Journal of Economic History* 49, 4: 803–32.

Nunan, David. 2003. "The Impact of English as a Global Language on Educational Poli-cies and Practices in the Asia-Pacific Region." *TESOL Quarterly* 37, 4: 589–613.

O'Leary, Brendan. 1989. "The Limits to Coercive Consociationalism in Northern Ire-land." *Political Studies* 37, 4: 562–87.

———. 2010. "Thinking About Asymmetry and Symmetry in the Remaking of Iraq." In *Asymmetric Autonomy and the Settlement of Ethnic Conflicts*, ed. Marc Weller and Katharine Nobbs. Philadelphia: University of Pennsylvania Press.

O'Leary, Brendan, Ian Lustick, and Thomas Callaghy, eds. 2001. *Right-Sizing the State: The Politics of Moving Borders*. Oxford: Oxford University Press.

O'Leary, Brendan, and John McGarry. 2012. "The Politics of Accommodation and Inte-gration in Democratic States." In *The Study of Politics and Ethnicity: Recent Ana-lytical Developments*, ed. Adrian Guelke and Jean Tournon, 779–116. Leverkusen, Germany: Barbara Budrich.

O'Neill, Jim, Dominic Wilson, Roopa Purushothaman, and Anna Stupnytska. 2005. "How Solid Are the BRICs?" Global Economics Paper 134. New York: Goldman Sachs.

Offe, Claus. 1999. "How Can We Trust Our Fellow Citizens?" In *Democracy and Trust*, ed. M. Warren. Cambridge: Cambridge University Press. 42–87.

Oliver, J. Eric, and Janelle Wong. 2003. "Intergroup Prejudice in Multiethnic Settings." *American Journal of Political Science* 47: 567–82.

Olson, Mancur. 1965. *The Logic of Collective Action: Public Goods and the Theory of Groups*. Cambridge, Mass.: Harvard University Press.

———. 1993. "Dictatorship, Democracy, and Development." *American Political Science Review* 87: 567–76.

Orlando Sentinel. 1993. "Miscommunication Requires Yes or No Answer." April 11.

Osborne, Milton. 1997. *Southeast Asia: An Introductory History*. St. Leonards, N.S.W.: Allen and Unwin.

Ostler, Nicholas. 2006. *Empires of the Word: A Language History of the World*. New York: HarperPerennial.

———. 2010. *The Last Lingua Franca: English Until the Return of Babel*. New York: Walker.

Ostrom, Elinor. 1990. *Governing the Commons*. New York: Cambridge University Press.

Paulston, Christina Bratt. 2003. "Language Policies and Language Rights." In *Sociolin-guistics*, ed. C. B. Paulston and G. R. Tucker. Malden, Mass.: Blackwell. 472–82.

Pavlenko, Aneta. 2006. "Russian as a Lingua Franca." *Annual Review of Applied Linguis-tics* 26: 78–99.

Penders, C. L. M., ed. 1981. *Mohammad Hatta, Indonesian Patriot: Memoirs*. Singapore: Gunung Agung.

Pepinsky, Thomas. 2009. *Economic Crises and the Breakdown of Authoritarian Regimes*. New York: Cambridge University Press.

Pepinsky, Thomas, R. William Liddle, and Saiful Mujani. 2010. "Indonesian Democracy and the Transformation of Political Islam." Paper presented at Annual Meeting of the Association for Asian Studies, Philadelphia.

Poe, Steven C., and C. Neal Tate. 1994. "Repression of Human Rights to Personal Integrity in the 1980s: A Global Analysis." *American Political Science Review* 88: 853–72.

Poe, Steven C., C. Neal Tate, and Linda Camp Keith. 1999. "Repression of the Human Right to Personal Integrity Revisited: A Global Cross-National Study Covering the Years 1976–1993." *International Studies Quarterly* 43: 291–313.

Pool, Jonathan. 1991. "The Official Language Problem." *American Political Science Review* 85: 495–514.

Portes, Alejandro. 1998. "Social Capital: Its Origins and Applications in Modern Sociology." *Annual Review of Sociology* 24: 1–24.

Posner, Daniel N. 2004. "Measuring Ethnic Fractionalization in Africa." *American Journal of Political Science* 48: 849–63.

Pourgerami, Abbas. 1991. "The Political Economy of Development: An Empirical Investigation of the Wealth Theory of Democracy." *Journal of Theoretical Politics* 3: 189–211.

Przeworski, Adam, Michael E. Alvarez, Jose Antonio Cheibub, and Fernando Limongi. 2000. *Democracy and Development*. New York: Cambridge University Press.

Przeworski, Adam, and Fernando Limongi. 1993. "Political Regimes and Economic Growth." *Journal of Economic Perspectives* 7: 51–69.

———. 1997. "Modernization: Theories and Facts." *World Politics* 49: 155–83.

Przeworski, Adam, and Harry Teune. 1970. *The Logic of Comparative Social Inquiry*. New York: Wiley-Interscience.

PuruShotam, Nirmala. 1998. "Disciplining Difference." In *Southeast Asian Identities*, ed. Joel S. Kahn. New York: St. Martin's.

Putnam, Robert D. 1995. *Making Democracy Work: Civic Traditions in Modern Italy*. Princeton, N.J.: Princeton University Press.

———. 2000. *Bowling Alone*. New York: Simon and Schuster.

———. 2007. "E Pluribus Unum: Diversity and Community in the Twenty-First Century." *Scandinavian Political Studies* 30: 137–74.

Quillian, Lincoln. 1995. "Prejudice as a Response to Perceived Group Threat: Population Composition and Anti-Immigration and Racial Prejudice in Europe." *American Sociological Review* 60: 586–611.

———. 1996. "Group Threat and Regional Change in Attitudes Toward African Americans." *American Journal of Sociology* 102: 816–60.

Rahim, Lily Zubaidah. 1998. *The Singapore Dilemma: The Political and Educational Marginality of the Malay Community*. Oxford: Oxford University Press.

Rahman Embong, Abdul. 2004. "Language, Nationhood, and Globalization: The Case of Malaysia." In *Globalization, Culture, and Inequalities*, ed. A. Rahman Embong. Bangi: Universiti Kebangsaan Malaysia.

Rahman Putra, Abdul. 1978. *Viewpoints*. Kuala Lumpur: Heinemann Educational Books.

—. 1986. *Political Awakening*. Petaling Jaya, Malaysia: Pelanduk.

Rajakumar, M. K. 2001. "Lim Chin Siong's Place in Singapore History." In *Comet in Our Sky: Lim Chin Siong in History*, ed. J. Q. Tang and K. S. Jomo. Kuala Lumpur: INSAN.

Rappa, Antonio, and Lionel Wee. 2006. *Language Policy and Modernity in Southeast Asia*. New York: Springer.

Rasiah, Rajah. 1997. "Class, Ethnicity and Economic Development in Malaysia." In *The Political Economy of South-East Asia*, ed. Garry Rodan, Kevin Hewison, and Richard Robison. Melbourne: Oxford University Press.

Regan, Patrick, and David Clark. 2010. "The Institutions and Elections Project Data Collection." http://www2.binghamton.edu/political-science/institutions-and-elections-project .html.

Reid, Anthony. 1974. *The Indonesian National Revolution, 1945–1950*. Hawthorn, Victoria: Longman.

Reilly, Ben. 1997. "The Alternative Vote and Ethnic Accommodation: New Evidence from Papua New Guinea." *Electoral Studies* 16: 1–11.

Reingold, Beth. 2008. "Women as Office Holders: Linking Descriptive and Substantive Representation." In *Political Women and American Democracy*, ed. Christina Wolbrecht, Karen Beckwith, and Lisa Baldez. New York: Cambridge University Press.

Reyna-Querol, Marta. 2002. "Ethnicity, Political Systems and Civil Wars." *Journal of Conflict Resolution* 46: 29–54.

Reynolds, Andrew. 2002. *The Architecture of Democracy*. New York: Oxford University Press.

Rice, Tom, and Brent Steele. 2001. "White Ethnic Diversity and Community Attachment in Small Iowa Towns." *Social Science Quarterly* 82: 397–407.

Ricks, Jacob I. 2008. "National Identity and the Geo-Soul: Spiritually Mapping Siam." *Studies in Ethnicity and Nationalism* 8: 120–141.

Riker, William. 1982. "The Two Party System and Duverger's Law." *American Political Science Review* 76: 753–66.

Rodrik, Dani. 1999. "Where Did All the Growth Go? External Shocks, Social Conflict and Growth Collapses." *Journal of Economic Growth* 4: 385–412.

Romer, Paul M. 1986. "Increasing Returns and Long-Run Growth." *Journal of Political Economy* 94: 1002–1037.

———. 1994. "The Origins of Endogenous Growth." *The Journal of Economic Perspectives* 8: 3–22.

Rosenbluth, Frances, and Ross Schaap. 2002. "The Domestic Politics of Banking Regulation." *International Organization* 57, 2: 307–36.

Ross, Michael L. 2001. "Does Oil Hinder Democracy?" *World Politics* 53: 325–361.

Rothstein, Bo, and Eric Uslaner. 2005. "All for All: Equality, Corruption and Social Capital." *World Politics* 58: 41–72.

Sadurski, Wojciech. 2008. *Equality and Legitimacy*. Oxford: Oxford University Press.

Safran, William. 2005. "Introduction: The Political Aspects of Language." In *Language, Ethnic Identity, and the State*, ed. William Safran and J. A. Laponce. New York: Routledge.

———. 2010. "Political Science and Politics." In *Handbook of Language and Ethnic Identity*, ed. Joshua A. Fishman and Ofelia García. New York: Oxford University Press.

Safran, William, and Amy H Liu. 2012. Nation-Building, Collective Identity, and Language Choices: Between Instrumental and Value Rationalities. *Nationalism and Ethnic Politics* 18, 3: 269–292.

Saguaro Seminar. 2001. *Social Capital Community Benchmark Survey.* Cambridge, Mass.: Saguaro Seminar of the John F. Kennedy School of Government at Harvard University.

SarDesai, D. R. 2010. *Southeast Asia: Past and Present.* Boulder, Colo.: Westview Press.

Sartori, Giovanni. 1970. "Concept Misformation in Comparative Politics." *American Political Science Review* 64: 1033–53.

Scherer, Nancy, and Brett Curry. 2010. "Does Descriptive Race Representation Enhance Institutional Legitimacy? The Case of the U.S. Courts." *Journal of Politics* 72: 90–104.

Schmidt, Ronald. 1998. "The Politics of Language in Canada and the United States: Explaining the Differences." In *Language and Politics in the United States and Canada,* ed. Thomas Ricento and Barbara Burnaby. Mahwah, N.J.: Erlbaum.

Seawright, Jason, and John Gerring. 2008. "Case Selection Techniques in Case Study Research." *Political Research Quarterly* 61: 294–308.

Shaw, William. 1976. *Tun Razak: His Life and Times.* Kuala Lumpur: Longman.

Short, Philip. 2006. *Pol Pot: Anatomy of a Nightmare.* New York: Owl Books.

Shoup, Brian D. 2011. "Ethnic Redistribution in Bipolar Societies: The Crafting of Asymmetric Policy Claims in Two Asia-Pacific States." *Perspectives on Politics* 9: 785–802.

Simandjuntak, B. 1969. *Malayan Federalism 1945–1963.* Kuala Lumpur: Oxford University Press.

Skinner, G. Williams. 1958. "The Chinese of Java." In *Colloquium on Overseas Chinese,* ed. M. H. Fried. New York: Institute of Pacific Relations.

———. 1963. "The Chinese Minority." In *Indonesia,* ed. Ruth T. McVey. New Haven, Conn.: HRAF Press.

Skutnabb-Kangas, Tove. 1996. "The Colonial Legacy in Educational Language Planning in Scandinavia: From Migrant Labor to a National Ethnic Minority?" *International Journal of the Sociology of Language* 118, 1: 81–106.

———. 2000. *Linguistic Genocide in Education—or Worldwide Diversity and Human Rights?* Mahwah, N.J.: Erlbaum.

Slater, Dan. 2003. "Iron Cage in an Iron Fist: Authoritarian Institutions and the Personalization of Power in Malaysia." *Comparative Politics* 36: 81–101.

———. 2004. "Indonesia's Accountability Trap: Party Cartels and Presidential Power After Democratic Transition." *Indonesia* 78: 61–92.

———. 2010. *Ordering Power: Contentious Politics and Authoritarian Leviathans in Southeast Asia.* New York: Cambridge University Press.

Smith, Anthony D. 2000. *The Nation in History.* Hanover, N.H.: Brandeis University Press.

Solow, Robert M. 1956. "A Contribution to the Theory of Economic Growth." *Quarterly Journal of Economics* 70: 65–94.

Spate, O. H. K. 1942. "Factors in the Development of Capital Cities." *Geographical Review* 32: 622–31.

Stasavage, David. 2005. "Democracy and Education Spending in Africa." *American Journal of Political Science* 49: 343–58.

Staton, Jeffrey K. 2006. "Constitutional Review and the Selective Promotion of Case Results." *American Political Science Review* 50: 98–112.

Stepan, Alfred. 2000. "Religion, Democracy, and the 'Twin Tolerations'." *Journal of Democracy* 11: 37–57.

Stern, Bernhard J. 1944. "Soviet Policy on National Minorities." *American Sociological Review* 9, 3: 229–35.

Stokes, Donald E. 1966. "Some Dynamic Elements of Contests for the Presidency." *American Political Science Review* 60, 1: 19–28.

Strait Times (Singapore). 1982. "MENDAKI Can Make the Difference, But . . . 'No Quick Fix-It Says PM.' " May 29.

Stuligross, David, and Ashutosh Varshney. 2002. "Ethnic Diversities, Constitutional Designs, and Public Policies in India." In *The Architecture of Democracy: Constitutional Design, Conflict Management, and Democracy*, ed. Andrew Reynolds. New York: Oxford University Press.

Sugar, Peter F., Péter Hanák, and Tibor Frank. 1994. *A History of Hungary*. Bloomington: Indiana University Press.

Sunday Times (Singapore). 1959a. "Translating Done Free During L-Week." March 25.

———. 1959b. "Institute of Malayan Culture." August 23.

———. 1966. "Ong: There's No Language Issue." November 22.

Suny, Ronald Grigor. 1994. *The Making of the Georgian Nation*. Stanford, Calif.: Stanford University Press.

Tajfel, Henri, ed. 1982. *Social Identity and Intergroup Relations*. New York: Cambridge University Press.

Tajfel, Henri, and John C. Turner. 1979. "An Integrative Theory of Intergroup Conflict." *Social Psychology of Intergroup Relations* 33: 47.

———. 1985. "The Social Identity Theory of Intergroup Behavior." In *Psychology of Intergroup Relations*, ed. Stephen Worchel and William G. Austin. Chicago: Nelson-Hall.

Tan, Eugene K. B. 2007. "The Multilingual State in Search of the Nation: The Language Policy and Discourse in Singapore's Nation-Building." In *Language, Nation and Development in Southeast Asia*, ed. H. G. Lee and L. Suryadinata. Singapore: Institute of Southeast Asian Studies.

Tan, Siok Sun. 2007. *Goh Keng Swee: A Portrait*. Singapore: Didier Millet.

Taylor, Paul, Mark Hugo Lopez, Jessica Martínez, and Gabriel Velasco. 2012. *When Labels Don't Fit: Hispanics and Their Views of Identity*. Washington, D.C.: Pew Hispanic Center.

Taylor, Rupert. 2009. *Consociational Theory: McGarry and O'Leary and the Northern Ireland Conflict*. Abingdon: Routledge.

Tendler, Judith. 2002. "Small Firms, the Informal Sector, and the Devil's Deal." *IDS Bulletin* 33: 1–15.

Thapar, Romila. 2012. *Aśoka and the Decline of the Mauryas*. Oxford: Oxford University Press.

Thee, Kian Wie. 2010. "Indonesia's Economy Continues to Surprise." *East Asia Forum*, September 25.

Thelen, Kathleen. 2004. *How Institutions Evolve: The Political Economy of Skills in Germany, Britain, the United States, and Japan*. New York: Cambridge University Press.

Thibaut, John, and Laurens Walker. 1975. *Procedural Justice*. Hillsdale, N.J.: Earlbaum.

Tilly, Charles. 1975. "Reflections on the History of European State-Making." In *The Formation of National States in Western Europe*, ed. Charles Tilly and Gabriel Ardant. Princeton, N.J.: Princeton University Press.

Tocqueville, Alexis de. 1835/2002. *Democracy in America*. Ed. Harvey Mansfield and Delba Winthrop. Chicago: University of Chicago Press.

Tomz, Michael, Judith L. Goldstein, and Douglas Rivers. 2007. "Do We Really Know That the TWO Increases Trade?" *American Economic Review* 97: 2005–18.

Tsebelis, George. 1995. "Decision-Making in Political Systems: Veto Players in Presidential, Parliamentary, Multicameralism and Multipartism." *British Journal of Political Science* 25: 289–325.

———. 2002. *Veto Players: How Political Institutions Work*. New York: Russell Sage.

Tyler, Tom R., Robert J. Boeckmann, Heather J. Smith, and Yuen J. Huo. 1997. *Social Justice in a Diverse Society*. Boulder, Colo.: Westview Press.

Van Parijs, Philippe. 2011. *Linguistic Justice for Europe and for the World*. Oxford: Oxford University Press.

Vanberg, Georg. 2005. *The Politics of Constitutional Review in Germany*. New York: Cambridge University Press.

Vella, Walter F. 1978. *Chaiyo! King Vajiravudh and the Development of Thai Nationalism*. Honolulu: University of Hawaii Press.

Vo-Duc, Viviane. 2011. 2011. "West Valley City Proclamation Encourages Residents to Learn English." *Deseret News*, January 4.

von der Mehden, Fred R. 1963. *Religion and Nationalism in Southeast Asia: Burma, Indonesia, the Philippines*. Madison: University of Wisconsin Press.

von Hayek, Friedrich A. 1960. *The Constitution of Liberty Press*. Chicago: University of Chicago Press.

Waldron, Jeremy. 1995. "Minority Cultures and the Cosmopolitan Alternative." In *The Rights of Minority Cultures*, ed. Will Kymlicka. Oxford: Oxford University Press.

Wang, Gungwu. 2007. "Keynote Address." In *Language, Nation and Development in Southeast Asia*, ed. H. G. Lee and L. Suryadinata. Singapore: Institute of Southeast Asian Studies.

White, Andrew Dickson. 1898. *A History of the Warfare of Science with Theology in Christendom*, vol. 2. New York: Appleton.

White, Bob W. 1996. "Talk About School: Education and the Colonial Project in French and British Africa (1860–1960)." *Comparative Education* 32, 1: 9–26.

White, Matthew. 2011. *Atrocitology: Humanity's 100 Deadliest Achievements.* Edinburgh: Canongate.

White, Roger, and Bedassa Tadesse. 2008. "Cultural Distance and the U.S. Immigrant-Trade Link." *World Economy* 31: 1078–96.

Whiteley, Paul F. 2000. "Economic Growth and Social Capital." *Political Studies* 48: 443–66.

Wong, Cara, Andrea Campbell, and Jack Citrin. 2006. "Racial Threat, Partisan Climate, and Direct Democracy." *Political Behavior* 28: 129–50.

Woolcock, Michael. 2010. "The Rise and Routinization of Social Capital, 1988–2008." *Annual Review of Political Science* 13: 469–87.

World Bank. 1993. *The East Asian Miracle.* Washington, D.C.: World Bank.

"World Values Survey." 2013. http://www.worldvaluessurvey.org/wvs.jsp.

Wortham, Stanton, and Betsy Rymes, eds. 2002. *Linguistic Anthropology of Education.* Westport, Conn.: Praeger.

Wright, Joseph. 2008. "Do Authoritarian Institutions Constrain? How Legislatures Affect Economic Growth and Investment." *American Journal of Political Science* 52, 2: 322–43.

Wyatt, David K. 1969. *The Politics of Reform in Thailand.* New Haven, Conn.: Yale University Press.

Young, Robert A. 1994. "How Do Peaceful Secessions Happen?" *Canadian Journal of Political Science* 27, 4: 773–92.

Zagarri, Rosemarie. 1988. "Representation and the Removal of State Capitals, 1776–1812." *Journal of American History* 74: 1239–56.

Zamenhof, L. L., and Henry Phillips. 1889. *An Attempt Towards an International Language.* New York: Henry Holt.

INDEX

Page references containing "fig." and "t." indicate illustrations and tables respectively.

ACKNOWLEDGMENTS

It seems both fitting and ironic that for a book about languages, I struggle to find the right words to say thank you. The phrase "thank you" just seems too routine. It is something you are supposed to say out of common courtesy: when someone holds a door for you when your hands are full; when someone gives you change when you're short a penny; or when someone retrieves your belongings for you when you've tripped. Yet, at the same time, its simplicity is appropriate. While I was writing this book, countless people have held open doors for me, given me much needed two cents, and picked me up.

Two individuals who deserve a "thank you" in every language are Tom Remington and Rick Doner. I always felt like a black sheep in that I did neither parties and institutions in Eastern Europe nor development and state capacity in Southeast Asia, but I never perceived any less care from either one. I also benefited immensely from Jen Gandhi and Jeff Staton. They not only read countless drafts, but they also taught by example what the career of an assistant professor should look like. Together these four—from Boston to Bangkok, from Madrid to Mexico City—have been selfless with their time and advice. While at Emory, I was also blessed with great colleagues. Terry Chapman, Amanda Murdie, and Jake Ricks have never stopped challenging me, supporting me, and laughing with me.

Before Emory, at Smith, I had two mentors, Mlada Bukovansky and Dennis Yasutomo, who steered me toward Singapore in spite of my personal affinity for Eastern Europe, taught me the fundamentals of social science research and the art of grant writing, and encouraged me to dream big.

At the University of Colorado, I benefited from having great colleagues. David Bearce, Moonhawk Kim, Anand Sokhey, and Jenny Wolak never complained [to me] about me barging into their offices, drinking their beer or eating their candy, and letting me brainstorm out loud. Andy Baker, Carew Boulding, David Brown, Joe Jupille, and Sarah Wilson Sokhey all took the time to read parts of—if not the entire—manuscript. And, of course, there was also Bill Safran, who despite his emeritus status never ceased to be a supportive mentor and a cherished friend.

Field research in Southeast Asia was made possible by a Department of Education Fulbright-Hays Doctoral Dissertation Research Abroad Fellowship and various research funds from Emory University and the University of Colorado. Many thanks to Peter Agree and Alison Anderson at the University of Pennsylvania Press for making this book possible. I am humbled by the enthusiasm Brendan O'Leary has always shown toward this project, and I am equally grateful to Bill Finan for guiding me through the unfamiliar terrain of book publishing.

While writing this book, I was blessed to have a group of good friends, both near and far, who never ceased to make life fun: Molly Butler, Arleen Chuang, Sofia Cunha-Vasconcelos, Bari Handwerger, Heather Kroger, Keleigh Peck, and Lily Welch. I was also fortunate that I had countless opportunities to dust off my passport, journey to lands afar, and be reminded of why I am interested in language politics. Mike van Opstal was a frequent travel buddy; at other times, people welcomed me into their world and sometimes literally their homes: Mica Bareto [Timor-Leste], the Bokuchava family [Azerbaijan and Georgia], Selima Chagra [Tunisia], Anamika Chakravorty [Austria], Hyelim Cho [Korea], Jay Chua and Amanda Lim [Singapore], Dave and Karen Cupery [Ecuador], the Petrov family [Moldova and Romania], Lindsey Richardson and Joe Vance [Guatemala], and the Somogyi family [Hungary].

Finally, this book would not have happened without the love of my family. My husband, Scott, has been arguably my biggest cheerleader since we met our first year at Emory. My two sisters, Liz and Mary, have been my sounding board, my moral compass, and my role models—despite the terror I unleashed upon them when I was younger. And of course, my parents, Chaonan and Huang Hei, have never stopped supporting me. Over three plus decades and across three plus continents, they have always been there. Their unwavering insistence that I learn to speak, read, and write Chinese is perhaps one of the most valuable gifts they have ever given me.

It seems that maybe the only word in the English language that can capture all these feelings of gratitude and love is simply "thank you."